Reading
Paradise Lost

Reading
Paradise Lost

ROBERT CROSMAN

INDIANA
Bloomington UNIVERSITY *London*
PRESS

Library of Congress Cataloging in Publication Data
Crosman, Robert, 1940–
  Reading Paradise lost.
  Bibliography: p.
  1. Milton, John, 1608–1674.   Paradise lost.   I. Title.
PR3562.C68   821'.4   79–3035
ISBN 0–253–15156–2 cl.   1 2 3 4 5 84 83 82 81 80
ISBN 0–253–20249–3 pa.

183085

To Christopher, who taught me how to read;
to Inge, who gave me time to write;
and to Herb and Adelaide, who gave me everything else,
this book is lovingly dedicated.

Contents

To the Reader

This book was very nearly called *The Experience of Reading Paradise Lost*, until John Reichert pointed out that I could cut three words from its title. The economy was irresistible, but what remains is still meant to suggest the idea that a work of literature is neither a document nor an artifact but an experience. Most modern criticism of *Paradise Lost* is historical, formalist, or an amalgam of the two approaches. Historical criticism, which tries to reconstruct the context in which the poem was first read, has done a great deal to improve our sense of the relevance of what Milton wrote to the religious, intellectual, and political life of his day, as well as to his own personal life. Yet the sheer volume of historical research into Miltonic contexts has led to diminishing returns; as the more obvious sources are thoroughly sifted through and analyzed, contexts progressively more remote or improbable must be discovered. As historical materials become more voluminous, they support more and more different interpretations of the poetry, muddying the waters they were once intended to clear, and leading to a rush for *further* historical evidence and an infinite regress from the poem. Historical critics have finally become so concerned with the historical record that they are likely to be more interested in it than in the poetry it was meant to explain.

The corrective trend to this mountain of historical research has been the formalism of New Critics, neo-Aristotelians, and lately Structuralists, who, by focusing on the text itself rather than its contexts, have set limits on the distance readers may profitably go from the text they aim to understand and enjoy. Of course, formalist critics have drawn freely on the discoveries of literary and intellectual history, so that most of the best Milton criticism today is both historical and formalist.

It would be foolish for any critic to be ungrateful for the contributions of these two trends to his understanding of Milton's poetry. Yet as criticism proliferates year after year, one limitation has become painfully clear: professional study of literature has become a barrier between literature itself and the reading public. "All professions," as Bernard Shaw observed, "are conspiracies against the laity." As Milton's poetry is hedged progressively round by studies of historic background and a mumbo-jumbo of critical terminology, their sheer bulk suggests more and more forcefully that reading *Paradise Lost* is the special province of professional readers.

The natural life cycle of any discipline begins with a bold new vision that is progressively elaborated until, weighed down at last by a complexity of trivial detail, it is ready for a revolution and a bold new vision once again. I suggest that literary studies are in this situation now, and that the intense theoretical debate of the past few years shows we are in need of a new paradigm. This new approach will, I predict, not ignore the contributions of either formalism or historical research, but will absorb them into a new view that takes as its object of study not "literature" as we have hitherto understood the word, but the experience of literature: *reading*.

"Literature" is one of those empty abstractions that our grammar tricks us into thinking of as a stable entity, a *thing*, while "reading" is still transparently a process, a human activity. Most modern literary theory, being formalist, sees a poem as an *object*—intricate and beautiful, perhaps, but an object nonetheless, in a continuum of other objects, collectively called "literature." This view is neither accurate nor useful, since we live in a world not of objects, but of experience. To think of complex experiences like poems as objects seriously falsifies their nature, conferring upon them a sort of marble stasis, chilling the very passions and imagination that poems are trying to bring to life. The one advantage of this pernicious view is that it simplifies, or seems to simplify, the task of criticism: a literary object does not change with the reader—it is "objective." Unfortunately, such a view robs literature of much of the interest it has for us *as we read it*, for then we are involved with it in a number of personal ways that we can hardly claim are objective or (as we say) "in the text."

So I propose that we think of *Paradise Lost* not as an object but as an experience. Objects are complete in themselves; experiences happen *to* someone. To talk about them at all, we must mention the person having the experience. In this book, the person reading *Paradise Lost* clearly is me, the text bears traces of my presence that are usually omitted in critical writing. Now some of my experience of *Paradise Lost* is admittedly private, or even unconscious and unavailable, but I can with some confidence assume that the broad lines of my experience— negotiating as I read among conflicting ideas and emotions—are the same for other readers. The resulting account, though hardly identical to any individual experience of reading *Paradise Lost*, should get appreciably closer to that experience than do most books of criticism.

Why should criticism try to approximate the experience of a reader reading? Because "common readers," whether they come to literature as students or as leisure-time readers, are in search primarily of help in their own reading. Readers fall into certain broad categories, and I have tried to keep a certain kind of reader always before my eyes. He or she is serious, is attentive, and is trying to read *Paradise Lost*—for the first time or the tenth, it doesn't much matter. I myself have often been in this situation; usually I have been disappointed by the books I have gone to for help. Because there has been too great a distance between the experience of reading the criticism and the experience of reading the poem, the first has not helped me greatly with the second. Hence this book.

It would be dishonest of me to deny, however, that I have had a second kind of reader also in mind. Professional Miltonists, too, are "just readers," but they are something else as well: namely, guardians of the standards of the profession. With them in mind, I have admitted indebtedness for my ideas when I was aware of the debt, and in the notes I have also gone very occasionally into matters that are likely to interest only other professionals. Still, since I am arguing for a fresh look at *Paradise Lost*, I have not wanted this book to be armor-plated with scholarly apparatus. Although I am not ignorant of current trends in Milton criticism and critical theory, the task of writing a useful book on *Paradise Lost* implies ignoring whatever is not *in my view* useful. So, if Miltonists find me implicitly rejecting their own views of *Paradise Lost*, they may assume the oversight was intentional. I suggest that they forget controversy and just read.

I will not deny myself the pleasure of acknowledging some debts here. Hugh Richmond first showed me that *Paradise Lost*, far from being the compendium of stale ideas that I supposed it to be, was witty, challenging, and unorthodox. Under the guidance of Edward Tayler, I began to be able to follow the poem's evasions, subterfuges, shocks, and surprises; it was he who first taught me, as much as reading *can* be taught, how to read for myself. From the excellent books of Joseph Summers, Christopher Ricks, and Frank Kermode I learned much. Finally Stanley Fish, who taught me first on the page and then in the flesh, has been my last and best teacher. Although in what follows I have presumed to quarrel with some aspects of *Surprised by Sin*, I happily admit that it is a classic of literary criticism.

Other debts are more personal. John Reichert, Robert and Ilona Bell, and Inge Crosman all helped me when this project was an essay sorely in need of encouragement. Richard Ohmann liked and published that essay in *College English*; some of it is now incorporated in the Introduction. Richard Beck's enthusiasm for an early chapter helped me to continue. Robert Scholes believed in me and put me in touch with Indiana University Press. Joseph Wittreich performed a unique kindness: he made the book better. My gratitude and thanks go to them all, and to my family, whose love and respect have sustained me through difficult years.

Providence, R.I.
31 May 1979

Reading
Paradise Lost

Reading and Criticism

IT IS COMMON knowledge that we learn from our children. My son Christopher, who at this writing is almost five, has taught me something about how we read. Here is a sample lesson.

"*James and the Giant Peach*," I begin, "by Roald Dahl."[1]

"Who's he, Daddy?"

"The man who wrote the book."

"Oh."

"Chapter One," I continue. "'Here is James Henry Trotter when he was about four years old.'"

"Who's James Henry Trotter?"

"The little boy this story is about. See his picture?"

"Yes."

"'Up until this time, he had had a happy life, living peacefully with his mother and father in a beautiful house beside the sea.'"

"Here's the sea," says my son, pointing over James's shoulder. Even simple words are still a bit treacherous to him, and he's happy to confirm them with a picture.

"'There were always plenty of other children for him to play with, and there was the sandy beach for him to run about on, and the ocean to paddle in. It was the perfect life for a small boy.'" (I rather expect a question, but Christopher knows all about the beach, having just been there.) "'Then, one day, James's mother and father went to London to do some shopping, and there a terrible thing happened.'"

"*What* happened, Daddy?"

"Wait a second. The story tells us: 'Both of them suddenly got eaten up (in full daylight, mind you, and on a crowded street) by an enormous angry rhinoceros which had escaped from the London Zoo.'"

Here an absolute barrage of questions defeats my powers of report-ing. My listener wants to know how the rhinoceros escaped? why was he angry? was he caught? what was done with him when he *was* caught? do rhinos *really* eat people? if not, why not? and, oh, yes, what is London?

It is not really true that at this moment it first dawned on me that reading is not as passive a process as it seems. Much of the best aesthetic theory and literary criticism I have read in recent years—by Rudolf Arn-heim, E. H. Gombrich, Morse Peckham, Stanley Fish, Norman Holland, David Bleich, Jonathan Culler, Wolfgang Iser, Stephen Booth, and oth-ers—has argued precisely this view.[2] The work of art, they have all in one way or another maintained, whether "spatial" like a painting or "tem-poral" like a piece of literature, is less profitably thought of as an object than as an *event*, or series of events—a transaction between a perceptual field and a perceiver. Much of what we call "learning to read" is adding to our repertoire of expectations of what the next moment's perceptual field will bring. Old habits of thought die hard, however, and though I *knew* that the reader collaborates with his text, I had not really observed myself or anyone else doing so until I began reading to Christopher.

In this book I hope to throw some light on what we do as readers when we read *Paradise Lost*. I may as well say at once that description of the reading process—both in general and with reference to specific works of literature—is in my opinion the most important task facing contem-porary literary critics. The directionless wandering of literary studies to-day, amid a hubbub of competing critical "systems," will be ended, I be-lieve, only when we return to the level at which all literary experience begins—the act of reading.

What is clear from a small child's reactions is how eager the mind is to place the new and unfamiliar into a context of the old and familiar. Christopher—who is inclined to question everything—has not yet learned to relish uncertainties, or to wait happily for the surprises the author will spring on him, but his questions are really no different from those adults ask silently as they read. A good author counts on his reader to be asking questions—formulating, testing, and changing expectations at every moment.

Take the enormous angry rhinoceros who so horribly yet entertain-ingly gobbles up the elder Trotters and thus permits James to begin a new life as eventful as his old one was tranquil. Clearly this incident is designed to be as surprising as possible—not only sudden, but contrary to the known dietary habits of rhinos—yet Dahl telegraphs it by first saying "and there a terrible thing happened." This rhetorical flourish is by no means unnecessary. It announces that all expectations with respect to James's story will have to be radically changed, yet it gives us little idea of *what* change to make. For a moment the mind goes blank, which I am convinced is the reason for Christopher's agitation; his worry is not for the still rather anonymous Trotters but for his grasp of the story he is trying to follow. That moment of intellectual terror is Dahl's way of warning the reader that his grip upon things is dangerously incomplete. It makes the Trotters' fanciful demise not less but more surprising and effective.

"But," I can hear my reader objecting, "you are describing a, to put it gently, naive reader. Even granting some residue of similarity between a child's way of reading and an adult's, the task of criticism is not to describe these fumblings and mistakes but to give us the end product of the reading experience—an account of the messages an author is sending, his skill in sending them, and some mature judgment as to their value."

True, we normally distinguish sharply between reading and criticism, but I am uncomfortable with this antithesis. We cannot really separate them; we can only criticize what we have read, and as we read we inevitably criticize—interpret, judge, applaud, or disapprove. Yet conventionally we do distinguish these activities, conceiving of criticism as an act of reflection performed upon what has already been read, and of "reading" as a naive, unreflective, pre-critical activity.

Yet, by separating reading from criticism, and then ignoring the former, critics have unintentionally falsified the nature of the object described. Whatever mode of existence the poem has in itself, it is only *known* by reading it. The atom of literary study is not text alone but text-plus-reader. For us, a literary text is not marks on a page but an experience, or a succession of experiences, that happens to our intellects and emotions.

The act of reading is in its very nature interpretive, a making of decisions. The fact that we are not continually aware of our own active participation as we read is no disproof of this contention; like most activities, reading is performed best when it is not self-conscious. "Meaning based on mere learning or knowledge," says Rudolf Arnheim, "is at best secondary for the purposes of the artist. He must rely on the direct and self-explanatory impact of perceptual forces upon the human mind."[3] In discovering and explaining such forces, a critic would provide, either as a help for readers in difficulty or as an enhancement of their pleasure, *a mimesis of the reader reading*.

Such a mimesis is the method I propose for this book. The process it hopes to mirror has been described in its outlines by Wolfgang Iser:

> As we read, we oscillate to a greater or lesser degree between the building and the breaking of illusions. In a process of trial and error, we organize and reorganize the various data offered us by the text. . . . [It] is not a smooth or continuous process, but one which, in its essence, relies on *interruptions* of the flow to render it efficacious. We look forward, we look back, we decide, we change our decisions, we form expectations, we are shocked by their nonfulfillment, we question, we muse, we accept, we reject; this is the dynamic process of recreation.[4]

Recording the struggles of a reader to make sense out of what he reads has not generally been considered an important part of literary criticism, perhaps because literary works have been thought of as vehicles for propositions. If the point of the poem is to convey a "message," does it matter much what stages of comprehension the reader goes through on his way to uncovering it? The usual answer is "no," but I disagree. Most of literature's great messages are clichés—grandly true, perhaps, but stupefyingly familiar: pride comes before a fall; love is stronger than hate; death is certain. If we persist in reading works containing such propositions, we do so not for the sake of the bare message but for the *process* of arriving at it, a process of vicarious experience that is unique to art.

Take *Paradise Lost*. Although the poem argues the proposition that God's ways are just, no one reads it solely to discover this proposition, but rather to undergo a series of experiences designed to convince us of its truth. Milton's very words in the poem: "That to the highth of this great Argument I may *assert* Eternal Providence, And *justify* the ways of God to men,"[5] propose a rhetorical function for the poem—propose, that is, that (if such a division were possible) what the poem says is finally no more important than how the reader comes to understand it. Better: how a reader learns to understand *is* an important part of the "meaning." If I am right, then any criticism that does not try to relate meaning to process, what the poem says to what it does (to a reader), fails to some serious degree even to tell us what the poem means.

Hence the need for sequential reading. Since all criticism is aimed at enhancing a reader's pleasure and understanding, all criticism in a sense depicts a reader, the critic, making sense out of the text before him. But unlike you and me, unlike the critic himself when he began, this reader is usually depicted as seeing the whole text at once, able to cross-reference at will, and having open before him the very resource books that illuminate its dark corners and straighten out its ambiguities. From his vantage point the critic-reader tames and masters the previously unruly text, whose very imperfections he sees and forgives, and offers *his* reader nothing less than the same superior position, safely above the subjected plain where the less enlightened must labor in dust and heat. If the point of art is not the message alone, however, but also the process a reader undergoes in arriving at it—"a succession of actions," as Stephen Booth puts it, "upon the understanding of an audience"[6]— then criticism should normally trace those actions in sequential order, so that it might be a truer mimesis of the reader reading, and might put less distance between the critic-reader and the actual reader looking for help.

Of course an author can't tell everything at once—neither our language nor our minds work that way—but for that very reason *how* he arranges his story is of great importance and interest to the literary critic. Milton thought that the Bible itself was a progressive revelation of truth; can we doubt that he constructed his biblical poem to be the same?

If not, we cannot assume that Milton's "fit audience" is made up of a race of beings who, unlike us, already possess the wisdom he aimed to impart. Ignorant and benighted we may well be, but it is exactly for such readers that Milton wrote. Let us set such a reader down in front of *Paradise Lost*. Since the poem has a point to make, a lesson to teach which it presumes the reader to be in need of, every reader is in this sense "naive" with regard to Milton's epic, no matter how "sophisticated" he may be. He or she can't be totally innocent, of course. The poem's very length and seriousness demand a certain experience with literature and a general maturity that would deter all but the most eager pre-adult or nonreader. But whatever our naive reader has or has not read before, it is really impossible that he or she has not read stories of heroic adventure, is not familiar with the rudiments of the Christian faith, or has not given thought to the fundamental problems of moral existence, such as the nature of good and evil. To have grown up in our culture (or in any culture) really insures exposure to the basic issues and techniques of Milton's poem. As with every book we read, then, before we begin reading

Paradise Lost we have in a sense "begun" it. Expectations have been created by the poem's very name and length, by its reputation as the greatest long poem in the language, as well as by whatever we may have heard about its contents.

Whatever a specific reader expects to find in *Paradise Lost* then— and of course individual expectations vary considerably—there are two expectations he can hardly avoid having: he expects a Christian poem, and he expects an epic. He cannot escape knowing at least the rudiments of Christian doctrine: a single, omnipotent Creator; an evil Adversary; the story of how the first two human beings were seduced by that Adversary; the role of Christ in repairing their ruin. The opening lines of Milton's poem remind us of that story; the poet assumes that we know it already; and we do. To expect a Christian poem is to expect a story that makes God appear good and Satan evil, and that encourages the reader to look favorably upon a system of values that exalts humility, obedience to God, love of one's enemies, passivity, spirituality, and other-worldliness.

To expect an epic, on the other hand, is to expect a poem of physical action: wars, battles, and great deeds by active, martial heroes. We may never have read a Classical or Renaissance epic, yet we have read, heard, and seen heroic stories, and they all follow the same basic pattern—the struggle of a strong man against seemingly overwhelming opposition and his eventual victory. The problem is: how can this pattern express a system of Christian values? The story of Christ's life, for example, is the story of spiritual victories and physical defeats, climaxed by the discovery that it is necessary to lose this world in order to win the next. Worldly triumph is the theme of epic, while the Christian theme is one of worldly defeat as the necessary prelude to spiritual victory. Christian values are intrinsically and irremediably anti-epic.

For centuries Christian poets labored unsuccessfully to produce Christian epic, unable to appreciate the incompatibility of their means and their goals. Milton, however, perceived the contradiction between epic form and Christian values, and solved the problem in what seems now the only way possible: he made Satan his epic hero.

The effect of this innovation upon the reader is hard to overestimate. Art is a matter of transformations or recombinations of familiar things, characters, and situations into new and surprising configurations. One quality of superior art is its capacity to disorient the reader, to surprise him and undermine his preconceptions, without of course losing him completely. Dahl's hungry rhinoceros has this effect of intellectual terror, but only briefly. *Paradise Lost* is far more disorienting for a far longer time, because its unexpected configuration is not some detail of plot but its overall narrative structure. It proposes, in effect, to tell antithetical stories simultaneously: the story of God's ways justified, and the story of Satan's heroism. For much of the poem our naive reader is disoriented by this conflict—which story is he really reading?

Naturally a poet runs large risks when he sets out to confuse his reader so thoroughly. Like other "great books"—the *Divine Comedy*, for instance, or *Ulysses*—*Paradise Lost* is hard to read. This is not simply a matter of elevated diction or classical and biblical allusion, although they play their part. Primarily *Paradise Lost* is hard to read because it contradicts itself, both in small things—such as the almost obsessive oxymorons, like "darkness visible," that feed us self-contradictory information—and in great, such as the clash of images of God as the loving Creator ("Dove-like satst brooding on the vast Abyss And mad'st it pregnant," I, 21–22) and as the harsh punisher ("Him the Almighty Power Hurl'd headlong flaming from th' Ethereal Sky," I, 44–45)—occurring in this instance within twenty-five lines of each other! These contradictions, and innumerable others, all flow from the first and greatest contradiction: the attempt to celebrate Christian values in a form designed to celebrate their opposite.

If Milton had taken the course of his predecessors and tried to fuse epic and Christian virtues in a single hero—as he apparently contemplated doing in his projected but abandoned epic on King Arthur—his reader would not have been initially aware of their incompatibility, but we can guess that his poem would have disintegrated like the others. By making the contradiction explicit in the figure of a military hero named Satan, Milton exploited it. Satan as epic hero embodies many of the values that we as men and women of the world *must* prize: strength, pride, leadership, self-control, endurance. Yet Satan is a villain and is denounced as such by the poet. The apparent insolubility of this paradox produces in the reader the confusion that is his most reliable impression of Hell—the "hateful siege of contraries," as Satan calls it. Only after he has been thoroughly exposed to the delusions and self-contradictions of the traditional heroic stance is the reader led to a radically different conception of "heroism" embodied in the fallen but repentant Adam and

Eve. In effect the poem begins by putting the reader in a large hole that only the rest of the poem can pull him out of.

The experience of reading *Paradise Lost* is one of the most difficult and at the same time most rewarding experiences that literature has to offer. Amazingly, for a poem whose basic plot is known before we begin reading, *Paradise Lost* is consistently able to bewilder and surprise. At every bend in its road we find some new horizon that we had not anticipated—Satan attractive, God repellent, Eden apparently tainted, the Fall in part comic, regeneration humiliating. The reader can never be quite certain that he knows where he stands in *Paradise Lost*. But who is this "reader" of whom I speak? Since we will meet him frequently in the pages ahead, it will be helpful now to discover who he is.

To begin with, it is easier to say who he is not. He is neither of the two "readers" most frequently met with in Milton criticism, the "seventeenth-century reader" and the "ideal reader." These two critical inventions represent an attempt on the part of critics to prescribe responses: when the actual reader responds differently from the way in which a critic thinks Milton's "fit audience" would have responded, he is exhorted to correct himself. For example, B. Rajan, worried like many critics that modern readers may respond favorably to Satan, argues from the climate of the age against such a response:

> Our response [i.e., as modern readers] is, I imagine, one of cautious interest. . . . But with Milton's contemporaries the response was predominantly one of fear. If like Calvin they thought of Satan as "an enemie that is in courage most hardie, in strength most mightie, in policies most subtle, in diligence and celeritie unweariable, with all sorts of engins plenteously furnished, in skill of warre most readie," that was only so that they could stand guard more vigilantly against their relentless opponent.[7]

Like so many before and since, Rajan opposes the modern stock response of admiration for Promethean rebels with the stock response of seventeenth-century Satan hatred.[8]

Setting aside the extraordinary naiveté of thinking that all readers of *any* period read or respond alike, the great puzzle surrounding such an historical reader is why he is necessary. Even supposing that a certain group can be shown to read in a uniform way, why ought *we* to read that way (on the very next page Rajan uses such phrases as "meant to be" and "you are not supposed to")? The answer can only be that the response of seventeenth-century readers should be normative because Milton, writing with that audience in mind, *intended* such a response. Arguments based upon historical readers are, in fact, disguised arguments of authorial intention. Whatever the merits of prescribing to the reader the responses the author wished or asked for (example: "Laugh; I meant that as a joke"), there is no merit in disguising the author's prescription as something else and no need for the concept of "the seventeenth-century reader," except as a rhetorical flourish.

Since the text itself, however, does imply and often directly asks for certain attitudes on the part of the reader, there is another prescriptive version of the reader that I call the "ideal reader." Wayne Booth gives this idea memorable expression in *The Rhetoric of Fiction*:

> It is only as I read that I become the self whose beliefs must coincide with the author's. Regardless of my real beliefs and practices, I must subordinate my mind and heart to the book if I am to enjoy it to the full. The author creates, in short, an image of himself and another image of his reader; he makes his reader, as he makes his second self, and the most successful reading is one in which the created selves, author and reader, can find complete agreement.[9]

Responding to cues in the text, argues Booth, we as readers take on, or *try* to take on, the attitudes and values the author wishes us to adopt. Applied by Anne Ferry to *Paradise Lost*, this doctrine comes out as the following:

> We the readers are immediately included in the events of the narrative with the first line of the poem, because its subject is "Mans First Disobedience" (not "Adam's" or "the first man's") and in any context in which the word is used, we are included in "Man." . . . We are human beings, simply, and yet certain assumptions are implied about us *as* human beings. It is assumed that we loathe sin and love virtue, regret the loss of Eden and long for our restoration; that we can respond to divinely inspired music, that we are interested in the serious treatment of a serious subject, and that we are capable of rational attention to logical argument. Yet it is simultaneously assumed that as human beings we need divine inspiration because our minds cannot transcend the limits of our creaturely nature, and that as heirs of Adam we are fallen, bereft, miserable and mortal.[10]

Here, of course, is a full-blown argument of authorial intention. Booth makes no bones about it, and Ferry, though she seems elsewhere to be confused about whether the poet's intentions should govern the reader's responses, in general endorses such control:

> When we find complexity in our response to the behavior or speech of a character and to the statement of the narrator which interprets it, we must judge the character by the interpretation, not the interpretation by the character's words or acts. (p.16)

Since narrators are not always reliable, however, and since one test of reliability is whether their comments tally with the voices of other characters or with the dramatized action (the other test is whether they tally with what we presume or know the author believes), Ferry's unwillingness to doubt the authority of Milton's narrator must arise from a belief that his views coincide so closely with Milton's own that no irony is conceivable.[11]

Although she carefully hides the author behind his narrator, Ferry still assumes that the author-narrator's values must obliterate those of the reader. For this reason the Booth-Ferry notion of an actual reader necessarily transformed "for the sake of the experience" into the poem's ideal reader seems to me different in form but not in substance from the argument of authorial intention. In either case the reader is asked to repress his own responses in favor of those prescribed to him by an author, by the author's persona, or (more accurately) by a critic interpreting both.

As his subtitle suggests, it may have been dissatisfaction with this excessively docile "reader" that led Stanley Fish to write *Surprised by Sin: The Reader in Paradise Lost*. Fish saw that, as Ferry maintained, Milton's narrator tried to exert moral pressure on the reader to hate Satan, but he also saw that Satan's appeal for readers was a consequence of a rhetorical brilliance that was equally Milton's intention. So Fish concluded that if, in Booth's terms, Milton "created" his reader, then he did so as much with Satan's speeches as with the comments that "corrected" them, and that Milton's reader was accordingly not the serene character Ferry described. On the contrary, Fish maintains that:

> Milton consciously wants to worry his reader, to force him to doubt the correctness of his responses, and to bring him to the realization that his inability to read the poem with any confidence in his own perception is its focus.[12]

In effect Fish broadens Ferry's idea of an "ideal reader" by inferring *his* reader from the entire text of *Paradise Lost*, rather than from certain direct speeches of the narrator deemed more authoritative than the rest of the poem. In the process he enlarges the concept of an "ideal reader" until it sounds more like the "implied reader" described by Iser. Fish's reader can take no part of the poem, no voice in the poem, as definitive of how he should think or feel. Instead he must actively seek to harmonize or resolve discords, and when he cannot, he must suffer their conflict.

Accordingly, Fish describes the poem's method as a "programme of reader harassment" (p.4) and the poem itself as an obstacle course, complete with dead ends, reversed sign posts, and occasional ambushes. The reader, his understanding confounded and his soul tested, does not simply sit back watching others (Satan, Adam, Eve) make mistakes, but himself begins almost immediately to err, while the narrative voice makes him aware of the fact and "humiliates" him for it.

What is the purpose of such rough treatment? Briefly, to destroy aesthetic distance. Under pressure of the harassing narrator, the reader is forced not merely to contemplate the stories of Satan's fall and of Adam's fall-and-redemption, but to *participate* in them. Fish believes that Milton thought of his reader, no matter how good a Christian, as to some degree alienated from God. A justification of God's ways, therefore, demands not merely a formal demonstration but an emotional catharsis as well, in which the reader is first brought to recognize his own kinship to Satan and to fallen Adam, and is then gradually led not only to see a way out but to want to take it. Since the reader recapitulates in himself the experience of the poem's protagonists, the act of reading is a process of self-discovery.

Intriguing as Fish's model of "the reader" is in some respects, it has one grave weakness, for in order to persuade us of the importance of the pattern of fault and correction, Fish feels (I believe quite wrongly) that he has to construct an elaborate argument about the "seventeenth-century reader," which soon becomes more prescriptive than the usual critical assumptions about Milton's reader. Ferry, after all, asked of us only that we come to the poem with a generally Christian worldview; Fish suggests that Milton's fit reader come equipped with an entire baggage of seventeenth-century Puritan habits of mind. Fish's "reader" sees temptation everywhere and is constantly examining his own conscience with anxious attention. He is (to paraphrase Thwackum) not any reader but a

Christian one, nor yet any Christian reader but a seventeenth-century one, nor yet any seventeenth-century Christian reader but one of the Puritan persuasion.

In some contexts it is of course perfectly permissible to refer to an historical "reader"; one may properly say, for example, "the seventeenth-century reader would recognize the dolphin as an emblem of Christ," meaning only that in the seventeenth century the dolphin was a conventional symbol of Christ. It would do us no good to inquire who this reader is or how he acquired his knowledge, for he is a mere turn of phrase, easily dispensed with without altering meaning. But to say "the seventeenth-century reader would respond to this poem in such and such a way" is at best to give a modern reader a rhetorical nudge toward responding to cues in the text he may previously have overlooked. When, on the contrary, an audience is stipulated who would so respond, even in the *absence* of such cues, then criticism has broken down.

The pattern of fault and correction, as Fish describes it in *Paradise Lost*, is not always there for the attentive reader, for in perhaps half of his examples Fish relies unduly upon his imagined seventeenth-century reader. For example, when Satan makes his defiant speech near the beginning of Book I, Milton's narrator follows it with the laconic comment: "So spake th' Apostate Angel, though in pain, Vaunting aloud, but rackt with deep despair" (I, 125–26). Fish notes, as have others, a certain inconsistency between the genuinely defiant-sounding Satanic rhetoric and the narrator's revelation of Satan's inner despair. His explanation of that inconsistency is, however, original:

> The comment of the epic voice unsettles the reader, who sees in it at least a partial challenge to his own assessment of the speech. . . . We are angry at the epic voice, not for fudging, but for being right, for insisting that we become our own critics. (pp.5–9)

"We are angry at the epic voice" seems excessive, but Fish has rather a special "we" in mind:

> A Christian failure need not be dramatic; if the reader loses himself in the workings of the speech even for a moment, he places himself in a compromising position. . . . In this case, the failure (if we can call it that) involves the momentary relaxation of a vigilance that must be eternal. . . . Protected from one error (the possibility of listening sympathetically to a disguised enemy) we fall easily into another (spiritual

inattentiveness) and fail to read Satan's speech with the critical acumen it demands. (pp.12–14)

"The reader" must still be attentive, but now he must be something more: a Christian eternally vigilant against Satanic wiles, even while reading a poem. It is not impossible to imagine such a reader—a backwoods fundamentalist, say, unfamiliar with imaginative literature and hence unused to distinguishing between fictional characters (Milton's "Satan") and real ones (Satan). What is impossible to imagine is that Milton addressed his poem specifically to such readers. The usual seventeenth-century reader, I take it, like the usual twentieth-century one, might notice the inconsistency, but would not feel "humiliated" by the narrator's "rebuke" (Fish's words). As part of an often-repeated pattern, however, such an inconsistency does wonderfully imitate the fall-and-regeneration pattern that is Milton's theme.

Luckily, as often as not Fish's pattern of fault and correction needs no such reader as he imagines. Stripped of its religious trappings, it becomes simple trial and error. Reading *Paradise Lost*, or any text, is a process of making guesses, perceiving that some of these guesses are wrong, and then making improved guesses, which are in turn revised. It is to this process of reading that Fish does such ample justice, and for which he deserves the warmest praise. But if it cannot be shown that Milton wrote his epic exclusively for the kind of reader Fish has in mind, then his way of reading becomes not *the* way to read *Paradise Lost*, but simply *a* way. What is lost with Fish's historical "reader" is the illusion of objectivity.

Let me make it clear that, though not flawless, *Surprised by Sin* is in my opinion the best book ever written on *Paradise Lost* and has helped me better than any other to understand and to enjoy Milton's poem. But there can be no denying that Fish's Puritan "reader" has annoyed many of his own readers. A statement of this annoyance that is extreme only in its rhetoric is William Kerrigan's joke that Fish's reader has a "remarkable appetite for being duped."[13] Peter Berek makes the same objection more soberly when he says:

> Fish presupposes a reader at once so confused—in that he is unwilling or unable to parse out the plain sense of the poet's syntax—and so sophisticated—in a later willingness to review the poem again and again as though he were preparing for a Ph.D. examination—that I

cannot imagine any seventeenth-century man for whom *Paradise Lost* was not an assigned text responding in a fashion as complicated as Fish proposes.[14]

As we shall see in the chapters ahead, confusion has a vital part in the effects of *Paradise Lost*—whether or not we have an "appetite" for it, we feel it. But Fish has a penchant for overstatement that leads to the kind of reaction Kerrigan and Berek illustrate, just as he has a fondness for close analysis that slights the larger movements of narrative—plot, characterization, point of view—and that lends credence to Berek's complaint of overreading.

Anyone familiar with *Surprised by Sin* will see how much I have relied on it in the chapters ahead, both as a model and as a quarry. But I have diverged from it sharply in the matter of an historic reader. In my view, the invention of a supposed seventeenth-century reader is not only fallacious but, in its effect on many modern readers, unfortunate, since it asks us to inhibit our own responses in favor of certain official or objective responses. Fish's historic reader is as dead as the spiritual tradition from which he was exhumed. To the extent that he requires a response that modern readers (Christian and non-Christian alike) neither have spontaneously nor would wish to have, Fish has only managed to suggest with his model of the reader that *Paradise Lost* is a dead text.[15]

The "seventeenth-century reader," like the "ideal reader," is a fictitious person invented by the critic in an effort to impose on modern readers responses they might not otherwise adopt on the basis of their own reading of the text. Even if there were such a thing as this reader, it is hard to see that his responses, any more than authorial intention, should govern the responses of actual readers.[16]

Response is precisely the realm of freedom, the part contributed not by the author but by each individual reader. How we respond to a text cannot be prescribed by anyone, nor can we delegate our ability to respond to any surrogate. Our reactions are our own, whether we like it or not. Such reflections lead the critic to the edge of an abyss: if response is a key aspect of literary experience but is inescapably subjective, then criticism can have nothing to say about it. All responses are equally valid, and there is no "reader" of *Paradise Lost*, or of any other poem—there are only readers. If every reader's response is valid, then there is apparently nothing for the critic to do.

There is one alternative left, however. Instead of prescribing responses we can *describe* them. This is possible because of art's universality, and because of the common humanity all readers share. The poet, like any artist, wishes to produce an effect upon his audience. In this sense he is as much a rhetorician as any expository writer. Unlike the orator or the newspaper editorialist, however, his audience is not a narrowly defined one, either in time or space. His audience is as universal as is competence in the language he writes in, and it extends indefinitely forward in time to audiences yet unborn. Since he writes for an ill-defined audience, he must pitch his persuasiveness at as nearly "universal" a level as he can manage. He assumes that certain interests are more or less permanent in human beings: that we like to be told stories, enjoy surprises, are interested in human personality vividly portrayed, think more easily in concretions than in abstractions, and have an inevitable interest in certain basic human problems, such as love, death, immortality, and the fate of human desires and aspirations, among others.

Because art is aimed in large part at interests and faculties that all readers share, it follows that our responses to it have a great deal in common. Rhetorically speaking, the *purpose* of art is to address the basic human being, to make him see and feel not simply the local issues of a particular time and place, but the underlying problems that repeat themselves in changing forms throughout human history. If each of us lived in a private universe, untouched by the concerns of others, responding in his own idiosyncratic ways to life, then art would be impossible, since the artist's concerns would be of no interest to his audience. But such is not the case. No two of us may see the world in precisely the same way, speak exactly the same language, or respond in identical ways to works of art, but there is considerable overlap between us nonetheless. Discussion ordinarily focuses upon differences, but this fact should not obscure the existence of vast areas of basic agreement, which are seldom discussed because they are so easily taken for granted. Criticism might be addressed to the responses of this "basic reader," who, whatever his individual biases and particular situation in time and space, is still attuned to fundamental devices of art and to primary human concerns that change very little, if at all, over three hundred years.

This, then, is what I mean by "the reader" when I use the term in the pages that follow. My assumption is that poetry speaks fundamentally to the "universal man" in each of us—a pragmatic rather than a mystical idea whose presence I infer from the manifest similarities in the ways we feel, think, speak, and act. Whether this communal self is innate or is taught to each of us in our incessant commerce with our fellow human beings I do not know—probably it is both. If my assumption is correct, then the key to reading *Paradise Lost* with pleasure and understanding lies not in acquiring any extrinsic body of knowledge and expertise (valuable as these may be in themselves) but is already within the naive reader's grasp as he begins *Paradise Lost*. What each of us needs to do is to perform the active function of reader with more vigor and self-confidence than is usual in readers much beyond Christopher's age. The freedom implicit in the reader's collaborative role in the experience of poetry must be recognized and accepted if we are to perform that role to our own satisfaction.

Readers who know Milton well will recognize, in this relative independence of authority, in this reliance upon the text itself as illuminated by the "inner light" of common human understanding, Milton's own attitude toward reading, especially toward reading Scripture. In the preface to his religious treatise, *Christian Doctrine*, Milton writes:

> I decided not to depend upon the belief or judgment of others in religious questions for this reason: God has revealed the ways of eternal salvation only to the individual faith of each man, and demands of us that any man who wishes to be saved should work out his beliefs for himself. So I made up my mind to puzzle out a religious creed for myself by my own exertions, and to acquaint myself with it thoroughly. In this the only authority I accepted was God's self-revelation, and accordingly I read and pondered the Holy Scriptures themselves with all possible diligence, never sparing myself in any way.[17]

Milton does not reject the help of other interpreters—far from it—but he subjects their interpretations to the authority of his own most scrupulous reading of Scripture, rather than subjecting his judgment to theirs; and I have followed this principle in reading *Paradise Lost* (and venture to hope that my reader will, too): "Do not accept or reject what I say unless you are absolutely convinced by the clear evidence of the Bible" (*Christian Doctrine*, p. 124). For Milton's "the Bible" I substitute "the text," in this case *Paradise Lost*.

The book that tries to follow this principle is, I recognize, something of a hybrid, a blend of the professional and the popular that may not entirely please either audience. "Common readers," students, and other non-specialists may be irked by the attention I ask them to pay to Milton's text, or by the difficulties I describe them as having with the poem—isn't it my job, after all, to make reading seem simple and pleasant? Miltonists, on the other hand, may feel that I am simplifying unduly, as in my discussion of Calvinism and in my definitions of comedy and tragedy, or that I am forcing a beloved classic into a straitjacket of superfluous methodology.

I won't apologize for the method. It is not much more than common sense and common experience applied with determination. It deals with the poem's two salient properties—energy and ambiguity—far better, I believe, than any alternative method, and does so, by and large, in plain English. Throughout I have tried to write as clearly and as interestingly as my subject would allow, which means not elaborating definitions or doctrines beyond what is necessary for my argument, but not ignoring the poem's complexities either. What I have really done is to lavish attention on the poem's words (or more precisely on our experience of them) while stinting on backgrounds, scholarship, and criticism. Yet it is refreshing to hear voices other than the author's own, so I have used those of critics (both to agree and to disagree with), of Milton himself in his prose works, and even of assorted historical characters like Calvin and Du Bartas, as a way of promoting dialogue. If some of these men and women end up sounding foolish or limited, that is because I have made them characters in my play.

In the pages that follow I will try to describe not what the reader should feel but some—a little—of what he *does* feel as he reads *Paradise Lost*. Some of my readers will nonetheless object that I am being prescriptive, that behind my "is" lurks an "ought." Those who read my interpretation in that spirit will defeat its purpose, however, for my aim is not to bring forth one more (at best) ingenious and sensitive "reading" of Milton's epic, but to provide a mimesis of how a reader (myself) reads a poem. My aim is not to foist *my* interpretation onto other readers, but to show other readers that they are, inevitably, collaborating with Milton when they read, and that they could enhance their pleasure and comprehension by doing so with more vigor and self-confidence. The "reading" itself is provisional—every one of my readers will find it untrue of himself in some respects, as will I myself in five years' time. There is not one of my readers, I hope, who will not be able to improve upon it, not only from his own point of view but from mine. It does, nonetheless, provide a beginning for what is in some respects a new critical activity—the exhortation by example of readers to become not "seventeenth-century readers" or "ideal readers" but themselves, reading. It is by this standard that I should like what follows to be judged.

1

Milton's Great Oxymoron

> Like all great works of art, great literary works are dare-
> devils. They flirt with disasters, and at the same time,
> they let you know they are married forever to particular
> order and purpose. They are, and work hard at being,
> always on the point of one or another kind of incoher-
> ence, always on the point of disintegrating and/or of in-
> tegrating the very particulars they exclude, always and
> multifariously on the point of evoking suggestions of per-
> tinent but syntactically impertinent auxiliary assertions
> or even saying things they cannot want to say, things
> irrelevant or antipathetic to their arguments or just plain
> untrue.—Stephen Booth

MODERN CRITICS HAVE grown tired of the question of Satan's heroism. If many of Milton's lines seem to flatter Satan, many others show the
poet's hostility toward him, and nothing that Milton said or did in his life
lends support to the idea that he was consciously anti-Christian. Yet the
question of Satan will always recur as fresh generations read the poem,
because it is built into the structure of Milton's epic. As Dryden a few
years after the publication of *Paradise Lost* remarked, Satan is its structural hero.

William Blake's solution to the poem's inconsistent and shifting portrait of Satan—"Milton was a true poet, and of the Devil's party without
knowing it"—makes some sense, and should not be lightly dismissed.
Not only does it reflect a common judgment that Milton's Hell is a more
interesting place than his Heaven, but it points to a feeling of kinship or

sympathy that many readers feel with Satan. There is no reason, however, to think that such a sympathy was *unconscious* in Milton. As a serious Christian, Milton knew that he was "fallen," and, like it or not, had
a deep bond of kinship to Satan. And he wrote for an audience who could
also be expected to feel such sympathy.

Because Milton himself, his poem, and his audience (Christian or
not) are all divided between antithetical attitudes toward evil, the problem of Satan recurs afresh every time a new reader opens the volume.
Satan is a problem for all readers of *Paradise Lost*—not simply for a particular kind of reader or a particular age—and the poem's opening is designed to force this problem on the reader's attention. An initially strong
and attractive, but ultimately loathsome and self-destructive, Satan corresponds to the reality of our paradoxical universe, where evil, whether
personified or not, has these same traits:

> As therefore the state of man now is; what wisdome can there be to
> choose, what continence to forbeare without the knowledge of evill?
> He that can apprehend and consider vice with all her baits and seeming
> pleasures, and yet abstain, and yet distinguish, and yet prefer that
> which is truly better, he is the true warfaring Christian.[1]

The only dangerous, hence the only important, evil is that which we
do not recognize as such, or that which we recognize but find nonetheless
attractive. Milton's Satan, in order to be dangerous, *must* appeal. But
since Milton's Satan is merely part of a larger poetic whole from which he
cannot finally be separated, the problem of Satan is only the most salient
aspect of what we should be calling "the problem of *Paradise Lost*," or, in
Milton's view at least, "humanity's problem": given that evil is within us,
how do we learn to strive for good? Milton's answer is to immerse ourselves in the destructive element: "And perhaps this is that doom which
Adam fell into of knowing good and evill, that is to say of knowing good
by evill" (*Areopagitica*, p. 514; Hughes, p. 728).

That error, evil's image, is a way to truth is not merely *asserted* by
Milton's poem; it is also a fundamental principle of its design. Consistently, it confuses or misleads its reader into the very errors it condemns.
If, for example, the reader knew from the beginning that Milton was "Not
sedulous by Nature to indite Wars" (IX, 27–28), he would not be so easily
misled by Satan's apparent military virtues; nor, if he knew the true story
of the war in Heaven, would he believe Satan's account of it. In every

aesthetic choice he made—the selection of genre, the expansion of the Genesis account of the Fall to include the entire story of Satan's fall, the beginning in Hell, the use of a grand style—Milton, not Satan, exposed his readers to vice with all its baits, so that the reader would know error by erring, and in that sense might know evil in the poem as he knows it in life—by doing evil.

If this uncomfortable truth has been largely obscured by the efforts of critics anxious to save Milton from the charge of devil worship, then these efforts have been made easier by a general critical indifference to the principle of sequential reading. Like a great palindrome, *Paradise Lost* often seems to invite us to read it backward as well as forward, an invitation most critics accept. There is a danger, however, in criticism that flattens a work of art into its "meaning" without examining how that meaning comes about. Although no one would accept a statement like "the Fall was, perhaps, fortunate" as an adequate substitute for the experience of reading *Paradise Lost*, the tendency of much criticism is to "decode" the poem into some such philosophic proposition, leaving one to wonder why the poet bothered to encode it in the first place. The point, at least for poetry, is not the bare message, but the process of arriving at it. Like Joyce or Proust, Milton thrusts us into the midst of things; part of the reading experience is confusion, which prepares us for a fresher, better ordering than we have previously known.

Why confuse a reader? Why mislead him? The answer is that *Paradise Lost* adopts a paradoxical technique to portray a paradoxical universe. In the poem as a whole, and in every part of it, prime polarities of human experience are distinguished, confused, distinguished again at a higher level. Out of a dialectical struggle of opposites emerges, by a leap of faith, a higher, spiritual meaning of words, things, experience: in darkness there is light; we rise by falling; death is the gate of life; the blind have "inner sight"; God brings good out of evil. Such puzzling truths cannot be handed to a reader; they are inert unless and until they are lived through: misunderstood, rejected, perceived afresh, partially understood, gradually accepted. This is why a poem—and only a poem, in Milton's view—can justify God's ways to men. But before he can find his way, the reader must lose it.

> Of Man's First Disobedience, and the Fruit
> Of that Forbidden Tree, whose mortal taste

Brought Death into the World, and all our woe,
With loss of Eden, till one greater Man
Restore us, and regain the blissful Seat,
Sing Heav'nly Muse, that of the secret top
Of Oreb, or of Sinai, didst inspire
That Shepherd, who first taught the chosen Seed,
In the Beginning how the Heav'ns and Earth
Rose out of Chaos: Or if Sion Hill
Delight thee more, and Siloa's Brook that flow'd
Fast by the Oracle of God; I thence
Invoke thy aid to my advent'rous Song,
That with no middle flight intends to soar
Above th' Aonian Mount, while it pursues
Things unattempted yet in Prose or Rhyme. (I, 1–16)

The poem's propensity for confusing its reader begins with the opening lines, a "prologue" as famous and often-quoted as any passage of English poetry. I will not dispute the beauty of these lines, whose varied rhythm, sound, and diction, along with their syntactic complexity, create a breathless sense of energy and motion that is the best possible proof of their claim to begin something greater than literature has ever before attempted, nor will I deny their efficiency, both in portraying a "reliable narrator" worthy of Milton's great argument and in briefly foreshadowing the poem ahead. But explication falsifies the experience of reading unless it also points out the obverse of this prologue's virtues.

For Milton's opening is not only grand but grandiloquent: its sweep implies cursoriness; and its suggestiveness, vagueness. In promising to sing of so much the poet gives no specific idea of what, in fact, he is going to sing. The scores of published explications of these lines, the crabbed footnotes encroaching ever upward on the page toward the poem's text, are themselves backhanded testimony to critical fears that the unguided reader will be confused by all these poetic riches. The critic who deprives us of that confusion, by implying that Milton's "fit reader" does not grope a bit for the shepherd's name or hesitate between Oreb and Sinai, distorts by that much the experience of reading the poem. The periphrases, the hesitations are there; the footnotes are ours, not Milton's.

Classical epics begin by proposing to sing about "a man," or "the man"; Milton's epic proposes "Man," the entire human race. Vergil's plot summary moves from Troy to Italy, looks forward from Aeneas's career to the building of Rome; Milton's prologue sketches in a plot that spans all

time and extends physically to the whole Earth and beyond to Heaven
and Chaos. With so much compressed into so brief a space, events, men,
and objects rush past us in a blur. Biblical history is played out twice
before our eyes. Man's first disobedience and loss of Eden yield suddenly
to Christ and the Resurrection; then we are back with Moses on the
mountain, then with David or Isaiah or Jesus by the streams of Sion and
Siloa.

The reader's mind is kept racing after allusions—even though he
knows Moses and Parnassus, it will take a moment to name them men-
tally—while the syntactic units succeed each other in logical but complex
order, so that, like the narrator, it dips and soars, hovering but never able
to land. Who is singing: Milton or the Muse? What is he singing about:
Adam or Christ, Eden or the Holy Land? The poet keeps the prime
polarities of life—light and dark, rising and falling, death and life, bliss
and woe, creation and destruction—aloft simultaneously, like so many
juggler's balls.

Is this poet proud or humble? No sooner has he boasted of "Things
unattempted yet in Prose or Rhyme," than he is genuflecting humbly to
the Holy Spirit:

> And chiefly Thou O Spirit, that dost prefer
> Before all Temples th' upright heart and pure,
> Instruct me, for Thou know'st; Thou from the first
> Wast present, and with mighty wings outspread
> Dove-like satst brooding on the vast Abyss
> And mad'st it pregnant: What in me is dark
> Illumine, what is low raise and support;
> That to the highth of this great Argument
> I may assert Eternal Providence,
> And justify the ways of God to men. (I, 17–26)

Here at last the mind can alight; departing from his classical models, the
speaker prays. Stability comes partly from the shorter syntactic units,
partly from the familiar biblical phrases, partly from the dramatic setting
of prayer, as opposed to the flight of the previous sentence. Yet this se-
curity comes at the price of undercutting the conventions of classical
epic. The muse is no daughter of Zeus but God himself; he (she?) is
sought not on Parnassus or even Sinai but in the heart prepared to receive him; he flies while we kneel. The gods of Homer and Vergil are

notoriously fickle, but our God is above all a *creator*; his ways are just and justifiable. The poem, then, promises rather overtly to be not one to set beside previous epics but one to annihilate them.

The second part of Milton's prologue, by extending to the reader stability, clarity, and order, gives him a kind of reassurance, but in undermining the first part it complicates the reader's position still further. What Milton has done, after all, is to propose to sing of Truth in a genre whose basic conventions, he goes on to imply, are transparent fictions— exactly the position of the singer in "Lycidas," who, in order to ease the pain of death and loss, dallies with the false consolations of pastoral elegy. The prologue gives something (the imitation of classical epic) in order to take it away (denial of the truth of epic conventions) and finally promises to give something better—not an idle tale to kill time, but a saving Truth to redeem time. It both warns and reassures: warns us that this imitation of pagan fable is not to be taken at face value, and reassures us that within or behind or above that fable is an argument that asserts Eternal Providence. Read rightly, as has been well and often observed in other senses, the prologue is a microcosm of the experience of reading the whole poem: *through* confusing appearances ("on the secret top Of Oreb, or of Sinai . . . Or if Sion Hill Delight thee more") *to* the inner reality ("Instruct me, for Thou know'st"). Needless to say, however, that "inner reality" is not an object of cognition but an act of faith.

To cram so much (and more) into twenty-six lines of poetry is to risk confusion, although the reader is likelier to blame himself than Milton for his sense of disorientation. The plot summary, in its scope, promises that the story ahead will be as difficult to understand as it presumably will be to tell, while the prayer, though it gives both speaker and reader a sort of blind confidence, sheds little light on the shape of what is to come. Even more than the narrator, the reader is flying blind, aroused and excited about the great thing beginning, but with little inkling of what it really is. If he clutches at "Man's First Disobedience" he will find himself mistaken; that event is over eight books away. "Man" himself will not put in an appearance for twenty-five hundred lines. Small wonder if he seizes gratefully on the poet's question of causality, which seems to offer, in the promise of a definite and concrete answer, an end to uncertainty as to where this poem is headed, even though the answer, unaccountably, turns out to be "straight to Hell":

> Say first, for Heav'n hides nothing from thy view
> Nor the deep Tract of Hell, say first what cause
> Mov'd our Grand Parents in that happy State,
> Favor'd of Heav'n so highly, to fall off
> From thir Creator, and transgress his Will
> For one restraint, Lords of the World besides?
> Who first seduc'd them to that foul revolt?
> Th' infernal Serpent; hee it was, whose guile
> Stirr'd up with Envy and Revenge, deceiv'd
> The Mother of Mankind; what time his Pride
> Had cast him out from Heav'n. (I,27–37)

The reader's gratitude at being given a definite answer to a definite question may account for the ease with which he accepts what is, by standards of the poem's Christian doctrine, a very strange result indeed. For when Milton's narrator asks "what cause?" then rephrases the question as "Who first seduc'd them to that foul revolt?" he leaves the impression that the two questions are interchangeable. Yet any student of *Paradise Lost* knows that strictly speaking they are not, that Milton's justification of God's ways turns upon Adam and Eve's freedom to fall or not to fall. The word "cause" invokes determinism and denies that freedom, for which reason Milton avoids it in his discussion of the Fall in *Christian Doctrine*: "This sin was instigated first by the devil. . . . Secondly it was instigated by man's own inconstant nature, which meant that he, like the devil before him, did not stand firm in the truth" (pp. 382–83). To instigate an action is to provoke it, to push someone towards it; instigation, unlike causation, does not imply a foregone conclusion. Nothing, in Milton's view, caused man's free choice to revolt against God: not man's inconstant nature (God made that nature), and certainly not the infernal serpent. Any attribution of causes, though it may seem at first to focus the reader's hostility in the right direction, cannot logically stop until it reaches back to the First Cause, God himself.

Curiously, though, I have never heard or seen the word objected to by any reader of *Paradise Lost*. The reasons I believe are two. The first is that at this early point there is no reason for the reader to suppose that the issue of free will versus determinism is of so central an importance to this poem. The second is the easy assumption (which Milton encourages and takes advantage of) that epic conventions belong in *Paradise Lost* simply because they are part of the generic tradition. Apparently even the professional Miltonist, that expert rereader, sees in "what cause?" little more than a convenient transition to the *in medias res* opening in Hell. Yet Milton has used the reader's willingness to leave epic convention unquestioned as a way of fostering a misunderstanding: a poem that ultimately will teach that Satan was not the "cause" of humanity's ruin begins by suggesting that he is exactly that.

Speaking from the vantage point of hindsight, "what cause?" is one of Milton's most misleading moves, but as we encounter it in the poem it seems quite the opposite. In the midst of so much uncertainty, the epic question pronounces a clear and reassuring subtext—"this poem is an epic"—that seems to promise at least a partial stay against confusion. Epic convention, both in the broad sense of the norms of heroic story-telling and in the narrow sense of the devices of classical epic, becomes the reader's map of what lies ahead. But in handing him this map, Milton has—for the most serious of reasons—again tricked his reader.

Like "darkness visible" or "fortunate fall," "Christian epic" is in Milton's hands an oxymoron whose literal self-contradiction forces the mind to perceive a higher, super-logical level of meaning. The contradiction in this case lies in a Christian (ultimately Platonic) antithesis between art and truth. Art is fiction, fable, illusion, lies; Christianity is Truth. Realizing that art can often influence man's emotional nature in a way that bare truth cannot, even strict Puritans allowed some latitude for the arts of music and poetry to adorn the truths of religion. The tradition of classical epic, however, is much harder to square with Christian doctrine, since its very conventions embody a pagan view of life. Even in the *Aeneid*, that most spiritual and contemplative of the great ancient epics, the subject matter is war and killing, the philosophy is this-worldly, man is viewed as plaything of the gods.

The prestige of Homer and Vergil was such that Renaissance poets never abandoned their quest for a Christian equivalent, but the story of Renaissance Christian epic, based upon classical models, is, from Vida's *Christiad* to Cowley's *Davideis*, as uninspiring a chapter in literary history as one would hope to find, piety and poetry pulling in opposite directions with one (usually both) the clear victim. As E. R. Curtius has put it, with Miltonic scorn:

> Throughout its existence—from Juvencus to Klopstock—the Biblical epic was a hybrid with an inner lack of truth, a *genre faux*. The

Christian story of salvation, as the Bible presents it, admits no transformation into pseudo-antique form. Not only does it thereby lose its
powerful, unique, authoritative expression, but it is falsified by the
genre borrowed from antique Classicism and by the concomitant lin-
guistic and metrical conventions. That the Biblical epic could nevertheless enjoy such great popularity is explained only by the need for an
ecclesiastical literature which could be matched with and opposed to
antique literature. So a compromise was reached.[2]

Because of the Christian antithesis between art and truth, *Paradise Lost*
does not merely *contain* paradoxes, it *is* a paradox: a poem apparently at
war with itself. By bringing to the pagan heroic poem a radically different
notion of "heroism," (which is to say, an entirely different hierarchy of
values) it takes epic form apart at the seams, restitching it into a very
different garment.

In time, Milton's reader will discover this fact for himself. As Milton's narrator observes late in the poem, the classical epic genre is not
well suited to a view of life whose supreme hero is a mild and pacific
carpenter executed for preaching politically offensive doctrines. True
heroism, Milton says, is "Patience and Heroic Martyrdom" (IX,32); how
to celebrate such unepical virtue in epical form is, he implies, the problem that prevented him for so long from beginning his poem:

> Since first this Subject for Heroic Song
> Pleas'd me long choosing, and beginning late;
> Not sedulous by Nature to indite
> Wars, hitherto the only Argument
> Heroic deem'd. . . . (IX,25–29)

But the subject of classical epic *is*, primarily, "wars," or at least martial
virtue, as exemplified in Achilles, Hector, Odysseus, and Aeneas. Of Milton's predecessors, Torquato Tasso was perhaps alone in achieving a
Christian poem based upon classical models that succeeding ages did not
let die; but of course Tasso too indited wars; his poem stands condemned
with the *Iliad* and the *Aeneid* in the passage just quoted.

After the first two books, wherever *Paradise Lost* touches upon battle, combat, or men in arms, it does so to deflate them: whether in the
promised duel of Satan and Gabriel, which, because its issue has already
been decided in advance by God, anticlimactically fails to take place (end
of Book IV); or in the tedious havoc of the War in Heaven, which force of

arms cannot solve until the Son chases the rebels out of Heaven with
highly metaphorical thunder and arrows (end of Book VI); or in the example of Nimrod, whose great martial power achieves nothing but confusion and destruction (beginning of Book XII):

> Contemporary critical theory and practice have accustomed us to the
> notion of the "anti-novel" and the "anti-hero." It is now at last obvious
> what *Paradise Lost* is. It is the anti-epic. Wherever we turn we find
> the traditional epic values inverted. It closed the history of this poetic
> genre in England—the epic form as understood by Petrarch, Ronsard,
> Vida, or (for that matter) Boileau and Dryden. It closed the history of
> the epic (for you will not expect me to comment on the unspeakable
> labours of Blakemore, Glover, and Wilkie).
>   Never was the death of an art form celebrated with such a magnani-
> mous ceremony, splendid in ashes and pompous in the grave. The
> death of tragedy was a mere decline into a whine and a whisper. But
> the death of epic was, in Milton's hands, a glorious and perfectly staged
> suicide.[3]

When we say, then, that *Paradise Lost* is an imitation of the *Iliad*, of
the *Aeneid*, or even of *Gerusalemma Liberata*, we utter a half-truth, unless we add that it is very explicitly a trenchant *critique* of the values
those poems embody. Milton's poem is as much anti-epic as it is epic, and
formally it inverts many of the epic norms, as Dryden perceived when he
complained that in Milton's epic the dragon won the day and sent the
knight forth with his lady-errant.

But the reader, as he begins to read, does not know all this, and
Milton makes him read more than half the poem before telling him. The
poem's method, in other words, is to establish in the reader's mind an
initial view of things that can then be undermined gradually, until it finally collapses into its opposite. At the beginning the reader is given an
apparently martial poem to read and an apparent military hero to watch.
He is both relieved and apprehensive: relieved that after the confusions
of the prologue the poem has turned definite and specific, but apprehensive as to the direction of that turn. One does not expect, in beginning a
Christian poem, to find at its center a character named Satan. The
reader's normal propensity for involving himself with a story's chief character collides immediately with his clear understanding of the Christian
implications of such involvement.

The reader's first and biggest problem with Satan is how to react to him, a problem that is not an accident of history but a result of the poem's design: its ethical villain, Satan, is the poem's structural hero, at least for two, and arguably for six, books. We follow, with interruptions, Satan's progress from the burning lake, through Hell and Chaos, to Eden, and encounter Adam and Eve with him. When he leaves the scene Raphael arrives to tell Adam (and us) of Satan's earlier exploits in Heaven. Not until Book VII does the plot shift definitively to the poem's true subject, the relations between God and man.

In terms of characterization, too, Satan is unique; no previous literary experience can surely guide our responses. As the poem unfolds he comes more and more to resemble the stock devil of the medieval morality plays, but at least in Books I and II the two figures have almost nothing in common except a name. Initially Satan bears a much stronger resemblance to certain bad heroes of Renaissance drama, most notably to the blood-spattered Macbeth who strides over the blasted heath, surrounded by the mangled bodies of friends and enemies, muttering "So foul and fair a day I have not seen." A great sinner who incarnates on a heroic scale our own worse natures and suffers hugely for his heroic villainy, Satan is a bit like Macbeth; just as he is, in another way, like Aeneas, who is found shipwrecked and despairing on the coast of Africa at the opening of Vergil's epic.

What makes these parallels disturbing is that they seem to extenuate the Antichrist. Within the framework of the *Aeneid*'s values, Aeneas is a supremely good man. Macbeth himself, although heroically bad, is after all a *man*, and hence the worthy object of our compassion. The shocking thing about Milton's Satan is that although every reader knows Satan is not even human, he is persistently portrayed as though he were. The effect is, so far as I know, unique in literature and probably unrepeatable. The reader, who knows he ought not—must not—feel sympathy for or identification with this protagonist, is subjected—in every way a great poet can devise—to the temptation to feel precisely such sympathy and identification.

We normally identify with the main character in any story, and Satan has no rivals for our interest in Books I and II of *Paradise Lost*. He is cast in the mold of the epic hero, which demands of us certain positive responses to time-tested human virtues: courage, strength, endurance, leadership, eloquence, and self-esteem. In Books I and II Satan has, or seems to have, all of these qualities. Our knowledge of Satan's crimes is second-hand, and he puts them in a flattering light. Perhaps most important, Satan, although he is fallen and wicked, can count on a certain indulgence from his fallen, wicked audience. As in *Macbeth*, what is most horrifying is not his awful crimes, but our dawning sense of complicity in them.

However, unlike the audience at *Macbeth*, who must sort things out without benefit of explicit authorial intrusion, the reader of *Paradise Lost* has an authority to turn to, Milton's "reliable narrator," that friend and guide through the poem's complexities and pitfalls. Even before Satan speaks, as if to forestall the reader's impending ambivalence toward a protagonist-villain, the narrator introduces Satan by denouncing him:

> Who first seduc'd them to the foul revolt?
> Th' infernal Serpent; hee it was, whose guile
> Stirr'd up with Envy and Revenge, deceiv'd
> The Mother of Mankind; what time his Pride
> Had cast him out from Heav'n, with all his Host
> Of Rebel Angels, by whose aid aspiring
> To set himself in Glory above his Peers,
> He trusted to have equall'd the most High,
> If he oppos'd; and with ambitious aim
> Against the Throne and Monarchy of God
> Rais'd impious War in Heav'n and Battle proud
> With vain attempt. Him the Almighty Power
> Hurl'd headlong flaming from th' Ethereal Sky
> With hideous ruin and combustion down
> To bottomless perdition, there to dwell
> In Adamantine Chains and penal Fire,
> Who durst defy th' Omnipotent to Arms. (I,33–49)

This passage labels Satan as the villain of the poem, the object of the narrator's practically gloating scorn, but what it does not do is at least as important as what it does. It does not explain Satan's situation in terms of Christian ethics: God's goodness to Satan in giving him a preeminent place in Heaven; the absurdity of opposing Omnipotence; the fact that Satan's sufferings are the inevitable consequences of a creature's voluntary self-alienation from the Creator.

Instead, the issue between God and Satan is assimilated to the norms of the epic, in which worldly opponents battle each other for worldly gain or glory in a contest that is by Christian standards morally neutral, since each side is as bad as the other. The terms of this denunciation are recognizably those of epic—monarchs and rebels, wars and battles, the scoffing victor, the abject victim. The style, too, is appropriately grand and pompous, with protracted, rolling periods, exotic word order ("Battle proud"), hyperbole ("Adamantine Chains"), periphrasis ("the most High"), and emphatic sound effects that echo the hiss of lightning and rumble of thunder in lines like "Hurl'd headlong flaming from th' Ethereal Sky." After this passage, no reader need be in doubt that Satan is this poem's villain: deceitful, envious, vengeful, proud, and ambitious. But the epic terms of this denunciation make it vulnerable to the kind of self-defense Satan is about to make.

For Satan defends himself not by denying that he is envious, vengeful, proud, and ambitious but by attributing these traits to God as well. When the narrator fails to rebut these attributions, but rather seems to support them, the ethical lines of the story become hopelessly blurred. Although he clearly affixes the label of "villain" to Satan, he does so in a way that makes the word mean little more than "loser," a role that Satan turns to his own rhetorical advantage. Striking the posture of a hero rising from defeat, Satan tries to evoke both pity at his fall ("If thou beest hee; But O how fall'n," I,84) and admiration at his renewed determination to prevail ("What though the field be lost? All is not lost," I,105–106). What the epic voice denounced as villainous, Satan defends as heroic, and this obvious, almost operatic disagreement between the two distracts the reader from noticing that they otherwise agree, or fail to disagree, on everything else.

Both represent the issue between God and the fallen archangel as a power struggle; Satan's "so much the stronger prov'd He with his Thunder" (I, 92–93) simply echoes the narrator's "Him the Almighty Power Hurl'd headlong flaming from th' Ethereal Sky" (I, 44–45), a line that suggests Divine brutality and tyranny as effectively as anything Satan subsequently says. With the narrator's view of God as "almighty Power" and "Omnipotent," Satan has at this point no disagreement, since such epithets accord perfectly with his version of himself as the victim of superior force. And although the narrator does not refer to God as such, "adamantine chains and penal fire" are certainly what we might expect from a tyrant. So, while overtly condemning Satan, the narrator is also, though less obviously, corroborating a view of the War in Heaven that supports Satan's claim to be God's victim.

Book VI lies far ahead of us. What Satan asserts and the epic voice does not deny, we must, perforce, accept as true, however anxious and unhappy that "truth" may make us. The more Milton's narrator heaps on the flames and chains and tortures of Hell, the more appropriate seems Satan's resolution never to submit to divine *power*. As if unwittingly, the epic voice is making Satan's point for him; and when the narrator turns from denunciation to picturing the sufferings of Hell, going so far as to break out at one point "O how unlike the place from whence they fell!" (I, 75), he is again preparing the reader to feel the pathos of Satan's situation, which the latter exploits so brilliantly. The antidote to this pathos is not the narrator's previous bloodthirsty exultation over the superior force of God's armament, which simply makes us sorry for Satan, but the discovery we will make first in Book IV, that Satan's own spiritual condition *creates* Hell wherever he is ("myself am Hell"), that Hell is the creature's voluntary self-exile from his Creator.

But how can the narrator convey such inward, spiritual truths in a worldly, physical genre like the epic? He cannot—not directly, at any rate. Since Hell is his setting, it must be a physical setting (which means it must seem God's doing), just as Satan, as central character, must be the epic protagonist. A choice of form narrows all subsequent choices: not only how he says it, but what he says. The real conflict in *Paradise Lost*, despite the narrator's ostentatious hostility toward Satan, is not between narrative and dramatic voices, but between Christian and epic norms, which are—both intrinsically and by Miltonic fiat—irreconcilable, as Milton's decision to make Satan the archetypal warrior suggests.

We ordinarily come to literature to dispel the ambiguities of "real life"; in *Paradise Lost* we find them exacerbated. Tensions between Satan's devotion to evil and his heroic rhetoric, between the narrator's overt condemnation of Satan and his covert defamation of God, between the poem's epic form and Christian content, like the local, more obvious tensions of "darkness visible" and "evil be thou my good," all document how profoundly paradoxical Milton's method is. Two points of view—frames of reference, systems of value—are in overt and irreconcilable conflict. One sees God as just and good, and Satan as evil, weak, pitiful; the other sees God as a tyrant, and Satan as the heroic rebel against divine oppression. The two are in open conflict for the reader's loyalty—look upon this picture and this—but although the poem ultimately does ample justice to the first, in Books I and II it is merely asserted, in the briefest of fashions, and never demonstrated.

The reader, who can neither deny the truths of the Christian faith nor *apply* them to the story the narrator is telling, is forced into the extraordinary position of simultaneously affirming and ignoring the truth, which he can manage only because in the context of Hell Christian truth is always general and abstract. If the epic voice were to apply the Christian perspective concretely to the Satanic story, then not only would the poem's epic pretensions be punctured but the reader would be prevented from making the same mistakes as Satan, which, given Milton's purposes, would be a pity.

One does not expect to feel ambivalence toward the "Author of All Ill"; yet even before Satan speaks we are confused and disoriented in our feelings toward the victim of so much punishment, the sufferer of so much pain. Satan's own self-portrait is ambiguous, and it is impossible to read his speeches in Books I and II without feeling ambivalent. To prove that Satan is hateful we need hardly mention his calculation, his arrogance, his self-centeredness; the fact is, he *admits* he is bad. But those who say they hate him ignore his epic and tragic virtues—his resolution, his strength, his capacity to bear suffering:

> If thou beest hee; But O how fall'n! how chang'd
> From him, who in the happy Realms of Light
> Cloth'd with transcendant brightness didst outshine
> Myriads though bright. (I,84–87)

We neither like nor hate Satan; we do both, simultaneously, to our own intense discomfort.

The strength of Satan's self-defense lies where we would least expect it—in the large concessions he is able to make to Christian doctrine. He never dodges the label of "badness," yet he confuses the reader by associating the idea of "evil" with things attractive or admirable, while he associates "good" with things repugnant. In the passage quoted above, Satan's condition, shorn of heavenly light, is evidence of Christian reprobation, but Satan turns it into an occasion for pathos at the spectacle of a fallen hero—shipwrecked Aeneas, or bloody, fallen Hector. In this pathetic, fallen condition, Satan asserts his will to resist:

> What though the field be lost?
> All is not lost; the unconquerable Will,
> And study of revenge, immortal hate,
> And courage never to submit or yield:
> And what is else not to be overcome? (I,105–109)

Again there is a false note in "immortal hate" to keep us uneasy, but extreme situations call for extreme remedies. In the epic perspective it is humanly necessary and ethically right to continue to fight against an unrelenting enemy: the more hopeless the cause, the braver the resolution. "Immortal hate" bothers us, in other words, as much for what it says about God as what it tells us about Satan. Under the circumstances, why should Satan behave better than God?

> Fall'n Cherub, to be weak is miserable
> Doing or Suffering: but of this be sure,
> To do aught good never will be our task,
> But ever to do ill our sole delight,
> As being the contrary to his high will
> Whom we resist. If then his Providence
> Out of our evil seek to bring forth good,
> Our labor must be to pervert that end,
> And out of good still to find means of evil. (I, 157–65)

Ordinarily, when someone announces his hatred of the "good," he irrevocably alienates his listeners. Here, however, Satan's word "good" stands in apposition to Beelzebub's "eternal punishment," reminding us that, since God's will is, by definition, good, eternal punishment fits into the official Christian system under the rubric "good," while resistance to such punishment is, by stipulation, "evil." If God is indeed an "angry victor" (I, 169), as both Satan and the narrator suggest, if Christianity is a doctrine of infinite punishment for finite transgression, then rebellion is not only necessary but admirable.

The tension in *Paradise Lost* is not primarily between the misguided voice of Satan and the inspired voice of the blind bard, but *within* each, in their own self-contradictions. Neither Satan nor the narrator will let us side entirely with God or with his enemies. By making Satan in part attractive and God commensurately repellent, while all along insisting that the reader should not find them so, Milton is in effect both telling us that we are like Satan and making us feel the kind of confused resentment toward his conception of good and evil that proves his point. And by demanding that we recognize as good something that we cannot help disliking, the poem angers or humiliates us, undermines our self-confidence and self-esteem. Instead of contemplating Hell we are *enacting* it in our own minds and feelings, learning about the fallen condition by *feeling fallen*, feeling, that is, like Satan.[4]

If all I have said makes this book's reader uneasy, it may be because I have apparently ignored the capacity of Milton's reader to perceive or impose hierarchies. The common sense objection to what I have said so far is that epic pattern may make Satan *seem* a hero, but the reader's knowledge of the poem's Christian purpose will keep him from assenting to that impression. Repeatedly Milton's text asks the reader to choose between antithetical contexts, epic and Christian. Will responsible readers be able to make the right choice?

My belief is that they will not. Our first choice is between the dramatized words of Satan and the interpretations of the narrator. Not all of us will make the "right" choice here, since Satan's words are much more ample and vivid than those of the narrator. But even supposing we prefer the narrator's superior authority, we will still be forced to discriminate between ways of interpreting *his* words. For example, after Satan's first speech the narrator makes that comment we have already examined in the Introduction:

> So spake th' Apostate Angel, though in pain,
> Vaunting aloud, but rackt with deep despair. (I, 125–26)

To look only at diction, the word "Apostate" invokes a Christian frame of reference; "Vaunting" is part of the stock vocabulary of epic poetry, while such words as "pain" and "despair" fit either context, with a suitable adjustment of meaning. We know that Christian despair is the extremity of spiritual misery, while secular despair is an obstacle epic heroes must sometimes surmount by dissembling. Which context do we apply?

Despite the presence of "Apostate Angel," and no matter how determined the reader is to give "despair" its full Christian weight, the message is at best ambiguous, since the narrator himself continually endorses the epic context, as when he follows the two lines quoted above with a final "And him thus answer'd soon his bold Compeer" (I, 127). The world of bold compeers and inverted poetic syntax is, needless to say, not that of Christian truth.

The poet himself gives us a choice between a Satan who is coping heroically and a wretch who is unable to cope. We are under pressure from his ideology to read Satan one way, but under equal pressure from verbal and dramatic structures to read him the other way. Hierarchy keeps the reader uneasy, but it does not stop him from imagining what the poem invites him to imagine, especially since, if we give the narrator's utterances their full Christian weight, we will frequently find the poem's entire structure crumbling beneath it.

When Satan prepares to rise from the fiery lake, the narrator intrudes with a reminder of the implications of God's omnipotence:

> So stretcht out huge in length the Arch-fiend lay
> Chain'd on the burning Lake, nor ever thence
> Had ris'n or heav'd his head, but that the will
> And high permission of all-ruling Heaven
> Left him at large to his own dark designs,
> That with reiterated crimes he might
> Heap on himself damnation, while he sought
> Evil to others, and enrag'd might see
> How all his malice serv'd but to bring forth
> Infinite goodness, grace and mercy shown
> On Man by him seduc't, but on himself
> Treble confusion, wrath and vengeance pour'd. (I, 209–20)

That Satan could never have "ris'n or heav'd his head" without God's permission is impeccable Christian doctrine, yet it threatens the credibility of Books I and II entire: if Satan is God's helpless thrall, then no contest is possible between such hopelessly mismatched opponents. Yet what do Milton's first two books argue if not that Satan is God's potent adversary? This corrective comment threatens to cancel his entire epic canvas. In order to go on reading, we must ignore the implication.

Ignoring is not oblivion, however, and beneath the surface half-formed doubts are fermenting. Doubts such as: in letting Satan rise, God must foresee that he will commit "reiterated crimes"; will, in fact, seduce mankind, at which point God will forgive Satan's victims. Since one does not *forgive* a victim, however, God's treatment implies that we are, like Satan, culprits. Indeed, the news that human suffering ("all our woe") was brought into the world simply so that Satan "might see" how all his evil is turned eventually to good (Satan is instructed at mankind's expense) is ill-suited to allay a reader's suspicions that good and evil are not in this poem quite what he would have supposed. Worse yet, if Satan caused the Fall, and if God, foreknowing his success, permitted him to try, then God too caused the Fall, and is now graciously forgiving his own victims.

That such implications consciously occur to many readers seems unlikely. We are prevented from drawing explicit anti-Christian conclusions by our secure knowledge (fostered by the prologue) that the poem has a Christian purpose. If in the materialistic, fatalistic context of classical epic genre too much thinking about Christian truths twists them into wicked paradoxes, then the responsible reader will avoid thinking and will accept on faith. He sees Satan rising and is told to disbelieve what he sees; he sees a God who permits Satan to seduce mankind and is asked to think of that God as gracious and merciful. Corrective commentary is his first lesson in disbelief of the senses and in disbelief of reason. Yet Milton's poem has continually spoken, and will continue to speak, both to his senses and to his reason. As yet we see too much to be able to "see," a condition for which the poem, although itself responsible, seems to scold us; like other aspects of the poem we have already discussed, corrective commentary argues our strangeness to the ways of God, our kinship to Satan.

Corrective comments often precede another turn of the screw. As soon as we have been warned that Satan is God's helpless thrall, he (Satan) begins to grow in stature, and within a few lines he strikes his most heroic posture thus far:

> Farewell happy Fields
> Where Joy for ever dwells: Hail horrors, hail
> Infernal world, and thou profoundest Hell
> Receive thy new Possessor: One who brings
> A mind not to be chang'd by Place or Time.
> The mind is its own place, and in itself
> Can make a Heav'n of Hell, a Hell of Heav'n. (I,249–55)

Although "The mind is its own place" hints at the true nature of Satan's predicament ("myself am Hell"), in this context it asserts the same belief in the superiority of spirit over matter that is so important a tenet of Christianity itself. The physicality of epic poetry, the poet's apparently resolute determination to make Hell a *place* that can be spiritually transcended, rather than itself a spiritual condition, makes Satan seem not merely an epic hero, but a Protestant Christian one as well, whose vaunt echoes the poet's own boastful reliance on inner light and the inner voice.[5]

Pity for Satan is suppressed hereafter. Instead of appearing merely human, Satan will from now on appear superhuman, and we will be bracketed not with him but with his followers. At first mention the fallen angels are not only passive and apparently helpless, as was Satan when first described floating on the lake of Hell, but also, unlike Satan, seemingly small and petty, like "Autumnal Leaves" (I,302) or "scatter'd sedge Afloat" (I,304–305). Responding to Satan's dread voice, they rise up like "a pitchy cloud Of Locusts" (I,340–41), and, having landed, they are compared to the northern barbarians who invaded Rome. This progression of similes closes distance between human reader and fallen angels, who enter the poem imagined as barely animate and who then end the progression figured as human warriors. Milton's art, like an "Optic glass," brings them closer to us.

As with Satan, who is "described" principally in terms of likeness—like Leviathan, like a tower—or by side-glances at his shield and spear, the fallen angels are evoked either in superlatives that call forth no precise pictures—"Godlike shapes and forms Excelling human, Princely Dignities, And Powers that erst in Heaven sat on Thrones" (I,358–60)—or in similitudes, which seem always to have false bottoms. The progression from "Autumnal Leaves" to "Princely Dignities" makes us slightly uneasy, because it suggests that Milton can make us see the fallen angels any way he wishes, and this sense of unease is augmented by similes that liken Satan alternately to "Busiris and his Memphian Chivalry" (I,307) and to "Amram's Son" (I,339)—both to Pharoah and to Moses.

But the catalog of principal devils soon finds what appears both a safer and more vivid technique of description, one that rests not upon the "fables" of pagan mythology or of epic convention but upon Old Testament truth, as Satan's followers are described in terms of their future careers as corruptors of mankind:

> The chief were those who from the Pit of Hell
> Roaming to seek thir prey on earth, durst fix
> Thir Seats long after next the Seat of God,
> Thir Altars by his Altar, Gods ador'd
> Among the Nations round, and durst abide
> Jehovah thund'ring out of Sion, thron'd
> Between the Cherubim; yea, often plac'd
> Within his Sanctuary itself thir Shrines,
> Abominations; and with cursed things
> His holy Rites, and solemn Feasts profan'd,
> And with thir darkness durst affront his light. (I,381–91)

In the ensuing description of the subsequent careers of the fallen angels Milton has found a way of condemning Satan's followers that is neither fictional nor abstract but repulsively visual and concrete. The trouble is that as the pictures of Satanic evil become more direct and "truthful," it becomes harder to ignore the fact that we are being given pictures not of evil spirits but of evil human beings.

The first, and most horrifying, description is of Moloch:

> First Moloch, horrid King besmear'd with blood
> Of human sacrifice, and parents' tears,
> Though for the noise of Drums and Timbrels loud
> Thir children's cries unheard, that pass'd through fire
> To his grim Idol. (I,392–96)

This sentence, whose verbs avoid agency, is carefully stage-managed to conceal, or *almost* conceal, the true culprits. Yet when we ask who the actors in this ghastly scene are, the answer is clear. Not Moloch but his effigy, the product of human hands, presides "besmear'd with blood." The "god" himself is present not physically but in the hearts of his human worshippers, who in effect "are" Moloch, or become him in the horrid ritual of human sacrifice. Without them, Moloch would not have a name (I,361–65); hence, he would not even exist, at least as far as human beings are concerned.

But Moloch was worshipped long ago; we are insulated from him by vast reaches of time and space; while Belial, who ends the list, gives an image not merely of ancient vice but of modern vice as well. Moreover, Belial is not only an historic pagan deity but also the Hebrew word for "profligacy" or "worthlessness":

> To him no Temple stood
> Or Altar smok'd; yet who more oft than hee
> In Temples and at Altars, when the Priest
> Turns Atheist, as did Ely's Sons, who fill'd
> With lust and violence the house of God. (I,492–96)

If Belial is simply the Hebrew noun for a human trait, then Belial as fallen angel is not "truth" but "fiction," and the impressive roll call of fallen angels collapses into a portrait of the human race—Milton has drawn not their portrait but *ours*:

> In Courts and Palaces he also Reigns
> And in luxurious Cities, where the noise
> Of riot ascends above thir loftiest Tow'rs,

And injury and outrage: And when Night
Darkens the Streets, then wander forth the Sons
Of Belial, flown with insolence and wine. (I,497–502)

This is the subtext of the entire catalog of devils—the lust and hatred of
the human heart, figured first in a series of quaint Old Testament vignettes, which finally reach forward into the present tense, explicitly encompassing us as well.

Milton's epic catalog is another instance of his adopting an aspect of
classical epic form for purposes antithetical to those of his model. Homer's list of ships in the *Iliad* was a device for involving his audience in
his story by naming their own illustrious ancestors among the victorious
invaders of Asia Minor. Milton, too, involves his audience in the story by
providing a capsule history of *their* ancestors—not just "the greatest part
Of Mankind" (I,367–68) but the spiritual ancestors of seventeenth-century Protestants, God's chosen people:

For those the Race of Israel oft forsook
Thir living strength, and unfrequented left
His righteous Altar, bowing lowly down
To bestial Gods; for which thir heads as low
Bow'd down in Battle, sunk before the Spear
Of despicable foes. (I,432–37)

Such reminders humble rather than flatter Milton's audience, who are
compelled to see that he is describing not their ancestors' victories, but
their defeats, and not merely their ancestors' but their own defeats as
well. Every fallen man has bowed down to bestial gods; if not to Moloch,
then to Belial.

Like every aspect of his technique that we have examined thus far,
Milton's portrait of his audience is ambiguous; first warned that unlike
Satan we are the objects of God's "grace and mercy," we are then subjected to a pageant of biblical history that seems to prove the contrary. Of
course there are exceptions. In some of the vignettes there is a single,
just man—Josiah, Ely, Lot—who resists and thwarts the ungodliness of
his fellow men; yet the mere unemphatic naming of a few heroes of faith
is hardly an effective counterweight to this extended portrait of human
viciousness. The effect of Milton's catalog of devils is to bracket his reader
firmly and remorselessly with Satan's angelic followers: Behold Moloch,

Chemos, Baal and Astarte, Thammuz, Dagon, Rimmon, Osiris, Isis, Orus, Belial; O reader, *de te fabulo!*

Along with this degradation of the reader's self-esteem, Hell goes through a metamorphosis. The fallen angels, erstwhile autumn leaves and scattered sedge, become so large that the greatest human heroes are pygmies by comparison; and Satan stands "like a Tow'r" among them. Their legions regroup and regain their splendor. A palace is built; a council is held; a plan—crowned in our foreknowledge with success—is hatched. The uncertainty and apparent hopelessness of the Satanic condition give way to resolution and an apparent hopefulness. Not just Satan's words and actions but the narrator's method of presenting them also changes. In the multiple activities of a resurgent Hell, there is no time to reveal in narrative asides what the pageantry and spectacle are designed to conceal. Where previously the epic voice made us privy to Satan's inner feelings, as well as to facts beyond his ken, it now keeps resolutely to surfaces and exteriors. The verbs "seem" and "appear," as well as their synonyms and functional equivalents, become stock-in-trade for describing the fallen angels:

> and now
> Advanc't in view they stand, a horrid Front
> Of dreadful length and dazzling Arms, *in guise*
> Of Warriors old . . . ; (I,562–65)
>
> . . . .
>
> his form had not yet lost
> All her Original brightness, nor *appear'd*
> Less than Arch-Angel ruin'd . . . ; (I,591–93)
>
> . . . .
>
> cruel his eye, but cast
> *Signs* of remorse and passion to behold
> The fellows of his crime, the followers rather
> (Far other once beheld in bliss) condemn'd
> For ever now to have thir lot in pain . . . ; (I,604–608)
>
> . . . .
>
> Behold a wonder! they but now who *seem'd*
> In bigness to surpass Earth's Giant Sons
> Now less than smallest Dwarfs, in narrow room
> Throng numberless . . . ; (I,777–80)
>
> . . . .

> The Stygian Council thus dissolv'd; and forth
> In order came the grand infernal Peers:
> Midst came thir mighty Paramount, and *seem'd*
> Alone th' Antagonist of Heav'n, nor less
> Than Hell's dread Emperor with pomp Supreme,
> And God-like imitated State. (II,506–11; my italics)

By line 521 of Book I, Hell has made a spectacular recovery, due not only to the glamour and grandeur automatically conferred by epic genre, nor simply to the brave words and mighty deeds of the fallen angels, but perhaps most of all to the epic voice, who has not only arranged for Hell's illusions to strike the reader's mind with more imaginative force than does Christian truth, but has also used that very Christian truth as a way of subverting the reader's own self-respect, driving him nearer and nearer toward identification first with Satan, then with his followers and servants.

The reader never stands in precisely the same place at any two points in *Paradise Lost*. Every new event or new speech alters in some respect his relation to the poem; yet I think it fair to say that after the mention of Josiah, Ely, and Lot, Milton never again overtly invites him to step outside the framework of Hell and the Satanic poem. Corrective commentary becomes elliptical, at best the nagging undertone of a narrator disappointed in his audience:

> High on a Throne of Royal State, which far
> Outshone the wealth of Ormus and of Ind,
> Or where the gorgeous East with richest hand
> Show'rs on her Kings Barbaric Pearl and Gold,
> Satan exalted sat, by merit rais'd
> To that *bad* eminence. (II,1–6; my italics)

The resolute attention to surfaces and exteriors, the slight inappropriateness and inexactness of diction (wealth *per se* does not shine), the adjectival snubbing of the reader's predictably fallen responses ("*Barbaric* Pearl and Gold"), and above all the oxymoronic reversal of values implicit in "bad eminence" make this passage an epitome of Milton's treatment of Satan thus far. Like a scorpion, this passage carries its sting in its tail, setting the reader up with images of earthly magnificence and even spiritual value ("High," "Outshone") only to condemn, after the fact, responses it has worked hard to evoke. The casualness of the correction implies that by this time there is no more point in contending for the reader's sympathies; either he sees through Satanic magnificence by himself or no amount of scolding will make him do so.

The entire council scene is a good test of how far the reader has come toward accepting the bond between himself and the fallen angels. Until now the struggle in *Paradise Lost* has been between Satan and God, with man as a sort of interested onlooker. Now, suddenly, the plan of revenge that emerges is one of attacking not God but man! By rights we should now be alienated; in fact, before we ever reach this scene we have been involved in so many ways by Satan's predicament that to a large extent we have forgotten that we ourselves are not fallen angels.

The debate itself masterfully focuses upon a *problem*—how to resume the struggle with God; and the reader's mind becomes so preoccupied with its solution that he scarcely notices the way in which the focus of animosity shifts from God to man. Given the nature of the opposition, there is *no* solution. As Belial observes:

> what can force or guile
> With him, or who deceive his mind, whose eye
> Views all things at one view? He from Heav'n's highth
> All these our motions vain, sees and derides;
> Not more Almighty to resist our might
> Than wise to frustrate all our plots and wiles. (II, 188–93)

Belial's objection refutes not only Moloch's foolish proposal to resume open war, at which it is explicitly aimed, but also, by anticipation, the "plots and wiles" of Beelzebub's proposed sneak attack upon man. No matter: By the time we have heard Belial out, then Mammon, then Beelzebub, we have forgotten these sensible words from one whom the narrator makes a special point of calling a liar. The entire point of the council scene, so far as it advances the plot, is to make us believe, contrary to Belial's explicit testimony, that there is a solution to the fallen angels' insoluble problem.

The poem invites us to forget both the futility of the scheme and our proximity to its victims. The plot has ensnared us in the intriguing problem of how to war against the Almighty; the dazzling rhetoric of the council scene itself has raised our excitement to a fever pitch; and Satan's offer

to undertake the perilous mission fulfills our highest expectations of the
epic protagonist. Under such circumstances it is hard to recognize ourselves in the hapless targets Beelzebub specifies:

>   perhaps
> Some advantageous act may be achiev'd
> By sudden onset, either with Hell fire
> To waste his whole Creation, or possess
> All as our own, and drive as we were driven,
> The puny habitants, or if not drive,
> Seduce them to our Party, that thir God
> May prove thir foe, and with repenting hand
> Abolish his own works. (II,362–70)

Although we know, in some distant sense, that we are those "puny habitants," we would really rather not think about it. So deep by this time is
our imaginative involvement in the plight of the fallen angels, so loath
are we to quit our place at the council table to take up the charmless role
of puny habitants, that we settle into the stance of enemies to ourselves,
conspiring with a kind of grim relish at our own ruin. As the narrator
tangentially observes:

> O shame to men! Devil with Devil damn'd
> Firm concord holds, men only disagree
> Of Creatures rational, though under hope
> Of heavenly Grace; and God proclaiming peace,
> Yet live in hatred, enmity, and strife
> Among themselves, and levy cruel wars,
> Wasting the Earth, each other to destroy:
> As if (which might induce us to accord)
> Man had not hellish foes anow besides,
> That day and night for his destruction wait. (II, 496–505)

The portrait of mankind as the *self*-destructive race seems at this juncture
a bit gratuitous (since it clashes with the council scene's image of man as
hapless victim) unless we take it as a comment on what is happening to
the reader, who is identifying with his own worst enemy, while Milton's
narrator, with monstrous unfairness, assails us for assuming a stance that
the poet has worked hard to produce. Milton's narrative strategy has set
narrator against reader, and reader against himself, and then, lest the fact

escape us, has pointed it out. The previous promise of God's grace recedes, appropriately, to a *hope*.

A final example of how well the poem has accommodated the reader
to Hell is the scene of Satan's departure from it. In the intervening lines
Hell has been explored and has been discovered to be uniformly terrible,
"A Universe of death" (II,622); while Satan's encounter with those two
grizzly personifications, Sin and Death, has added little charm to the
picture. Yet when Sin unlocks the adamantine gates, Satan hesitates to
leave:

> So wide they stood, and like a Furnace mouth
> Cast forth redounding smoke and ruddy flame. (II,888–89)
> . . . .

>   Into this wild Abyss,
> The Womb of nature and perhaps her Grave,
> Of neither Sea, nor Shore, nor Air, nor Fire,
> But all these in thir pregnant causes mixt
> Confus'dly, and which thus must ever fight,
> Unless th' Almighty Maker them ordain
> His dark materials to create more Worlds,
> Into this wild Abyss the wary fiend
> Stood on the brink of Hell and look'd a while,
> Pondering his Voyage. (II,910–19)

With him, I think, the reader hesitates. Bad as Hell is, it has its apparent
compensations: stately palaces, good talk, and "proud imaginations." Milton has labored hard to make Hell diverting, and even at its most terrible
it is by now familiar, a known quantity. In contrast to the unknown terrors
of the "wild Abyss," the ruddy flame of a furnace mouth is a homey, almost a pleasant, image. And perhaps the reader senses, too, that Satan
will never be the same, that Hell's landscape, after all, flatters him. Satan
belongs in Hell, and, as the poem has been at pains to teach us, so to a
considerable extent do we.

Paradise Lost, a poem that fulfils no expectation we bring to it without first thwarting that expectation, is itself an oxymoron, simultaneously
on both sides of every issue, affronting, like every great work of art, our
cherished illusions of living in an orderly, rational, rectilinear universe.
The entire text of Books I and II is a tissue of contradictions, from the
most local of oxymorons—"bad eminence," "precious bane," "death

lives"—to the dramatic ironies of entire scenes—Satan's defiant first speeches, delivered while flat on his back, for example, or the council scene that systematically destroys all basis for hope while insisting that hope has been found. In Milton's Hell we "see" by errors or by truth that misleads—the poetic equivalent of darkness visible.

The best way to survive and benefit from the onslaught of Books I and II is not by an irritable reaching after fact and reason, but by a faith in Milton similar to the poet's faith in God: Whatever happens to us, it will be for our own ultimate good. Faith, in *Paradise Lost*, is surely the evidence of things not seen; and our faith in Milton's poem is sorely tested by its apparent Satanism. Yet even in our darkest hour Milton does not leave us entirely on our own, for, as we have already observed, into every scene, every speech, every simile, he has inserted some inaccuracy of diction or incongruity of detail that keeps the Satanic perspective from becoming comfortable. Taken together, these hints are part of what might best be called, borrowing the word from Geoffrey Hartman, a "counter-plot," an undercurrent of words, events, and images that contradict—illogically, unobtrusively—what the more obvious movements of the plot are saying.[6] As Milton's plot carries us in one direction, his counterplot carries us in the other; so that we are always at least faintly uneasy with the vision of reality the poet seems to be painting. Like an imperfect film print, Hell "flickers," and this flickering is an implicit message from the author, at first inconspicuous and yet cumulatively effective, not to take what he shows at face value.

Corrective commentary is the most obvious way in which Milton contradicts Satan and the Satanic plot, yet its overall tendency is to rein-force Hell's illusions. Even at its least ambiguous, corrective commentary demands that we *not* respond in ways that the poet has devoted consid-erable artistry to making certain we *will* respond. From the very begin-ning, these intrusions are implicit criticisms of the reader, and by Book II it is *we*, not Satan, who are being corrected ("O shame to men"). Cor-rective commentary divides the reader into two persons—an imaginative faculty that responds to the heroic Satan versus a conscience that is made to feel ashamed of such responses—and thus turns the reader's mind into a hateful siege of contraries. The more it nags, the more it helps the Satanic plot to make God appear repellent and Satan appealing.

Alienation from God is the essence of Milton's Hell. By touching that tangled knot of guilt, fear, and self-hatred that would rather blame

God than ourselves for our unhappiness, Milton pulls the Satanic stop in each one of us. Showing us Satan he teaches us to know ourselves. But of course such a feeling, no matter how subjectively real, is a mistake. God loves man and asks only that we wish to have his love. Hell then is an illusion—not in the sense that there are no damned souls, or no "place" for them to go, but because the place is of no importance. To reject God's love is to be in Hell, whatever our physical location. Hell is not punishment but *self*-punishment, as Satan acknowledges of himself in his first soliloquy (see IV,93–104). The "art" of Milton's epic, the whole charade of presenting Satan as a military hero, is, as the reader will discover in time, also an illusion. Although Milton wants us to believe that illusion for a while, he also wants to plant the seeds of our eventual disillusionment.

And so a pattern emerges in the poem, the true counterplot of Books I and II, that asks the reader to disbelieve both the reliable narrator and the evidence of his own senses. When Satan awakes upon the burning lake, he fails for a moment to recognize Beelzebub. After his comrade has answered his defiant speech with a realistically despairing one, Satan replies with "speedy words" (I,156)—the "winged words" of Homer's heroes, but also suggestive of a wish to silence Beelzebub's indiscretions. After more of Satan's declaiming, we are reminded that he is still incongruously lying flat on his back. Comparison of Satan to Leviathan introduces the apparently irrelevant story of the human pilot who moored his ship on the sea beast by mistake. A faint undercurrent of mistakes, miscues, incongruities, and stage management is being set in motion.

Meanwhile Satan is described as "in bulk as huge As whom the Fables name of monstrous size" (I,196–97), introducing not only the problematic question of the size of mythical beings, but also the whole issue of the relation in this poem between fable and truth. A few lines later, the poet encounters the same problem in another form: can earthly words represent Hellish facts?

> on dry Land
> He lights, if it were Land that ever burn'd
> With solid, as the Lake with liquid fire
> And such appear'd in hue. (I,227–30)

Hell "flickers" here for a moment, for to question the applicability to Hell of the word "land" is also by implication to question "lake," "chains," perhaps even "fire" itself.[7] For the first time since we entered Hell, Milton's poem has become self-referential, asking us to look not merely at a scene but at the words used to paint it. The implication, unstressed and probably unnoticed, is that Milton's Hell is a tissue of words, and that words should be approached with a certain skepticism.

Epic similes comparing Satan's spear and shield respectively to the moon and to a Norway pine make Hell seem indeterminate in a different way. The moon is large or small relative to where an observer stands. Viewing it through a telescope brings it artificially closer, a meaning emphasized by reference to Galileo as the Tuscan *artist*. The effect described in this simile is enacted in the next, as Satan's spear grows in the reader's mind to huge proportions, only to shrink to the size of a wand:

> His Spear, to equal which the tallest Pine
> Hewn on Norwegian hills, to be the Mast
> Of some great Ammiral, were but a wand,
> He walkt with. (I,292–95)

Satan's spear seems to "equal" a Norway pine, until the sentence's ending makes us retrace our steps to discover whether spear or pine has been likened to a wand. The reader may eventually sort out the meaning hidden in this tortuous syntax—spear is to pine as pine is to wand—but in the meantime he has had to juggle images of Satan as simultaneously great and tiny (which is of course the truth).[8]

The narrator is obscurely testifying against himself, warning us that the epic method is unreliable. Needless to say, the warning is unwelcome, since our only hope of arriving at "truth" in this poem seems to depend on the reliability of the narrator, the goodness of the poet. The pressure is great to dismiss these lines as simply badly written. The more worried we become that Milton will prove unequal to the demands of his art, or that we will prove unequal to its comprehension, the *less* likely we are to give such passages as this the attention they require. The logic of reading demands that we ignore details that do not fit our overall conception of what we are being told.

The power of art to delude emerges more explicitly in Milton's discussions of Hellish music. Music charms the pain of Hell for Satan's reassembled legions:

> Anon they move
> In perfect Phalanx to the Dorian mood
> Of Flutes and soft Recorders; such as rais'd
> To highth of noblest temper Heroes old
> Arming to Battle, and instead of rage
> Deliberate valor breath'd, firm and unmov'd
> With dread of death to flight or foul retreat,
> Nor wanting power to mitigate and swage
> With solemn touches, troubl'd thoughts, and chase
> Anguish and doubt and fear and sorrow and pain
> From mortal or immortal minds. Thus they
> Breathing united force with fixed thought
> Mov'd on in silence to soft Pipes that charm'd
> Thir painful steps o'er the burnt soil. (I,549–62)

Two kinds of "charming" are going on here. The martial song *in* the poem makes the devils forget about the pains of Hell, while the martial song that *is* the poem is doing much the same thing for the reader. Milton's simile is dishonest, using verbs and adjectives with ambiguous antecedents to conflate the fallen angels with "heroes old." Yet human warriors marching to battle "unmov'd With dread of death" are courageous in a way that spirits who are not subject to death, and are in any case not marching to battle, are not. The inconsistency of Milton's tenses ("Anon they move . . . ; Thus they . . . Mov'd on") makes it impossible to tell where the simile ends, hence impossible to distinguish heroes and devils. Hell flickers here, since devils who are/are not heroic are feeling/not feeling the pains of Hell; yet I doubt that the reader consciously learns to distrust the poem, since there seems no logical reason to connect the heavenly inspired song we are reading with the hellish music we are reading *about*. Only cumulatively will Milton's references to the dissimulative powers of music come to seem self-referential.

Music is joined to the arts of architecture and masque as the fallen angels build Pandaemonium, an ingenious "artificial" Hell in which both they and we take refuge for a while from Hell's savage "natural" landscape. Under Mulciber's direction molten ore fills an underground mold:

> As in an Organ from one blast of wind
> To many a row of Pipes the sound-board breathes.
> Anon out of the earth a Fabric huge

> Rose like an Exhalation, with the sound
> Of Dulcet Symphonies and voices sweet,
> Built like a Temple . . . . (I,708–713)

Pandaemonium's sudden emergence is faintly stagy, like one of the elaborate, insubstantial sets conjured up by Inigo Jones in the opulent court masques of Milton's youth. A palace, no matter how solid we are subsequently assured it is, is bound to flicker momentarily in our mind's eye when we are told that it was built "from one blast of wind." Even more remarkable, though, is the power of Milton's poetry to suggest, irrationally, that Pandaemonium is not merely (like Troy and Camelot) built *to* music, which is all these lines literally say, but *is* music: it emerges "like an Exhalation" from a sort of subterranean organ, to the sound of symphonies and voices. A stage-set palace is insubstantial enough, but a palace that is merely a blast on the organ seems hardly there at all.

If giving architecture the properties of song suggests a similarity between Satan's palace ("Built like a Temple") and the poem we are reading, then the lesson is, once again, not to read uncritically:

> The hasty multitude
> Admiring enter'd, and the work some praise
> And some the Architect . . . . (I,730–32)

Hell is illusion, but so is fiction; Satan tells lies but so do poets. The honest poet is the one who reminds us that he lies:

> Men call'd him Mulciber; and how he fell
> From Heav'n, they fabl'd, thrown by angry Jove
> Sheer o'er the Crystal Battlements: from Morn
> To Noon he fell, from Noon to dewy Eve,
> A Summer's day; and with the setting Sun
> Dropt from the Zenith like a falling Star,
> On Lemnos th' Aegaean Isle: *thus they relate*,
> *Erring*; for he with this rebellious rout
> Fell long before; nor aught avail'd him now
> To have built in Heav'n high Tow'rs; nor did he scape
> By all his Engines, but was headlong sent
> With his industrious crew to build in hell. (I,740–751; my italics)

This is of course another place in which Milton connects art and the artist with Hell, but my interest is now less with the matter than with the manner of this fable's telling. No narrative device is more familiar to the reader of earlier books of *Paradise Lost* than that of the picture first lovingly painted and then canceled, as if to teach us the delusive powers of art. This passage offers us two pictures of the same event, then tells us that the more beautiful is false. We must read poetry with care, it suggests, since poetry's most attractive and appealing aspects may be the most delusive, yet (it goes on to suggest) within the lie there may be a truth, if we learn to read rightly—Mulciber did fall, just as pagan myth, that cracked image of truth, suggests.

The rhythm of the counterplot is accelerating, as Milton brings closer and closer to consciousness the contradictions in our apparently direct view of Hell. Pandaemonium's windy solidity and Mulciber's truthful fictitiousness lie within a few lines of each other; their separate contradictions resonate with each other, making it harder for the reader to ignore the relevance of the proposition that art is untrustworthy. The question of the size of the fallen angels arises again, but this time neither fancifully (as in the similes surrounding Satan's shield and spear) nor abstractly, but dramatically, before the reader's eyes, as the fallen angels enter Pandaemonium:

> As Bees
> In spring time, when the Sun with Taurus rides,
> Pour forth thir populous youth about the Hive
> In clusters; they among fresh dews and flowers
> Fly to and fro, or on the smoothed Plank,
> The suburb of thir Straw-built Citadel,
> New rubb'd with Balm, expatiate and confer
> Thir State affairs. So thick the aery crowd
> Swarm'd and were strait'n'd; till the Signal giv'n,
> Behold a wonder! they but now who seem'd
> In bigness to surpass Earth's Giant Sons
> Now less than smallest Dwarfs, in narrow room
> Throng numberless . . . . (I, 768–80)

Pandaemonium, a palace built huge in order to augment the fallen angels' sense (and our sense) of their own stature, ironically dwarfs them. Entering by thousands they become "as bees" swarming around a hive, and the devils again metaphorically shrink. Then, overgoing his classical models, Milton makes the ground of *his* comparison no mere trope of rhetoric. Life imitates art as the devils "really" shrink in size (we should by now be a trifle suspicious of such a formulation): the line between fiction and truth, between figurative and literal language, is being rubbed out before the reader's eyes.

What is most perplexing about this awkward piece of stage business is that it seems at first so unnecessary. The reader, who has never been given a precise notion of the size of the fallen angels, nor of Pandaemonium, would have had no trouble imagining the palace as large enough to contain all of them. By shrinking his fallen angels, Milton hasn't solved the problem of scale so much as he has pointed out that the problem exists. What this "wonder" does is to cast doubt upon all previous descriptions of the fallen angels as great or huge. If incorporeal spirits can assume whatever size and shape they wish, then their size at a particular moment—large as Leviathan, small as a bee—has no special significance. As Raphael warns Adam in Book VIII:

> Great
> Or Bright infers not Excellence: the Earth
> Though, in comparison of Heav'n, so small,
> Nor glistering, may of solid good contain
> More plenty than the Sun that barren shines . . . . (VIII,90–94)

The metamorphosis into bees argues the same lesson as Raphael's, but in far more veiled a manner. For what has the constant emphasis in Book I on Satan's stature and still-potent brightness argued but that great and bright *do* imply excellence? To shrink the fallen angels suddenly to pygmy size is, in this context, shocking enough to the reader's sense of knowing where he stands; to shrink them first "poetically," through the epic device of simile, and then immediately to shrink them "literally," is to suggest that there *is* no literal level in *Paradise Lost* upon which we can absolutely depend; it is all metaphor, none of it literally true. The poet requires us to look not merely at this scene, but at the techniques of its rendering.

Again, as in the fable of Mulciber that followed the "magical" creation of Pandaemonium, Milton follows a dramatic example of Hell's illusory nature with a seemingly irrelevant story that casts an obscure light on the same topic:

> they but now who seem'd
> In bigness to surpass Earth's Giant Sons

Now less than smallest Dwarfs, in narrow room
Throng numberless, like that Pigmean Race
Beyond the Indian Mount, or Faery Elves,
Whose midnight Revels, by a Forest side
Or Fountain some belated Peasant sees,
Or dreams he sees, while over-head the Moon
Sits Arbitress, and nearer to the Earth
Wheels her pale course; they on thir mirth and dance
Intent, with jocund Music charm his ear;
At once with joy and fear his heart rebounds. (I, 777–88)

Read allegorically, as Milton's similes often require, this puzzling tableau holds up a distorting mirror in which we may briefly glimpse ourselves as readers misled by a poem. Under the influence of poetry (the moon is the patroness of magicians, poets, and madmen) the reader is shown, or perhaps only imagines he is shown, the entertaining activities of fallen angels conjuring up palaces and swarming like bees. Milton's music is "jocund," yet it cannot entirely prevent the reader's mixing his joy at the performance with his fear of what is being performed. At this climax of Milton's counterplot, the poem obscurely invites the reader to see himself, not merely in the general guise of fallen man, but specifically as the victim of fallen art, not only manipulated into approving what he should abhor, but tricked into seeing what may not be there at all.

Milton is teaching the one lesson his reader is least prepared to learn: distrust of the very poem he is reading. Our only defense is to miss the point; hence this simile produces bewilderment. By breaking the first rule of reading—"you can believe what I say"—the counterplot risks being ignored by the logical reader. Yet in our bewilderment Milton's whole poem noticeably flickers.

Flickers, perhaps, but does not go out. No amount of verbal conceit and dark allegory can reverse or even much deflect the direction in which Milton's authoritative plot and vivid characterization are carrying us. Despite aery Pandaemonium and fabled Mulciber, elfin angels and deluded peasant, Hell is still as great and as real for us as Milton wishes to make it. When he has done with his games, he returns to serious business and to Satan, who is, we are told, as huge as ever:

> But far within
> And *in thir own dimensions like themselves*
> The great Seraphic Lords and Cherubim

> In close recess and secret conclave sat
> A thousand Demi-Gods on golden seats,
> Frequent and full. (I,792–97; my italics)

The final irony is that we read these lines with no irony.[9]

Milton's counterplot finally surfaces, late in Book II, by joining the plot. That readers have been, from the first, vocally disgruntled with his introduction of allegorical characters into a "true" story demonstrates their reluctance to believe what the counterplot has been saying all along—that the story is a fiction (how many of us realize, or bother to remember, that Belial and Mammon are equally allegorical?). Sin and Death tastelessly dramatize what has hitherto been kept from us—Hell's unheroic "lowness"—and also elicit from Satan a kind of behavior that cannot be squared with his earlier lofty poses. Most of all, though, by turning epic into mock epic, Milton causes the reader to doubt the credibility of the poem he has been reading, not by implication but directly.

Satan's meeting with his progeny is a comedy of mistaken identities ineptly disguised as an epic confrontation. Sin's scaly, serpentine nether parts, with barking hellhounds kenneled in her womb, revolt Satan as much as they do the reader, and he prepares for combat with her grim companion with a salvo of puissant insults:

> Whence and what are thou, execrable shape,
> That dar'st, though grim and terrible, advance
> Thy miscreated Front athwart my way
> To yonder Gates? through them I mean to pass,
> That be assured, without leave askt of thee:
> Retire, or taste thy folly, and learn by proof,
> Hell-born, not to contend with Spirits of Heav'n. (II,681–87)

When we learn the facts of Death's paternity, Satan's taunts of "miscreated" and "Hell-born" will seem funny. At present, though, Satan seems to be offering what heroic poems are supposed to provide: brave deeds to equal his brave words. Those words may seem stagy, but the narrator's answering bombast reassures us that we are meant to take them seriously:

> Incens't with indignation Satan stood
> Unterrifi'd, and like a Comet burn'd,
> That fires the length of Ophiucus huge

In th' Artic Sky, and from his horrid hair
Shakes Pestilence and War. Each at the Head
Levell'd his deadly aim; thir fatal hands
No second stroke intend, and such a frown
Each cast at th' other, as when two black Clouds
With Heav'n's Artillery fraught, come rattling on
Over the Caspian, then stand front to front
Hov'ring a space, till Winds the signal blow
To join thir dark Encounter in mid air:
So frown'd the mighty Combatants, that Hell
Grew darker at thir frown, so matcht they stood. (II,707–20)

The cloud-wind-air vehicle of the second simile plays an obscure, deflat-
ing (or inflated) counterpoint to the seeming grandeur of this confrontation; "Hell grew darker" is nonsense. But can there be any doubt that the
epic reader, who came for exactly this kind of effect, is carried along
by it?

But no sooner have the mighty combatants squared off, spirit versus
abstraction, than Sin intercedes, revealing to Satan the unwelcome fact
that they are family. Satan naturally demurs—"I know thee not, nor ever
saw till now Sight more detestable than him and thee" (II,744–45)—but
Sin's story of her own birth and nuptials, although compromising to Satan, is perforce convincing: "such joy thou took'st With me in secret, that
my womb conceiv'd A growing burden" (II,765–67). With every line of
this speech, Satan looks worse.

The incongruity of Sin's high style to her low matter marks her as a
character of mock epic, but the same can now be said of Satan himself,
who does a sudden, comic *volte-face* on learning that Sin holds the key
to the gates through which he must presently pass:

She finish'd, and the subtle Fiend his lore
Soon learn'd, now milder, and thus answer'd smooth.
Dear Daughter, since thou claim'st me for thy Sire,
And my fair Son here show'st me, the dear pledge
Of dalliance had with thee in Heav'n, and joys
Then sweet, now sad to mention, through dire change
Befall'n us unforeseen, unthought of, know
I come no enemy . . . . (II,815–22)

The abruptness with which Satan changes his tone is one of this serious
poem's genuinely funny moments. We knew all along, of course, that he

was a liar (although exactly what his lies were was never clear), but now we have caught him in a situation no epic hero—or epic villain for that matter—can afford; Satan looks not so much evil as merely ridiculous.

Accidents of plot have conspired to give us, for the first time, the chance to gauge for ourselves the distance between the true facts and Satan's rendering of them, to glance for once behind the scenes of Milton's infernal theatre, where "sights detestable" are painted and costumed as "Dear Daughter" and "Fair Son," and the monstrous product of incest is tricked out as "the dear pledge Of dalliance." We are at last learning by experience what the counterplot has hitherto only hinted at in asides and seeming irrelevancies, that epic convention and epic diction are themselves instruments of deception. The discovery is of course momentous, teaching us that Milton's narrator, as the fable of Mulciber obscurely hinted, is reliable only if read with the utmost wariness:

> So frown'd the mighty Combatants, that Hell
> Grew darker at thir frown, so matcht they stood;
> *For never but once more was either like*
> *To meet so great a foe*: and now great deeds
> Had been achiev'd, whereof all Hell had rung,
> Had not the Snaky Sorceress that sat
> Fast by Hell Gate, and kept the fatal Key,
> Ris'n, and with hideous outcry rush'd between. (II,719–26; my italics)

A small but important bit of truth redeems, if we know how to read aright, this dishonest bluster of mighty combatants and fatal keys, and the demonstrated dishonesty of Satan's grandiloquence provides us with the clue to unlock the ultimate secret of Milton's grand style. The narrator's own pompous tone is punctured by its lack of fidelity to the dramatized comedy. We recognize that he is wearing a mask of epic grandeur that is at last beginning to slip. The action is in effect "correcting" the narrator.

The difficulty in describing the oxymoronic force of *Paradise Lost* is that it makes the poem seem absurd. Although literature is addressed not to the intellect alone but to the whole reader, the conventions of criticism insist upon making a poem appear rational. But once we recognize that absurdity in *Paradise Lost* is not a flaw but a deliberate poetic strategy, we can stop loyally ignoring it and can begin asking why it is there. The reason is that neither Milton, nor his audience, nor the world they live in, nor the language they speak, is wholly rational. Reason is only one of man's faculties, and (since the Fall) not the one normally in control:

> For Understanding rul'd not, and the Will
> Heard not her lore, both in subjection now
> To sensual Appetite, who from beneath
> Usurping over sovran Reason claim'd
> Superior sway . . . . (IX,1127–31)

A poet speaks not to an audience of saints or of disembodied intellects but to flesh-and-blood human beings, "to those especially of soft and delicious temper who will not so much as look upon Truth herselfe unlesse they see her elegantly drest," as a younger Milton put it. [10] Yet, since there is no way to "dress" Truth without disguising her, a holy poet is one who brings us from an initial admiration of the elegant costume to a more awful and wonderful contemplation of naked Truth.

The problem, ultimately, is the nature of truth itself:

> When we talk about knowing God, it must be understood in terms of man's limited powers of comprehension. God as he really is, is far beyond man's imagination, let alone his understanding. [11]

But this limitation upon our comprehension applies not only to God but to the other characters in *Paradise Lost* (except Adam and Eve after the Fall) and to most of its places as well—Heaven, Hell, and unfallen Eden. Milton's solution was, as it had to be, first to clothe supernatural beings in the images of this world, and then to lead his reader progressively from deluding ornaments to the truth itself. Gradually we learn to look *beyond* fallen words and pictures to the ineffable truth behind them.

Can we call a narrator "reliable" who misleads us as Milton's narrator does in Books I and II? To answer this question we must distinguish between a literal and a higher sense of the word "reliable." To mislead initially in order to lead more truly is to be, in the higher sense, "reliable." For Milton the Bible itself was proof that God revealed himself gradually, in ways accommodated to the understandings of his hearers. Thus Genesis does not reveal the true identity of the tempter; and thus the Decalogue was given to men to show that they could not keep it. In each case, in order to lead mankind it was necessary first to mislead them. For Milton the entire rhythm of human history, as recorded in the

Old Testament, was a sequence of foreshadowings, progressively less obscure, of the arrival of Christ; yet that history was not understood until
Christ's appearance. In Books XI and XII, Adam himself learns gradually,
by mistake and correction, how to "read" human history: not judging by
appearances, but looking beneath the surface for signs of God's forgive-
ness. Hell is illusion, but so is art; Satan tells lies, but so do poets. The
honest poet is the one who admits he lies—who teaches you to find, as in
the fable of Mulciber, the dull nugget of truth amid the glitter of false-
hood.[12]

   Paradise Lost is, in a real sense, a divided poem, inviting antithetical
responses. If we choose to believe what the epic says, then we are untrue
to Christian doctrine; yet if we really wish to remain pure, then we had
best throw the book away—it is too seductive. In other words, the poem
offers us a *choice*, but in the first books it throws nearly all of the re-
sources of art onto the side of error. A truly saintly reader may avoid
these snares entirely, just as a consciously Satanic reader may not wish to
escape them; but such readers, if they exist at all, are not the ones who
need to see God justified. Surely the middling reader—who is most of
us, mixture of good and bad—cannot escape the overwhelming force of
poetry and narrative urging upon him a Satanic perspective, even as a
still, small voice, at first unwelcome, prepares a reversal in the books
ahead.

   The first half of *Paradise Lost*, organized narratively around Satan's
story, from insurrection in Heaven to first temptation of Eve, is chrono-
logically disordered to put Satan's best foot forward. Focused structurally
upon Satan, it is no wonder that the first half of the poem, and especially
Books I and II, do him such ample justice. Yet Satan is finally irrelevant.
The true conflict in Milton's epic is not between God and Satan, or even
between Man and Satan, but between Man and God. The reader's early
feelings of alienation from God, evoked not only by the darkness of Hell
but by the blinding, humiliating light of Heaven in Book III, and his
progressively more positive responses to the concrete *evidence* of God's
goodness in the beauties of Eden, the nobility of Adam and Eve, and the
love evidenced in the Creation, converge upon the moment of the Fall.
Eve and Adam are free to fall or not to fall, the issue being between them
and God, and Satan is only a pretext. From there on, until he disappears
entirely in Books XI and XII, Satan becomes only a cartoon figure, and
the major exemplar of wickedness is not Satan but fallen man.

Milton's epic addresses itself to a contradiction in Christian belief: how can a loving, omnipotent deity have created a universe in which men suffer? Milton did not "solve" this problem—nor have we—but he transcended it in a leap of faith. His poem prepares us for a leap of our own, but our preparation is not purely intellectual. The method of *Paradise Lost*, aimed as it is at an audience not wholly rational, is itself not wholly rational. "Justification" of God includes not simply exonorating him from Adam's sin, nor explaining his plan of redemption, but also consists of setting in motion in the reader's breast those feelings and perceptions that lead him to expect God's love and to reciprocate it. Much of the poem, being beyond rational analysis, must be experienced rather than merely thought about. Like an oxymoron, *Paradise Lost* flickers, sending contradictory messages that demand an intuitive leap to a truth beyond words. No one has ever entirely understood it, and no one ever will.

2

Light Invisible

We boast our light; but if we look not wisely on the sun
itself, it smites us into darkness.

——*Areopagitica*

Why is everything rational in *Paradise Lost* so profoundly unreasonable?

——Northrop Frye, *The Return of Eden*

"*PARADISE LOST* IS supposed to justify God's ways," says Joan Webber;
"instead it seems perpetually to call them into question."[1] Remote as Hell
is from the Almighty, Milton's omnipresent deity is implicit in every line
of Books I and II, and the evidence is far from flattering. The God of
these books is primarily a God of Wrath; how can he elicit our love? Still,
until now our view of God has been remote and inferential. Whatever we
learn of him directly in Book III is bound to be more compelling. The
"Heavenly Council" scene, set in obvious contrast to the "Infernal Council" of the previous book, is Milton's chance to reverse the current of
feeling running against his deity. Yet the consensus among readers is that
the poet has failed.

Some critics argue that Time rather than Milton is responsible for
their failure to love Milton's God. "If we cannot always find the Father a
more attractive speaker than Satan," says Peter Berek, "we can at least
understand why Milton might have expected his ideal reader to do so."[2]
Marjorie Nicolson makes the same point more bluntly: "A modern reader
of Book III feels rebuffed and repelled when he first meets Milton's

God."[3] Berek's antithesis between actual readers ("we") and ideal readers, like Nicolson's implicit distinction between modern readers and seventeenth-century ones, posits a change in poetic sensibility between Milton's day and our own.

Since Renaissance and seventeenth-century poems are today generally considered among the greatest in the language, what Berek and Nicolson are suggesting is not a general change in poetic sensibility but a shift in attitudes toward God and religious doctrine that would affect the way readers respond to their presentation in verse. Perhaps, for example, earlier readers did not really understand that an infinite deity cannot be represented as if he were a finite human being. This falsification of God is what Nicolson objects to:

> If God is truly "ineffable," He should neither speak nor be spoken to. If He is, as the Angels hymn him in Book III (372 ff.) "omnipotent, immutable, immortal, infinite, eternal," how can Infinity be expressed in finite terms, Spirit clothed in body and localized—even on a Throne in Heaven? Milton is inconsistent with himself. (p. 223)

Nicolson finds Milton's portrait of God too direct, too reductive, inconsistent with itself, and (by demonstration) productive of resentment rather than of adoration. These are her responses, but she rules them out of court as the peculiar problem of *modern* readers: Milton must have intended us to adore the God of Book III, she implies, but time has turned his gold to lead.

Blaming history for the poem's deficiencies is at best a pyrrhic victory. Although we exonerate Milton from the charge of writing badly, we make the poem no better for the only audience who really matters: ourselves. But in fact history will not support the claim that Milton and Milton's age were unaware of the difficulties of speaking about God in human terms, as Milton's theological treatise *Christian Doctrine* clearly demonstrates. Along with the Reformation generally, Milton knew that God "as he really is" was far beyond human comprehension. It was of course necessary that men have some knowledge of God, and for this reason God had revealed himself in the Bible. But in the Bible itself "God is always described or outlined not as he really is but in such a way as will make him conceivable to us."[4]

This amounts to saying that when God portrays himself in the Bible in anthropomorphic terms ("For I am an angry God," etc.) he is himself in effect a "poet," using metaphor and personification to suggest what lies beyond the power of words to state. But a good poet, whether he be Milton or God himself, selects his literary tools with an eye to the effect he wishes to produce in his audience. Since God is portrayed in a variety of ways in *Paradise Lost*, as he is in the Bible, there is every reason to suppose that the personified God of Book III is as conscious a literary "device" as any other feature of the poem, and one for which Milton bears full artistic responsibility. If he made a mistake, "history" is not to blame.

The judgment that Milton erred in personifying God rests on the assumptions that the God of Book III was meant to appeal, and that until recently he did appeal. Actually there is little evidence that the Heavenly Council *ever* gave pleasure. Readers as far back as Alexander Pope have disliked Milton's personified God as a sermonizing "school divine," while defenders of Book III rarely go beyond constructing hypothetical readers who are *imagined* as responding to it with pleasure. Actual readers feel resentful instead. According to Nicolson:

> A modern reader of Book III feels rebuffed and repelled when he first meets Milton's God. If he does not "believe in God," he might have been appreciative enough of literature to have risen with Beatrice and Dante to the great light in the center of the rose, but it is not likely that Milton's God would have converted him from unbelief to belief. If he "believes in God," he has even more difficulty, since he starts off with specific prejudices *pro* and *con* the positions God goes out of His way to expound. (p. 225)

Since the objection here is to God's "expounding positions" and ineptly trying to "convert," it is clear that Nicolson dislikes Milton's God not simply for speaking, but for haranguing, and perhaps for what He says as well. There is no reason why this objection should be limited to "modern readers." Whether Milton's God attracts or repels, and why he does so, are questions to be settled not by reference to a hazy conception of *Zeitgeist* but by close examination of the text and of readers' responses to it.

From St. Paul to Paul Tillich, from Dante to Dostoyevsky, the Christian image of man is of a divided being, a mixture of light and dark, a battlefield between God and Satan. *Paradise Lost* embodies and mirrors that conflict. As the clash of plot and counterplot illustrates, we are in an ambiguous and anxious relationship to the materials of this poem. Standing with one foot in sanctity, one in profanity, the poem itself, like Hell, is an oxymoron, asking us to discriminate between false and true messages, both of which it is sending. The narrator, too, if ultimately reliable, is capable of at least *seeming* to say things that are wrong. So far the experience of reading *Paradise Lost* has not only argued but elicited the reader's ambivalence; whether we come to Satan prepared to love him or hate him, Books I and II give us reason to doubt our preconceptions.

Stepping out into the chaos beyond Hell's gates, Satan immediately shrinks to a small figure in a large landscape, nor does the dramatized hypocrisy of his flattery of Sin and Chaos do anything to augment his ethical stature. But still the quest is Satan's, the obstacles impressively great, and our interest is accordingly engaged in how he is to succeed. Since he is portrayed in ways that both attract and repel us, we are free to follow our own predilections and to call Satan either hero or buffoon, but neither label fits comfortably. The narrator concludes Book II with a final slur:

> Thither full fraught with mischievous revenge,
> Accurst, and in a cursed hour he hies. (II, 1054–55)

But such melodramatic touches as this scarcely negate either our naive interest in Satan's adventures or our sophisticated worries about who has provided Sin with her fatal key and Satan with his cursed hour. The opening books have thrown a shadow over the reader's conception of God, while insisting that no such shadow should exist. Hell's discomfort comes from its ambiguity, the crossfire of conflicting "truths" in which the reader is caught. We come to Book III in sore need of certainty. The question is, do we get it?

Book III, signaling a new beginning, opens with the second of the poem's four prologues (the others begin Books VII and IX). Each of these prologues provides commentary on the text from the point of view of the poet, dealing with the special difficulties of writing it—and, by implication, the special difficulties of reading it as well. The contradictions and disparities of the first prologue, for example, obscurely suggested the tensions between epic form and Christian matter. But no amount of preparation, I have argued, can replace the reader's own painful process of learning that in this poem, though he must perforce judge by appearances, they will often play him false.

The second prologue develops the theme of readerly circumspection a little less obscurely than its predecessor. Its subject is the adequacy of the image "light" to symbolize Christian truth. To counter Hell's darkness, Book III offers Heaven's light, especially the metaphoric "light" of God's providential plan for Man's redemption, to contrast with and undo Satan's dark plans for man's destruction. But Christian truth is not easy to grasp, since it involves contradictions beyond the power of men's minds to resolve. Why, for example, does God not simply stop Satan from tempting Adam, instead of unfolding an elaborate scheme for his eventual reinstatement, in the process of which millions of souls will be condemned to eternal punishment? Such "light" is, at this point at least, far beyond our understanding. It is the task of the prologue to teach us to look behind the image of light—and, by implication, behind other important words, images, and ideas in the poem—to paradoxical truths of Christianity that must be intimated not as they really are, but in such a way as will make them conceivable to us.

This dark purpose explains, I think, why a passage whose subject is light is so hard to understand. Once we were used to it, Hell's darkness proved remarkably visible; Heaven's light smites us into blindness:

> Hail holy Light, offspring of Heav'n first-born,
> Or of th' Eternal Coeternal beam
> May I express thee unblam'd? since God is Light,
> And never but in unapproached Light
> Dwelt from Eternity, dwelt then in thee,
> Bright effluence of bright essence increate.
> Or hear'st thou rather pure Ethereal stream,
> Whose Fountain who shall tell? before the Sun,
> Before the Heavens thou wert, and at the voice
> Of God, as with a Mantle didst invest
> The rising world of waters dark and deep,
> Won from the void and formless infinite. (III,1–12)

The center of this turning world of doubts and questions is the proposition that "God is Light," indubitable, since biblical, but puzzling nonetheless since God "created" light on the First Day—also according to the Bible. Whether God *is* light or *made* light is the sort of problem that delighted (and delights) anti-Christian rationalists, since it makes the whole religion seem absurd. For example, Smerdyakov, in *The Brothers Karamazov*, cites the absurdity of God's creation of light before the sun as proof of Christianity's errors. Perhaps subtle distinctions can be drawn between the light God is and the light God made, but phrases such as "Bright effluence of bright essence increate" only make our heads spin. Better to recognize humbly that we don't fully understand than to try to wrap our incapacity in grandiloquence.

The poet acknowledges his limitations by his hesitations and unanswered questions. Then, after failing to imagine precisely how God is Light, he turns to the light God makes. Even here, of course, there is a question of how literally we are to take the word "light." The light God made on the First Day was doubtless real, visible light (even without a radiant source), but he was also imparting some aspect of his own Being to the created world. If the connection between the creation of the world and the creation of Milton's poem, already suggested in the first prologue, is hinted at again in lines 9–12, then the light that invests the "rising world" of Milton's poem is divine truth and inspiration, as well as visible light. But when the poet announces he is "revisiting" light after long sojourn in the "Stygian pool," the hinted admission that he has dallied with error is all but eclipsed by the literal sense of his words. Having "been" in Hell, he was in darkness; having left Hell, he is now in light:

> Thee I revisit now with bolder wing,
> Escap't the Stygian Pool, though long detain'd
> In that obscure sojourn, while in my flight
> Through utter and through middle darkness borne
> With other notes than to th' Orphean Lyre
> I sung of Chaos and Eternal Night,
> Taught by the heav'nly Muse to venture down
> The dark descent, and up to reascend,
> Though hard and rare: thee I revisit safe,
> And feel thy sovran vital Lamp. . . . (III,13–22)

But now, at the moment when "light," in the tactile image of "feel thy sovran vital lamp," comes closest to meaning something purely physical, we make the only real narrative discovery of the entire passage—the poet is blind!

>   but thou
> Revisit'st not these eyes, that roll in vain
> To find thy piercing ray, and find no dawn:
> So thick a drop serene hath quencht thir Orbs,
> Or dim suffusion veil'd. (III,22–26)

There is of course an irony in the fact that the would-be celebrator of light is himself blind. If he "revisits" the realms of light, in what sense can he be said to "see" them, when he sees nothing? The triumphant strains of a rise out of Hell to Heaven suddenly and unexpectedly modulate to a very different tone. The movement from dark to light is reversed by one from sight to blindness; the cosmic scope and high abstraction of the opening lines shrink to the painful limitation of blind eyes rolling in vain to find a single ray.

Paradoxically, though, when the blind poet begins to talk about himself, the verse suddenly becomes more visual, as the grand but hazy imagery of ethereal fountains and worlds rising out of chaos is replaced by the experiences of a man like ourselves in a world we know well:

> Yet not the more
> Cease I to wander where the Muses haunt
> Clear Spring, or shady Grove, or Sunny Hill,
> Smit with the love of sacred Song; but chief
> Thee Sion and the flow'ry Brooks beneath
> That wash thy hallow'd feet, and warbling flow,
> Nightly I visit. . . . (III,26–32)

These springs, groves, hills, flowers, and brooks are not the "real thing," as the adverb "nightly" poignantly reminds us, but their images in verse and song, above all biblical verse and song, seen with the inward eye of the imagination. Through "sacred Song" our blind poet lives in a world as visually rich as any we could wish for ourselves.

And thus the grand imaginative journey out of Hell's darkness into celestial light is paralleled by a more personal, far humbler, metaphoric "journey" of the poet from physical blindness to inner sight. The mention of "sacred Song" reminds him that many of the greatest songs were sung by men blind like himself—epic poets, visionaries, and prophets—whose affliction was a mark not of divine punishment but of divine election:

> Nightly I visit: nor sometimes forget
> Those other two equall'd with me in Fate,
> So were I equall'd with them in renown,
> Blind Thamyris and blind Maeonides,
> And Tiresias and Phineus Prophets old. (III,32–36)

What follows is one of the most splendid effects in the poem. In an adumbration of the Fortunate Fall, the poet's very deprivation of light is

seen as the sign of his possession of, or by, "light." He no sooner speaks
of singing than he begins to sing lines that have brought me closer to
tears than any in the poem:

> Then feed on thoughts, that voluntary move
> Harmonious numbers; as the wakeful Bird
> Sings darkling, and in shadiest Covert hid
> Tunes her nocturnal Note. Thus with the Year
> Seasons return, but not to me returns
> Day, or the sweet approach of Ev'n or Morn,
> Or sight of vernal bloom, or Summer's Rose,
> Or flocks, or herds, or human face divine;
> But cloud instead, and ever-during dark
> Surrounds me, from the cheerful ways of men
> Cut off, and for the Book of knowledge fair
> Presented with a Universal blanc
> Of Nature's works to me expung'd and ras'd,
> And wisdom at one entrance quite shut out. (III,37–50)

The tears are simultaneously those of grief and joy—grief that a man who
knows the full value of sights of earthly beauty will never see them again,
and joy that in his deprivation he can nonetheless make us see them so
well. His song enacts in our imagination what it says to our reason, that
the words light and sight have several senses, that these senses may in
human experience conflict (to see we must be blinded) but that in "sacred
Song" all losses will be restored:

> So much the rather thou Celestial Light
> Shine inward, and the mind through all her powers
> Irradiate, there plant eyes, all mist from thence
> Purge and disperse, that I may see and tell
> Of things invisible to mortal sight. (III,51–55)

Beautiful in itself, the prologue to Book III is also strictly functional,
teaching as it does a lesson in how to understand the image "light." Like
all the important words and ideas of *Paradise Lost*, the word is used
paradoxically and requires from the reader a process of trial-and-error, as
the narrator leads us through an elaborate series of reversals. An attempt
to speak directly of "holy Light" leads only to contradiction, pomposity,
and unanswerable questions, blinding us with too direct an approach to
light, while the poet's shift from generality to personal experience, which
promises to make the experience of light more concrete and intelligible,

ends in paradox: "Thee I revisit . . . but thou Revisit'st not these eyes" (III,21–23). Revisiting light, the poet is apparently excluded from it. By another reversal, however, when our gaze is directed *away* from holy light toward the experience of blindness, we begin to see. Thus, in human experience at least, light can mean several things. Ideally these things should be found together, as they are in God. For us, however, the presence of one may mean the absence of the other.

The prologue ends by drawing an explicit distinction between visible light and "inner light," as the poet's loss of physical sight is taken as a sign of his enhanced powers of spiritual vision. In the figure of the blind poet may lie an invitation to the reader to "blind" himself to the sights of the visible world in order to see Christian truth more clearly, but it is difficult if not impossible at this point for the reader to imitate the poet. After all, although this prologue is the nearest thing so far to an overt warning not to take at face value the poem's physical descriptions of spiritual beings and situations, it is neither sufficiently explicit nor sufficiently impressive, relative to the length of the poem itself, to make the reader abandon the reading habits of a lifetime.

Primarily by rooting his difficult message in the concreteness of personal human experience, the poet teaches a lesson in the ambiguity of words like "light" and "sight" and thereby gives us an inkling of the depths of paradox behind the story he is telling. But it would be foolish to suppose that such a lesson is readily grasped at this point in the poem. The phrase "Things invisible to mortal sight" may be intended as a suggestion that we distrust our senses, but in context it seems to lead to something quite different—a splendid vista of the universe from the best seat in the house:

> Now had th' Almighty Father from above,
> From the pure Empyrean where he sits
> High Thron'd above all highth, bent down his eye,
> His own works and their works at once to view:
> About him all the Sanctities of Heaven
> Stood thick as Stars, and from his sight receiv'd
> Beatitude past utterance; on his right
> The radiant image of his Glory sat,
> His only Son; On Earth he first beheld
> Our two first Parents, yet the only two
> Of mankind, in the happy Garden plac't,
> Reaping immortal fruits of joy and love,

Uninterrupted joy, unrivall'd love
In blissful solitude; he then survey'd
Hell and the Gulf between, and Satan there
Coasting the wall of Heav'n on this side Night
In the dun Air sublime, and ready now
To stoop with wearied wings, and willing feet
On the bare outside of this World, that seem'd
Firm land imbosom'd without Firmament,
Uncertain which, in Ocean or in Air. (III,56–76)

As we might suspect after our lesson in the ambiguity of the words "light" and "sight," there are two antithetical ways of reading this passage. First, as a description of God's physical vision, the passage is breathtaking. God's vision includes literally *everything*—all of the places and all of the major characters in the poem. As if through God's eyes we see a vertical diagram of reality, starting at the top with the Son and the angels, descending to Earth and to Adam and Eve in the Garden, then dropping to Hell and rising again, as if following the course of Satan's journey up to light. Though "distances" between Heaven, Earth, and Hell are "inexpressible By Numbers that have name" (VIII,113–14), God's view is undiminished by distance. Hence, though we seem to see Satan from a great distance, we also see him with perfect accuracy and immediacy. But God not only sees his creatures perfectly; he sees into them as well: he sees the angels' beatitude; Adam and Eve's bliss; and most strikingly, he sees Satan's weariness and uncertainty.

But though at this moment we seem to see splendidly from God's "prospect high," here is our first chance to apply the lesson we have just learned—to look *behind* the poem's words for their spiritual significance, rather than *at* them for their misleading appearance. If we do so, then we will find upon examination that this passage, while seeming to give a picture of the physical universe, actually gives something far different. The phrase "uncertain which" is perhaps the most striking reminder in the passage that we are not seeing as clearly as we might suppose. Satan can't see whether the created universe floats in water or in air, but of course poet and reader share his incapacity. Looking back, we find a number of other details that in blocking our visual imaginations warn us to distrust that imagination. "High Thron'd above all highth" suggests that our normal notion of height is not adequate to understand God's location (does God have a "location"?), and "Beatitude past utterance" also suggests the inadequacies of our minds and of our language. "The radiant image of his Glory" gives no real image, nor are "immortal fruits of joy and love" really fruits—in both cases what promises to be a picture develops into an abstraction. Only Satan is given a setting that seems genuinely pictorial, until we reach the vitiating "uncertain which."

What we have, then, is not really a view from God's "prospect high" at all, but an emblematic tableau of the eternal relationships between God, Man, and Satan: Man and Woman at their daily tasks; Satan above them ready to pounce; and high above all God bending in concern over his creatures. Such things are invisible to mortal sight not because they exceed our visual powers, but because they are, quite simply, not visible. By suggesting that they *are* visible, that with the aid of Milton's telescope we will see God face to face and gain an intellectual understanding of his ways to men, this tableau leads the suggestible reader away from the profounder meanings of "inner light" back toward the mistaken impression that in Book III he will see and hear God "as he really is." The phrase "uncertain which," coming near the end of the passage, implicitly challenges, but in its unemphaticness fails to destroy, the premise upon which the entire passage rests—that God's vision of reality can be mediated to man—by suggesting that, on the contrary, this description has been pure sleight of hand. Although God sees things "as they really are," any image the poet can give us of God's vision will be, no matter how true *in spirit*, ultimately less than the whole truth.

The proper function of poetry, however, is precisely to make us "see" with the inner eye of the imagination—"Yet not the more Cease I to wander where the Muses haunt Clear Spring, or shady Grove, or Sunny Hill, Smit with the love of Sacred Song" (III,26–29). We cannot totally distrust what the poet shows us and yet go on reading, and so we discount the lesson on light invisible. In these pages, at least, (we mistakenly think) we will see as well as the poet sees, and without the inconvenience of being blinded first. Thus, like Satan or Œdipus, we hasten toward our own undoing.

For any defense of God's ways to occur in *Paradise Lost*, it must first be clear what God's ways are. Milton, for all we know, may have weighed alternative methods of bringing the Divine Plan before his audience, but in retrospect it is hard to imagine that he could have done other than to make God himself enunciate it. God is of course the prime actor in Milton's universe; to deny him a substantial speaking role in *Paradise Lost* would be falsely to minimize his active role in the events of the epic, to make it seem as if he were a "watchmaker God" who set the universe running according to immutable laws and then turned his back on it. By devoting his first three books to extraterrestrial events, Milton clearly wants us to see his human actors in the cosmic framework of God's will, and of its apparent antithesis, Satan's will.

Still, the device of a Heavenly Council scene, in which the fate of mortals comes from the mouths of the gods themselves, is a device of classical epic, whose gods and goddesses really *are* persons, neither omnipotent, immutable, infinite, nor eternal. The sustained personification of the Christian God in a speaking role is bound to create contradictions that pagan epic was not subject to.

In the first place God is eternal. For him there is no difference between what has happened and what will happen in the poem's time sequence. But for God to speak in the future tense about a Fall that has not yet taken place in the poem is to give the impression that the Fall is a foregone conclusion: "Man will heark'n to his glozing lies" (III,93). And when God announces the dire consequences of man's disobedience, it sounds (to the time-bound reader) that he is judging mankind in advance of their crime.

Further, since God is omnipotent, it requires some intricate argument on his part to demonstrate that he did not *cause* that Fall:

> Man will heark'n to his glozing lies,
> And easily transgress the sole Command,
> Sole pledge of his obedience: So will fall
> Hee and his faithless Progeny: whose fault?
> Whose but his own? ingrate, he had of mee
> All he could have; I made him just and right,
> Sufficient to have stood, though free to fall. (III,93–99)

Here, almost casually, the Father brushes aside the whole tendency of the first two books to blame Satan for man's Fall. His assertion is that it is man's *own* fault that he fell (will fall), and yet the balance of this longish speech is devoted to refuting Satan's charge that fallen beings (the fallen angels, strictly speaking, but the argument applies equally to fallen humanity) are *God's* victims.

The Father counters this charge by asserting that he gave his creatures free will:

Freely they stood who stood, and fell who fell.
Not free, what proof could they have giv'n sincere
Of true allegiance, constant Faith or Love,
Where only what they needs must do, appear'd,
Not what they would? what praise could they receive?
What pleasure I from such obedience paid,
When Will and Reason (Reason also is choice)
Useless and vain, of freedom both despoil'd,
Made passive both, had serv'd necessity,
Not mee. They therefore as to right belong'd,
So were created, nor can justly accuse
Thir maker, or thir making, or thir Fate;
As if Predestination over-rul'd
Thir will, dispos'd by absolute Decree
Or high foreknowledge; they themselves decreed
Thir own revolt, not I: if I foreknew,
Foreknowledge had no influence on their fault,
Which had no less prov'd certain unforeknown.
So without least impulse or shadow of Fate,
Or aught by me immutably foreseen,
They trespass, Authors to themselves in all
Both what they judge and what they choose; for so
I form'd them free, and free they must remain,
Till they enthrall themselves: I else must change
Thir nature, and revoke the high Decree
Unchangeable, Eternal, which ordain'd
Thir freedom: they themselves ordain'd thir fall. (III, 102–28)

Predestination versus free will is of course one of the famous cruxes of
Christian theology, and it is a crux precisely because it cannot be resolved. Omnipotence means "all power"—all power belongs to God. If a
stone falls to the ground, for example, it does so because God wills it so.
The "law of gravity" is simply a manifestation of God's will, which can
accordingly change at any time God wills it changed. Logically God's
omnipotence excludes free will in his creatures, for to give *some* power
to his creatures (even the power to make up their own minds) is to take
some away from God, which renders him no longer omnipotent. But of
course like any moral system Christianity rests upon free will, since it
assumes that human beings are free to choose between good and evil.
There is no point in exhorting people to love their neighbors if that choice
is not theirs, if they are simply automata. The easiest way to put this
problem is that Christianity as an ethical system is logically at odds with
Christianity as a metaphysical system.

The Father, needless to say, does not give a logical account of how these incompatibles, divine omnipotence and creaturely free will, can coexist. He simply asserts their coexistence in three or four different ways (e.g., "if I foreknew, Foreknowledge had no influence on their fault," etc.) and explains why it is necessary that men and angels be free: "Not free . . . what praise could they receive? What pleasure I from such obedience paid?" In other words, omnipotent God *ordains* their freedom, whether or not that freedom is logically consistent with his omnipotence. This is a mystery that the human intellect will never fathom, since (to human reason, at least) it is absurd. We can accept human freedom on faith and understand why it is both necessary and beautiful, but we will never really understand how it is possible: the Divine Will transcends the limits of our understanding. But if God's will can supersede logic itself, why does God pretend that he is subject to the laws of consistency?

> I else must change
> Thir nature, and revoke the high Decree
> Unchangeable, Eternal, which ordain'd
> Thir freedom. (III, 125–28)

All we can say is that God, who (to human apprehensions) inconsistently gave men and angels free will in the first place, *chooses* not to be inconsistent a second time by removing the unhappy consequences of that freedom. Perhaps he foresees good results coming from that choice.

Nor does God's promise of "grace," though it works to our advantage, make any more sense:

> The first sort by thir own suggestion fell,
> Self-tempted, self-deprav'd: Man falls deceiv'd
> By th' other first: Man therefore shall find grace,
> The other none: in Mercy and Justice both,
> Through Heav'n and Earth, so shall my glory excel,
> But Mercy first and last shall brightest shine. (III, 129–34)

Moral responsibility in Milton's world is elsewhere everywhere unitary— "whose fault? Whose but his own?" There is no such thing as partly willing a sin, or willing part of a sin. One either obeys God's will or disobeys it, and before the Fall man has the power to will either way: "I made him just and right, Sufficient to have stood, though free to fall." To extenuate Adam's sin by saying he was "deceiv'd" violates human logic (in Book IX the narrator tells us Adam falls "not deceiv'd," line 998). God's decision to show man mercy is another mystery that we can gratefully accept but not understand.

A third difficulty that the reader encounters with a personified God is in the distinction of two persons, Father and Son, both of whom are in some sense "God." In the abstract it is not easy to understand the precise differences between them. The Son as "radiant image of his Glory" is scarcely more imaginable than light as "bright effluence of bright essence increate," but the relationship the words suggest is one of complete congruence, if not identity. When they speak, however, there seems to be a sharp distinction between them, as the Son expands the Father's closing glance at "mercy" for mankind into a critique of his justice:

> O Father, gracious was that word which clos'd
> Thy sovran sentence, that Man should find grace;
> For which both Heav'n and Earth shall high extol
> Thy praises, with th' innumerable sound
> Of Hymns and sacred Songs, wherewith thy Throne
> Encompass'd shall resound thee ever blest.
> For should Man finally be lost, should Man
> Thy creature late so lov'd, thy youngest Son
> Fall circumvented thus by fraud, though join'd
> With his own folly? that be from thee far,
> That far be from thee, Father, who art Judge
> Of all things made, and judgest only right.
> Or shall the Adversary thus obtain
> His end, and frustrate thine, shall he fulfil
> His malice, and thy goodness bring to naught,
> Or proud return though to his heavier doom,
> Yet with revenge accomplish't and to Hell
> Draw after him the whole Race of mankind,
> By him corrupted? or wilt thou thyself
> Abolish thy Creation, and unmake,
> For him, what for thy glory thou hast made?
> So should thy goodness and thy greatness both
> Be question'd and blasphem'd without defense. (III,144–66)

This answering speech, although it enlarges upon the Father's closing promise of mercy, strikes many readers as critical of what the Father has just said. As John Peter puts it:

The Son's first speech is largely, if inadvertently, at his Father's expense, and it tends to confirm our incipient hostility towards God. "O Father, gracious was that word which clos'd Thy sovran sentence," he begins, as if like us dissociating himself from God's other "words," and he proceeds to describe the praises that will accrue to God if he is merciful. Poetic speech is to be judged by its effects, not its intentions, and here the effect is very close to tactful bribery. The Son's speech is suasive, as if he has to work on God to prevent him from changing his mind and delivering a sterner sentence. . . . The real difficulty is that he is obliged to state what must be God's own reasons for saving Man, but as if urging them upon his Father, to whom they might not otherwise have occurred. Two divinities cannot discuss what must be known to them both like this without at least one of them appearing fallible.[5]

As a matter of fact, Milton did believe that the Son was, if not exactly "fallible," at least not omniscient: "The Son also teaches that the attributes of divinity belong to the Father alone, and that even he himself is excluded from them. First, omniscience. . . ."[6] A time, therefore (if we can call it time), when the Father's plan for mankind was communicated to the Son must have occurred, however unimaginable the *form* of that communication may be. Whether by previous knowledge or by intuition, however, the Son knows that God will not let evil overwhelm good, so he has no difficulty proving that God, to be God, must be merciful. Milton's subordination of the Son to the Father does give the interchange dramatic force that it otherwise would lack, since the Son is not omniscient but has to *infer* God's intentions from his knowledge of God's goodness, and since his apparently wheedling tone is explainable as deference to the Almighty from his junior and inferior, but the drama would be justified even without such a reading.

Milton's presentation of God's plan for mankind is rendered in dialogue not simply because a "dramatic" presentation heightens our interest (as Peter's reaction demonstrates, that "hightened interest" may work *against* the reader's acceptance of God's ways) but because that plan can look either attractive or forbidding depending upon how we look at it. Milton's God is dialectical, unfolding his plan not only in steps but by progressive stages, each of which reverses the current of feeling in the previous stage. Milton read the Bible in this way, and it is my belief that he wrote *Paradise Lost* in this way, too. Thus the Father begins the revelation of his ways by an almost uncompromisingly harsh pronouncement that "justice" demands no help be given to creatures who have freely rejected his love. But the Son knows how to "read" the Father's words, and the secret is a simple one. The Son knows that however harsh God's words may sound, his love for his "youngest son" (the implied comparison between man and the Son is surely not inadvertent) is such as to prevent his dealing in any but the kindest way with man. For the Son the one word, "mercy," shines like a beacon from the lowering storm clouds of God's apparent anger—light out of darkness. That single word, combined with faith in God's goodness, turns a threat into a promise. His answer is of course not "wheedling," nor is God even making up his mind by stages, but it *seems* so to our time-bound apprehensions, since this is the way *we* think things out and the way human language represents them. Father and Son are putting on a dramatic performance for the benefit of creaturely intellects—ostensibly for the angels, actually for us.

That the Son speaks the Father's thoughts is asserted both by the poet: "in him all his Father shone Substantially express'd" (III, 139–40), and even more explicitly by the Father himself:

> O Son, in whom my Soul hath chief delight,
> Son of my bosom, Son who art alone
> My word, my wisdom, and effectual might,
> All hast thou spok'n as my thoughts are, all
> As my Eternal purpose hath decreed. (III, 168–72)

Here God affirms that the Son's critique of divine justice is not simply one he agrees with but is *his own* critique. Perhaps the reader would come to see it that way too, if the Father did not so soon reinstate eye-for-an-eye justice again:

> Man disobeying,
> Disloyal breaks his fealty, and sins
> Against the high Supremacy of Heav'n,
> Affecting God-head, and so losing all,
> To expiate his Treason hath naught left,
> But to destruction sacred and devote,
> He with his whole posterity must die,
> Die hee or Justice must; unless for him
> Some other able, and as willing, pay
> The rigid satisfaction, death for death. (III, 203–12)

This is the kind of pound-of-flesh legalism for which Reformation Christianity is so deservedly infamous, and it arises precisely from the Reformation's desire to make the ways of God seem logical and consistent: if Christ has been sent to "redeem" mankind, then it must be that God, like a pawnbroker, demands that debts be redeemed, even if he reaches into his own pocket to do so. That Milton believed in this doctrine of redemption is clear from *Christian Doctrine*, but that he saw it as in need of extenuation is clear from *Paradise Lost* itself. Otherwise the naked truth of God's exacting justice might blind the reader with doubt and despair to God's (logically inconsistent) mercy and goodness.

The sense in Book III that God's justice and God's mercy clash with and contradict each other is not simply the result of a dramatic method of presentation. God's justice and God's mercy really *do* clash with one another, at least to our human apprehensions, and it is to Milton's credit that he does not try to hide their logical incompatibility. In God's second speech, the door of mercy, flung open wide by the Son, is squeezed partly shut again by the Father:

> Man shall not quite be lost, but sav'd who will,
> Yet not of will in him, but grace in me
> Freely voutsaf't. (III, 173–75)
> . . . .

> Some I have chosen of peculiar grace
> Elect above the rest; so is my will:
> The rest shall hear me call, and oft be warn'd
> Thir sinful state, and to appease betimes
> Th' incensed Deity while offer'd grace
> Invites; for I will clear thir senses dark,
> What may suffice, and soft'n stony hearts
> To pray, repent, and bring obedience due.
> To Prayer, repentance, and obedience due,
> Though but endeavor'd with sincere intent,
> Mine ear shall not be slow, mine eye not shut.
> And I will place within them as a guide
> My Umpire Conscience, whom if they will hear,
> Light after light well us'd they shall attain,
> And to the end persisting, safe arrive.
> This my long sufferance and my day of grace
> They who neglect and scorn, shall never taste;
> But hard be hard'n'd, blind be blinded more,
> That they may stumble on, and deeper fall;
> And none but such from mercy I exclude. (III, 183–202)

Lines 183–84 are perhaps more in need of extenuation than any in the poem. For Milton's God states explicitly what I have argued is implicitly true of other portions of the Heavenly Council, that there are mysteries in Providence beyond the power of man's rational mind to understand: "Some I have chosen of peculiar grace Elect above the rest; *so is my will.*" A Calvinist reader, and those readers who fear that Milton is a Calvinist, might well suspect that the category of those who, not among the elect, still endeavor sincerely to repent and thus in the end are saved, is in fact an empty category. Again we have to look outside the poem for reassurance, a procedure which suggests that the poem itself is raising problems in the reader's mind that it does not satisfactorily answer, at this point at least.

Milton, as we know from *Christian Doctrine*, rejected the Calvinist doctrine of predestination by arguing that God was no "respecter of persons"—that is, that God did not predestine *particular people* for salvation or damnation.[7] Calvin's position was, on the face of it at least, the more logical, since an omnipotent, omniscient, and eternal God can hardly *not* be ultimately responsible for *all* of his creatures' acts, including their decision to believe or disbelieve. But Milton, as we have already seen, takes refuge in the mystery of free will in order to save the Christian moral system from absurdity. Thus we may say that Calvin is ultimately no more logical than Milton; in choosing to be consistent with Christian metaphysics, he (Calvin) makes Christian morality a mystery of faith:

> Because it seems absurd . . . that some men should be preferred to others without merit, human effrontery enters into controversy with God, as if He showed more respect to some persons than was right.[8]

Calvin's idea that God rewards some men with Heaven and allows others to roast in Hell—not on the basis of "merit" but simply at his own pleasure—is hardly one that would encourage us to think of God as either just or reasonable. Calvin's God commands sinners to believe, while making it impossible for them to do so; Milton prefers a God who is morally consistent to one who is metaphysically consistent.

What the Father is saying in his second speech seems to be the following: Although God does favor, for his own inscrutable reasons, some sinners more than others ("Some I have chosen of peculiar grace"), *all* sinners will have full opportunity to be aware of their sin (hence the "Umpire Conscience") and to repent. Repentence is not in the power of fallen man, however; hence the need for grace to "soft'n stony hearts." But God's gift is not automatic: men must *want* to repent ("Though but *endeavor'd* with sincere intent"), and those who do not want grace will not have it.

Milton's poem argues that God's will is not to exclude anyone *arbitrarily* from grace, but to exclude those who will not have it. This doctrine tries to meet an obvious objection to Christian doctrine—that although Christ came to save mankind, not all men are saved—by answering that men must first *want* to be saved, or at least (such powers of volition being beyond the capacity of most fallen men) they must *want* to want it. Even so, the goodness of Milton's God is not beyond impugning. After all, countless souls are consigned by God to everlasting perdition simply because God has ordained their wills to be free. If God will not *make* his creatures love him (since to compel love violates free will) would it not be kinder simply to annihilate them than to allow them to remain in eternal torment? It is perhaps to answer this possible objection that Milton made Belial affirm the desire of the fallen angels to continue existing ("for who would lose, Though full of pain, this intellectual being . . ," II,146–47). Eternal torment, says Belial, is preferable to annihilation. But the claim is highly debatable and hardly reassuring to those readers who would rather not suffer for eternity. God's final justification of the condemnation of souls to endless torment is that he has ordained free will—but is such an ordinance really consonant with the hypothesis of God's perfect goodness?

Trying to follow the logic of the Father's words we are, like the fallen angels of Book II, "in wand'ring mazes lost" (II,561). This is precisely my point. It is frequently maintained that in Book III God's ways, however hard to accept, are at least logical and intelligible.[9] My impression is precisely the opposite: that the harder we stare at the Light, the more blind we become. I cannot pretend that many readers will spend so long or pry into so many murky corners as I have, but I do maintain that the harder the reader tries to see God's ways as the God of Book III presents them—that is, as rationally consistent—the more confused he will get. God's logic is not our logic; his light is our darkness:

> Dark with excessive bright thy skirts appear,
> Yet dazzle Heav'n, that brightest Seraphim
> Approach not, but with both wings veil thir eyes. (III,380–82)

The humbler reader, who does not aim to get to the bottom of every mystery but relies on his general impressions, is better off, but not by much. The word "mercy" has been explained and the way up to Heaven revealed, but that way looks hard and seldom traveled: "Man shall not *quite* be lost. . . . *Yet not of will in him* but grace in me Freely voutsaf' t"(III,173–75). By stressing that it is God, not man, who provides the will power to repent, the Father depicts man as a creature of very feeble capacity indeed, yet this same nearly paralysed will is expected to perform resolutely ("And to the end *persisting*" III,197).

The tone is still overpoweringly negative. Not one line pictures the joy and bliss that await the redeemed, while line after line insists upon the difficulty of the road, stresses the sinner's unfitness to undertake the journey, and suggests that few indeed will ever reach the goal. God clearly expects profound and sustained efforts from the sinner in his own behalf, yet he pictures man as so helpless ("how frail His fall'n condition is," III,180–81) that it must take great faith and fortitude on our part not to give a hollow laugh when God makes what in this speech is his final clarification of what "mercy" means:

> This my long sufferance and my day of grace
> They who neglect and scorn, shall never taste;
> But hard be hard'n'd, blind be blinded more,
> That they may stumble on, and deeper fall;
> And none but such from mercy I exclude. (III,198–202)

None but such! Surely with such a task before him and so meager a capacity to undertake it, not one sinner in ten million will reach port and taste God's "mercy." God's mercy is a sentence of death: "He with his whole posterity must die, Die hee or Justice must" (III,209–10). The reader knows that the Son will offer to ransom man, but he also knows that each of us is born under a sentence of death. Whatever ransom has been paid, the sentence remains unchanged.

The Heavenly Dialogue baffles the intellect and troubles the emotions by not delivering what it seems to promise. The promise of a superhuman view of God's Truth ends in doubts and paradoxes, while our expectation of a supremely good God is disappointed by a character who seems either indifferent or actually angry toward mankind. His first two speeches in Book III amply confirm the impression given by Books I and II that he is tyrannous and willful, meting out, even in advance of the transgression, an inflexible justice that is insufficiently palliated by a "mercy" hedged round with conditions and exceptions. An omnipotent God *should* be impartial, serene, imperturbable, and consistent, but when he is imagined as a human being these qualities can easily seem to be coldness, derision, indifference, and implacability. What is missing from God's words is a declaration of love for his erring creatures, some reassurance of his unerring good will that would make us—at each ambiguous or threatening point in the Divine Plan—pick the alternative most consistent with his loving kindness.

Here is where the character and role of the Son is so important. Not that his voice of itself can compensate for the Father's omissions, nor as a matter of fact does the Son declare love for mankind either, although we should observe that his promised *actions* imply such love in the highest degree. What he does is discover behind God's words a benevolence that the words themselves do not adequately express, as if the Father were concerned to understate his love for man. The Son, that is, trusts not the appearances of words, but his own faith in God's love:

> Father, thy word is past, man shall find grace;
> And shall grace not find means, that finds her way,
> The speediest of thy winged messengers,
> To visit all thy creatures, and to all
> Comes unprevented, unimplor'd, unsought?
> Happy for man, so coming; he her aid
> Can never seek, once dead in sins and lost;
> Atonement for himself or offering meet,
> Indebted and undone, hath none to bring:
> Behold mee then, mee for him, life for life
> I offer, on mee let thine anger fall;
> Account mee man; I for his sake will leave
> Thy bosom, and this glory next to thee
> Freely put off, and for him lastly die
> Well pleas'd, on me let Death wreck all his rage. (III,227–41)

In this second speech, the Son exemplifies precisely the spirit in which God's words are to be read: first, the spirit of submission ("Father, thy word is past, man shall find grace; And shall grace not find means?") and humility ("Behold mee then, mee for him, life for life I offer, on mee let thine anger fall"); second, the capacity to look beyond the menacing exteriors of words to their secret promise. For God's harshest threat— "Die hee or Justice must"—is in actuality, read rightly, a promise. The Son discovers that the word "death" has a spiritual as well as a literal meaning: man can never seek the aid of Grace, he says, "once dead in sins and lost." Since one can be physically alive and yet spiritually dead,

"dead," like "blind" in the prologue, is a paradoxical term that, looked at with the eyes of faith, becomes attractive rather than forbidding:

> thou has giv'n me to possess
> Life in myself for ever, by thee I live,
> Though now to Death I yield, and am his due
> All that of me can die, yet that debt paid,
> Thou wilt not leave me in the loathsome grave
> His prey, nor suffer my unspotted Soul
> For ever with corruption there to dwell;
> But I shall rise Victorious, and subdue
> My vanquisher, spoil'd of his vaunted spoil;
> Death his death's wound shall then receive, and stoop
> Inglorious, of his mortal sting disarm'd. (III,243–53)

Looked at through the eyes of faith, death becomes, as regenerate Adam discovers near the poem's end, its opposite—"the gate of Life" (XII,517), a meaning that the Father himself marks with the seal of his authority in Book III:

> So Man, as is most just,
> Shall satisfy for Man, be judg'd and die,
> And dying rise, and rising with him raise
> His Brethren, ransom'd with his own dear life. (III,294–97)

The dialogue in Heaven has led to a radical shift away from the will and purposes of the Father to those of the Son. Milton's God is a *progressive* deity, one who unfolds in stages, and there is even the suggestion, in his last speech, that he means to "abdicate" in favor of his Son:

> because in thee
> Love hath abounded more than Glory abounds,
> Therefore thy Humiliation shall exalt
> With thee thy Manhood also to this Throne;
> Here shalt thou sit incarnate, here shalt Reign
> Both God and Man, Son both of God and Man,
> Anointed universal King; all Power
> I give thee, reign for ever, and assume
> Thy Merits; under thee as Head Supreme
> Thrones, Princedoms, Powers, Dominions I reduce:
> All knees to thee shall bow, of them that bide
> In Heaven, or Earth, or under Earth in Hell. (III,311–22)

The idea of eternal, omniscient Omnipotence abdicating is one that the mind cannot easily accept. What it suggests is that Father and Son are indeed "one," that their separate persons are masks we are meant to see through; and that as God's plan of redemption progresses, he will have less and less reason to show himself as hard and just. The mild and merciful face of the Son will henceforth become the face of God, and the guise of "Father" will be abandoned.

Far from being exempt from change, Milton's God himself submits to a process of evolution—the Father first gives way to the Son, who will in turn give way:

> Then thou [i.e., the Son] thy regal Sceptre shalt lay by,
> For regal Sceptre then no more shall need,
> God shall be All in All. (III,339–41)

In this vision of ultimate democracy, Heaven and Earth will merge; Father, Son, angels, and men will all be part of an encompassing Godhead. In tract of time, all human souls (all except the damned!) will become, or will discover they always were, "God." That time is not yet, but the Father finishes by suggesting that Father and Son at least ought to be thought of as essentially the same being:

> all ye Gods,
> Adore him, who to compass all this dies,
> Adore the Son, and honor him as mee. (III,341–43)[10]

These are abstruse hints, however, which most readers have never noticed. For the purposes of the narrative action in Book III, Father and Son are separate persons, and the Son is first of a series of dramatized "readers" of God's words, looking between the lines of Old Testament harshness to find Christian tenderness and compassion. The Son is the narrative "mediator" in Book III, as he is the spiritual mediator between God and man in Christian redemption. By responding as he does to God's apparently harsh pronouncements, he teaches us to do the same. If we close the eye of the senses and of that sort of reason that insists upon proof, if we are content not to get to the bottom of each of God's mysteries, then our eyes will be opened and we will see, through the eyes of faith, God's perfect goodness, less in his words than in his *actions*—actions which however are yet to be, both in the poem and in the world Milton's readers inhabit.

But a lesson such as this, teaching the superiority of concrete experience over abstract theorizing, cannot be taught in the theoretical and abstract manner of the Heavenly Dialogue. Instead of a refutation of Satan's charge of arbitrariness, we find it confirmed. God's vaunted logic is the logic of *a priori* rectitude: God is right because he is God. Getting close to God, we find how far we are from him. Favored by God, we are favored with temptation; forgiven by God, we are consoled with death—and all, ultimately, for his greater "Glory." From the final mutual admiration of Father and Son, man is excluded, like the charity case invited to eat downstairs with the help.

The gross narrative function of the Dialogue in Heaven is to make God a felt presence in the poem, and in terms of "message" to give God's ways as clear as exposition as their mysterious nature and our own limitations allow. The effect upon the reader is, however, humiliating, and to that extent alienating. By denying us at this point in the poem the kind of emotional experience that alone would enable us to accept the difficult fate that God foresees for man, it prevents us from seeing his ways as justified. But in so doing it suggests why the rest of the poem is necessary. Only through *experience* can God's love be felt—this is what makes the rest of human history, and the rest of the poem, necessary. The Dialogue in Heaven succeeds by failing.

3

Points of View in Paradise

> "We are not provided with wisdom, we must dis-
> cover it for ourselves, after a journey through the wil-
> derness which no one else can take for us, an effort
> which no one can spare us, for our wisdom is the point
> of view from which we come at last to regard the world."
> — Marcel Proust, *Remembrance of Things Past*

LIKE ANY STORY with more than one character, *Paradise Lost* is built
out of multiple points of view: Satanic, Divine, Angelic, Innocent,
Fallen. The presence of different and often conflicting perspectives implies that we are being offered a choice—that Milton permits and indeed
requires us to choose between good and evil, between God and Satan.
This is not surprising, since the subject of Milton's epic is freedom, its
conditions, and its uses:

> Many there be that complain of divin Providence for suffering Adam to
> transgresse, foolish tongues! when God gave him reason, he gave him
> freedom to choose, for reason is but choosing.[1]

Milton's God gives each of his rational creatures freedom of choice—
"Reason is also choice" (III,108)—and it is not fanciful to think that the
poet himself imitated God's respect for the autonomy of the individual
human soul when he wrote *Paradise Lost*.

Hence the particular strategy of Milton's "great argument." It takes
no special skill or wisdom to announce dogmatically that Satan is bad and
God good, that sin is to be avoided and virtue loved. If men were so

easily made good then the whole problem of evil would long since have
been solved and forgotten. On the contrary, Milton sets out to justify
God's ways because they so clearly need such justification if we are to
accept our difficult situation as God's creatures. Despite the sufferings
God has "favored" us with, we must love God and expect his love if we
are to be saved. But love cannot be compelled: it must be freely given.
"Not free," says the Father:

> what proof could they have giv'n sincere
> Of true allegiance, constant Faith or Love,
> Where only what they needs must do, appear'd,
> Not what they would? (III,103–106)

The burden of freedom must be borne. Milton's job in *Paradise Lost* is to
persuade us that God is good; our job is to make our very best effort of
understanding, without surrendering our freedom, if Milton fails, not to
be persuaded.

Of course such justification is not simply (or even primarily) a matter
of logical demonstration. Milton regarded a holy poet like Spenser as "a
better teacher than Scotus or Acquinas" not because poetry is more
suited to rigorous philosophic proof but because the "justification" he
aims at is a matter of seeing and feeling as well as of thinking. His poem
does not compel us to love God and hate Satan—how could it?—but
neither does it give us a raw choice without guidance; that we have without reading the poem. It offers us, rather, a *pattern* of logic, vision, and
affect that teaches us, if we are willing to learn, how to make that choice.

In terms of narrative art, that pattern is built up out of the clash and
resonance of different points of view. At no point in the poem are we
entirely subjected to a single, monolithic perspective upon events: Satan
has his interlocutors, as does God, and Milton's "narrative voice," as we
have seen, rings a complex series of changes on the role of commenta-
tor—sometimes supporting Satan, sometimes condemning him, thrust-
ing himself forward *in propria persona*, then effacing himself behind his
characters, simultaneously leading and misleading in a multitude of different ways and combinations that ultimately defeat rational classifica-
tion. If we remember that, as Wayne Booth has argued, all speaking characters are "narrators," too, then it is clear that Milton's narrative art is
polyphonic, with a constant interplay of "voices" variously reinforcing and
contradicting each other.[2]

However, it is also clear that in the first three books large blocks of narrative are effectively dominated by a single point of view. Beelzebub and the other fallen angels speak Satan's thoughts, just as later the Son speaks the Father's. Even when their interlocutors seem to contradict Satan or God, they do so only to bring out latent inconsistencies, as when Beelzebub's initial dejection brings out some of the futility in Satan's posturing, or when the Son contradicts God's justice with God's mercy. Most important, although the narrator's point of view often stands in opposition to Satan's in Books I and II, and is also sharply distinguishable from God's in Book III, that opposition is neither consistent nor emphatic. Until Book IV opposition *within* each section of the narrative is not fully dramatized but is provided *sotto voce* by the epic voice, who at moments speaks his own views, only to turn at other moments to projecting those of dramatized characters.

It may be this nearly monolithic predominance of a single point of view that leads to the reader's feeling of being overpowered and bludgeoned by the poem's first three books, of being unequal to the demands either of Milton's God or of the poem devoted to him. We are accustomed to seeing things in two lights: "pure" evil and "pure" good are equally puzzling and perplexing, which is perhaps why we persist, against the epic voice's avowed wishes, in seeing a double image of God and Satan, much as after staring too long at the sun we see a dark sun projected against our eyelids.

"The very essence of truth is plainness and brightness," says Milton the epistemologist; but Milton the phenomenologist adds: "the darkness and crookedness is our own."[3] Truth may be simple and clear, but the double mind of fallen man sees a more complicated picture. A fallen world is at once the image and the product of a fallen mind, as Andrew Marvell argues in one of his seriously witty meditations upon gardens:

Luxurious Man, to bring his Vice in use,
    Did after him the World seduce:
And from the fields the Flow'rs and Plants allure,
    Where Nature was most plain and pure.
He first enclos'd within the Gardens square
    A dead and standing pool of Air:
And a more luscious Earth for them did knead,
    Which stupifi'd them while it fed.
The Pink grew then as double as his Mind;
    The nutriment did change the kind.[4]

The technique of the opening books seems intended more to exacerbate than to heal the doubleness of our minds. Mind-wrenching imperatives like "Evil be thou my good," "Die hee or Justice must," and even "Be thou in Adam's room," are puzzling and frightening; they darken and confuse our responses to Milton's theme. The epic poet's art seems one more veil drawn between our eyes and the plain, clear truth we expected, or at least hoped, to find. As we shall shortly see, Books IV and V introduce techniques designed to remedy the reader's sense of anguished dualism, but at the beginning of Book IV Milton is content to reintroduce and even to aggravate the contradictions that have bothered us so in the first three books.

> O for that warning voice, which he who saw
> Th' Apocalypse, heard cry in Heav'n aloud,
> Then when the Dragon, put to second rout,
> Came furious down to be reveng'd on men,
> *Woe to the inhabitants on Earth!* that now,
> While time was, our first Parents had been warn'd
> The coming of thir secret foe, and scap'd
> Haply so scap'd his mortal snare. . . . (IV,1–8)

In the opening lines of Book IV of *Paradise Lost*, the epic voice overtly questions God's justice in allowing Satan to tempt Adam and Eve. The poet's stance is complex, since the reference to St. John anticipates Satan's ultimate defeat, but for the moment the narrator is content to reestablish the image of Satan as a great and mighty enemy of God and man. Caught between opposing supernatural forces who both seem to wish his downfall (Satan actively; God by inaction) man is once again the helpless "puny habitant" of Book II, victim of forces beyond his control. As we shall discover, Adam and Eve *are* warned of their secret foe, and the narrator's stumbling over the anticipated consequences of such a warning—"and scap'd Haply [i.e., "perhaps"] so scap'd his mortal snare"— shows that he doesn't quite believe what he is saying. The immediate effect upon the reader, however, is to return us to the deterministic world of pagan epic, in which fallen beings are victims, and in which the contest between good and evil is a power struggle at which mankind is a helpless spectator. The narrator has returned us, in short, to the Satanic perspective.

Ironically, though, Satan himself has been undermining that perspective. Since leaving Pandaemonium he has been subjected to various

perspectives that belittle and distance him. Consistently a large and imposing figure in the flattering confines of Hell, he seems far less so as he
wanders through chaos, or when God bends down his eye to find him
"coasting the wall of Heav'n" in Book III. More important, his claims to
heroic character have been smirched in encounters with Sin and Uriel.[5]
Our image of Satan the haughty rebel has been gradually undermined by
the image of Satan as opportunist, who says and does whatever he must
to get ahead. Add to this the snubbing Satan gets in God's first speech in
Book III, and the reader is bound to take a more skeptical view of Satan.
Having seen more of the universe he inhabits, we are simply less willing
to believe what he says.

Yet at precisely the moment when, seeing through his lies, we have
achieved some distance from him, Satan opens his heart and begins to
tell the truth! Rhetorically addressing the Sun (IV,32–41), Satan speaks
his inner thoughts, stripped of all need to conceal or embellish. He is in
the wrong and says so:

> Ah wherefore! he deserv'd no such return
> From me, whom he created what I was
> In that bright eminence, and with his good
> Upbraided none; nor was his service hard.
> What could be less than to afford him praise,
> The easiest recompense, and pay him thanks,
> How due! (IV,42–48)

Satan sees precisely what God sees, but we cannot for this reason say that
the Satanic and Divine Perspectives are the same. In *Paradise Lost* truth
exists and is the same for all viewers, but point of view determines the
perceiver's response to that truth.

With Angelic intelligence Satan cannot fail to perceive God's hard
truths, but since they make his position absolutely untenable, he must
perpetually deny or ignore them as soon as he sees them. Thus he admits
that "all his good prov'd ill in me" (IV,48), but he still tries to find some
way of blaming God. Perhaps (Satan thinks) divine love itself can be accused of being insufficient:

> whom hast thou then or what to accuse,
> But Heav'n's free Love dealt equally to all?
> Be then his Love accurst, since love or hate,
> To me alike, it deals eternal woe. (IV,67–70)

But he knows that nothing God has done determined his fall; Satan *chose* damnation: "Nay curs'd be thou; since against his thy will Chose freely what it now so justly rues" (IV,71–72). The result is a spectacle at once painful and absurd, illustrating the narrator's prefatory observation that "within him Hell He brings, and round about him, nor from Hell One step no more than from himself can fly By change of place" (IV,20–23).

This inner dialectic, the charge and counter-charge of a soul at war with itself, is the style Milton reserves for fallen beings. In *Paradise Lost* only Satan and fallen Adam soliloquize, as if to demonstrate that only divided beings can speak to themselves. This self-division in fact may be not merely the emblem of Hell but its essence, as the narrator suggests when he likens "the Hell within" Satan to a cannon recoiling upon its gunner:

> his dire attempt, which nigh the birth
> Now rolling, boils in his tumultuous breast,
> And like a devilish Engine back recoils
> Upon himself. (IV,15–18)

In planning evil for Adam and Eve, Satan is tormenting himself, and each unsuccessful attempt to blame God for his sufferings merely makes his load of self-reproach greater:

> Me miserable! which way shall I fly
> Infinite wrath, and infinite despair?
> Which way I fly is Hell; myself am Hell;
> And in the lowest deep a lower deep
> Still threat'ning to devour me opens wide,
> To which the Hell I suffer seems a Heav'n. (IV,73–78)

Satan is (or seems to be) going through precisely the spiritual struggle that the Father outlined in Book III as the product of "Umpire Conscience":

> The rest shall hear me call, and oft be warn'd
> Thir sinful state, and to appease betimes
> Th' incensed Deity while offer'd grace
> Invites. . . . (III,185–88)

The narrator refers to conscience, too, in Satan's case (IV,23–24), raising the interesting question: could Satan at this moment repent? Christians have traditionally assumed that he cannot, a view that God seems to endorse when he says "Man therefore shall find grace, The other [i.e., Satan] none" (III,131–32). However, the paradoxes surrounding God's foreknowledge and omnipotence prevent us from knowing whether this is a command or a prediction.

To apply a human sense of justice to the situation demands that Satan be given the same chance of repentance, even though God foresees that Satan will never use it. If so, then the latter part of Satan's soliloquy is not a grisly example of how God twists the knife in a wounded spirit but a vivid drama of how the soul chooses its own damnation:

> O then at last relent: is there no place
> Left for Repentance, none for Pardon left?
> None left but by submission; and that word
> Disdain forbids me, and my dread of shame
> Among the Spirits beneath, whom I seduc'd
> With other promises and other vaunts
> Than to submit, boasting I could subdue
> Th' Omnipotent. Ay me, they little know
> How dearly I abide that boast so vain,
> Under what torments inwardly I groan:
> While they adore me on the Throne of Hell,
> With Diadem and Sceptre high advanc'd
> The lower still I fall, only Supreme
> In misery; such joy Ambition finds. (IV,79–92)

Although Satan chooses not to repent, he does seem to believe at this point that he *could* be pardoned if he were to submit. Yet he immediately, inconsistently, asserts that he is *beyond* all hope of salvation, taking refuge in precisely the same excuse that every sinner gives himself when tortured by conscience—I have no choice:

> But say I could repent and could obtain
> By Act of Grace my former state; how soon
> Would highth recall high thoughts, how soon unsay
> What feign'd submission swore: ease would recant
> Vows made in pain, as violent and void.
> For never can true reconcilement grow
> Where wounds of deadly hate have pierc'd so deep:
> Which would but lead me to a worse relapse,
> And heavier fall: so should I purchase dear
> Short intermission bought with double smart. (IV,93–102)

The absurdity, the illogic of Satan's position is finally clear to the reader—
Satan is damned because he *chooses* to be: "And none but such from
mercy I exclude" (III,202).

The effect of Satan's soliloquy is to change our view of him profoundly, for he in effect acknowledges everything God said about him
earlier. In previous books he blamed God for his revolt; now he accuses
himself. Previously he had struck the pose of heroic independence; now
he confesses to being confused and despairing. The pomp and circumstance of Hell in large part obscured testimony that Satan was neither so
grand nor so bold as he claimed; now Satan's own voice joins those testifying against him.

But the truth-telling, tormented Satan we now see is in some ways
a more involving character than the earlier epic hero. Lines like "from
what state I fell, how glorious once above thy Sphere" (IV,38–39), *mean*
something to us by now; through long association with Satan we can feel
their pathos as well as their egotism. And no one to whom the issues of
damnation and salvation are, or have become, important can fail to be
fascinated and appalled by Satan's sufferings and self-deceptions, as he
veers toward repentance and then away again. Wracked by contraries,
tortured by conscience, he is, like each of us, a suffering sinner. His view
of things may be both painful and irrational, but it is terribly familiar.
Entering the Garden with Satan, we first discover in the blind bard's own
presentation of Eden, how much like Satan's our view of it must be.

Eden before the Fall should be an image of perfect goodness; yet
even if Milton's double mind could conceive of such a place, how could
our ambiguous language express it; and what reader would be pure
enough to understand? Ambivalence is the mind's normal state: we are
intolerant of ambiguity precisely because we are so vulnerable to it, so
aware that the native hue of resolution is apt to be sicklied o'er with the
pale cast of thought. Fallen human beings must feel ambivalent about
Milton's portrait of Eden: it ravishes us and yet brings to our remem-
brance from what state we fell.

Hence the problem that has most bothered modern critics with respect to Milton's Eden—why does innocence appear so *fallen*?—is partly
answered by the simple reminder that there is *no* way for Milton, or for
any other poet since Adam's fall, to present an Eden untinged with de-

fect. Since we bring impurity into the world, we bring it also to Milton's Eden; even if we were to enter Eden before Satan, he would enter with us. As Marvell's poem argues, fallen minds perceive fallen gardens, just as fallen hands *produce* fallen gardens. Since Milton could not escape this fact, he exploited it.

Faced with the goodly prospect of the newly created universe, Satan has momentarily wavered between good and evil. So does the narrator. The "pure air" of Eden, he says, is "able to drive All sadness but despair" (IV,155–56). Even at this delightful moment the word "despair" raises the possibility of an antithetical perspective on Eden's pleasures, a suggestion Milton echoes when he then tells us Satan is "better pleased" with the perfumes of Paradise "Than Asmodeus with the fishy fume" (IV,168). "The poet's principal intention," remarks Frank Kermode, "is simply to get into the context a bad smell."[6] Not entirely. Through the bad smell we also participate in Satan's sense of Eden's potential for corruption. The fishy fume helps define our point of view. Milton obliges us, like Satan, to smell Eden's innocence going bad; unlike Satan, we take no pleasure in the change.

This clash of perspectives is absolutely characteristic of the style of Book IV. Milton's overall technique in approaching Eden is to alternate impressions of innocence, purity, and delight with their opposite: "pure air" with "fishy fume." There is a kind of impropriety here, since Eden itself is pure delight; the reader who expects sensual gratification alone is apt to be disgruntled:

> [Eden's river] now divided into four main Streams,
> Runs diverse, wand'ring many a famous Realm
> And Country whereof here needs no account,
> But rather to tell how, if Art could tell,
> How from the Sapphire Fount the crisped Brooks,
> Rolling on Orient Pearl and sands of Gold,
> With mazy error under pendant shades
> Ran Nectar, visiting each plant, and fed
> Flow'rs worthy of Paradise which not nice Art
> In Beds and curious Knots, but Nature boon
> Pour'd forth profuse on Hill and Dale and Plain,
> Both where the morning Sun first warmly smote
> The open field, and where the unpierc't shade
> Imbrown'd the noontide Bow'rs: Thus was the place,
> A happy rural seat of various view. . . . (IV,233–47)

Here a fresh country landscape of flowers poured profusely and with natural randomness is juxtaposed to a heavily artificial scene of sapphire founts and sands of gold, an artificiality that is underscored by two mentions of "art" as both inappropriate to Eden and inadequate to its description. But even the denial makes present in the reader's mind what Milton seems to be trying to exclude: "not nice Art In Beds and curious Knots" calls up before the reader's mind a picture that he can't quite cancel. If Milton's purpose were to present an innocent, pastoral Eden, he need only have omitted such tainted details. By leaving them in, along with self-conscious phrases like "if art could tell," he seems unable, as F.R. Leavis claims, to portray an unfallen Eden:

> as the laboured, pedantic artifice of the diction suggests, Milton seems here to be focussing rather upon words than upon perceptions, sensations or things. . . . In this Grand Style, the medium calls pervasively for a kind of attention, compels an attitude towards itself, that is incompatible with sharp, concrete realization; just as it would seem to be, in the mind of the poet, incompatible with an interest in sensuous particularity. He exhibits a feeling *for* words rather than a capacity for feeling *through* words.[7]

Leavis's criticisms underline a crucial fact about Milton's "art"; despite the show of concreteness, we are not actually seeing Eden at this point with "sensuous particularity." Not daffodils, pansies, and marigolds but "flowers" are poured out on no particular landscape but on a generalized "Hill and Dale and Plain." No viewer stands at a particular spot at a particular time, but rather the narrator shows us an "average" view, including a variety of geographical features at a variety of times of day, both morning and noontime. The "Sapphire Fount" and "crisped Brooks" are a bit more particular, perhaps, but they have a staleness of diction, a bookish quality that Milton seems to be apologizing for when he reminds us that "Art" is inadequate to their description. The apology is worse than useless and simply breaks whatever illusion there was that we were looking at Eden instead of at words.

One aspect of this verbal self-consciousness that has received considerable attention is the way a line like "With mazy error under pendant shades" suggests a fallen perspective:

> *Error* here is not exactly a pun, since it means only "wandering,"—but the "only" is a different thing from an absolutely simple use of the word, since the evil meaning is consciously and ominously excluded.

Rather than the meaning being simply "wandering," it is "wandering (not error)." Certainly the word is a reminder of the Fall, in that it takes us back to a time when there were no infected words because there were no infected actions.[8]

By having two meanings, one obvious but inappropriate, the other appropriate but hidden in etymology, the word "error" enacts in the reader's mind the mental process he must go through on his way back to Eden— rejecting first responses in favor of a more discerning second response ("Error. No: wandering, not error"). And since every other word in the line requires an analogous sifting of innocent and guilty meanings— mazes and shades are prominent Miltonic symbols for Hell, and even "pendant" suggests falling—"With mazy error under pendant shades" represents a considerable challenge to the fallen reader not to see a fallen Eden.

Although the line is replete with Empsonian ambiguity, the effect of each detail is to subtract from rather than add to the effect of "sharp, concrete realization." The effect is precisely as Leavis describes it: "In this Grand Style, the medium calls pervasively for a kind of attention, compels an attitude towards itself." The attitude called for is one of skepticism: in rejecting one meaning of "error" for another, we learn (as with "light" in the prologue to Book III) to scrutinize Milton's words more carefully.

But we must go further, for the pattern implicit in "wandering (not error)" is the structural principle upon which the entire set description of Eden as Satan "views" it is built. Like the drawing of a woman at a dressing-table mirror, that as the eye moves suddenly becomes a death's head, Milton's Eden flickers in Book IV between suggestions of innocent pleasure and fallen pain. The narrator first situates the garden geographically, but in terms of places that are yet to be in the poem's present and that are no more in Milton's present, or in ours:

> Eden stretch'd her Line
> From Auran Eastward to the Royal Tow'rs
> Of great Seleucia, built by Grecian Kings,
> Or where the Sons of Eden long before
> Dwelt in Telassar. . . . (IV,210–14)

Mesopotamia has modern cities whose locations could have been used as coordinates for Milton's Eden, and although Auran, Seleucia, and Telassar have an evocativeness that Baghdad perhaps lacks, the question remains: evocative of what? Of vanished glory, I would suppose. Milton invites us to imagine Eden by offering names barely less fabulous, so that it will shimmer in our minds over a not-quite-visible topography in a remote and unfamiliar section of the world. If his list of vanished cities evokes anything, it is feelings, not pictures, and this is true of other passages as well:

> in this pleasant soil
> His far more pleasant Garden God ordain'd;
> Out of the fertile ground he caus'd to grow
> All Trees of noblest kind for sight, smell, taste;
> And all amid them stood the Tree of Life,
> High eminent, blooming Ambrosial Fruit
> Of vegetable Gold; and next to Life
> Our Death the Tree of Knowledge grew fast by,
> Knowledge of Good bought dear by knowing ill. (IV,214–22)

The garden is "pleasant," the Tree of Life is "noble," "eminent," and its fruit is "Ambrosial" (tastes and smells good), but this small grain of sensuous particularity is eclipsed by the problematic "vegetable Gold," an Edenic oxymoron. Some readers have felt the word "gold" hardens and denatures "vegetable," while others argue that the adjective softens and vivifies the noun. Since both responses are logical and spontaneous, it seems likely that, like other oxymorons, this paradoxical image calls forth contradictory responses in the reader's mind. We see the fruit simultaneously in antithetical ways, and Eden flickers.

The mention of "Art" in a passage we have already looked at (IV,233–47) is a reminder of where Milton has gone for many of his details:

> Groves whose rich Trees wept odorous Gums and Balm,
> Others whose fruit burnisht with Golden Rind
> Hung amiable, Hesperian Fables true,
> If true, here only, and of delicious taste. (IV,248–51)

Since pagan fables were for Milton the cracked images of biblical truth, we might expect him to claim that Ovid's Hesperides was actually a racial memory of Eden. Actually he is much more tentative: Hesperian fables may be simply false; perhaps Eden's fruits were not golden. Milton does not "see" clearly in Eden, and neither do we:

> Betwixt them Lawns, or level Downs, and Flocks
> Grazing the tender herb, were interpos'd,
> Or palmy hillock, or the flow'ry lap
> Of some irriguous Valley spread her store,
> Flow'rs of all hue, and without Thorn the Rose. (IV,252–56)

The delighted eye dances quickly here from one delight to the next but sees none of them with clarity or precision save perhaps the proverbial thornless rose. Our minds are made to hover between images, profuse but cursory, all more or less appropriate, none definitive.

Then, finally, comes an extraordinary series of cancellations:

> Not that fair field
> Of Enna, where Proserpin gath'ring flow'rs
> Herself a fairer Flow'r by gloomy Dis
> Was gather'd, which cost Ceres all that pain
> To seek her through the world; not that sweet Grove
> Of Daphne by Orontes, and th' inspir'd
> Castalian Spring might with this Paradise
> Of Eden strive; nor that Nyseian Isle
> Girt with the River Triton, where old Cham,
> Whom Gentiles Ammon call and Lybian Jove,
> Hid Amalthea and her Florid Son,
> Young Bacchus, from his Stepdame Rhea's eye;
> Nor where Abassin Kings thir issue Guard,
> Mount Amara, though this by some suppos'd
> True Paradise under the Ethiop Line
> By Nilus head, enclos'd with shining Rock,
> A whole day's journey high, but wide remote
> From this Assyrian Garden, where the Fiend
> Saw undelighted all delight. (IV,268–86)

Here the mind is subjected to an extended version of the same experience provoked by "Fables true, If true, here only," and "wandering (not error)"—that is, we are given a series of details (mythic gardens) known to be literally false, and asked to find the grain of truth in each: in this case, that Eden is like each but far lovelier.

Each garden named, however, has two defects. First, each comes bearing its train of inappropriate fallen associations. In one the Ethiopian king imprisons his sons; in another a bastard son is hidden from the anger of a wife; in a third pagan prophecy is practiced; and in the most famous, a goddess is kidnapped and taken down to Hell. The second problem with these gardens is that, never having existed, their relationship to Eden is infinitely problematic, a puzzle that is emphasized by the negatives that introduce them. The paradox can perhaps be put most succinctly this way: "the fairest images you have of gardens are both untrue and inadequate; now that you have imagined them, *stop* imagining them." Art, it seems, *cannot* describe Eden, and thus the long set description of Eden ends with a thunderous series of negations and irrelevancies that wipe the slate clean, as it were, and prepare us for a fresh start.

Yet it would be perverse to claim that this great set description of Eden conveys no impression beyond confusion and uncertainty. Auran, Seleucia, and Telassar evoke excitement, impressions of fabled grandeur, as well as conflicting impressions of loss. "Ambrosial fruit" and "vegetable Gold" may be hazy as images, but they have the charm of fabulous, dreamlike perfection: which of us has tasted ambrosia, yet who doubts that it is exquisite? Milton's sensuous images of Eden are always a bit beyond our reach, but in making us strain to see, hear, smell, or taste them, he involves us in their creation. "We are his organ," says C.S. Lewis. "When he appears to be describing Paradise he is in fact drawing out the Paradisal Stop in us."[9]

Moreover, Eden is conveyed in a series of active, humanizing verbs that make it a place of life and participated process as well as a gallery of picturesque views. God "planted" Eden (IV,210) and "had thrown" (IV,225) the mountain over Eden's river. The unemphatic verbs for that river's movements—"went," "Pass'd," "Water'd," "fell," "Runs,"—match its own calm movements; but when it emerges to make a fountain, it does so "through veins Of porous Earth with kindly thirst up-drawn" (IV,227–28). Its water, so delicious it is called "Nectar," "rolls" over golden sands, "visiting" and "feeding" the plants and flowers, which "Nature boon Pour'd forth profuse" (IV,242–43). Everywhere there is purposeful, solicitous, *nurturing* activity: the "Sun first warmly smote," "the unpierc't shade Imbrown'd." We *feel* these images as much as see them, and the impression they give is one of humanized, *active* benevolence toward mankind, supplying direct intuitions of the kindliness of the unseen Creator, visible in these his works.

Paul Alpers is extremely good on this aspect of Milton's Eden, as he is on many others:

Note the importance of word order and line division in "Both where the morning sun first warmly smote / The open field." "First warmly smote": we feel the sun shining down on us rather than merely observe it shining elsewhere. Similarly the next detail, "and where the unpierced shade / Embrowned the noontide bowers," assumes that we are engaged in the normal cycle of a pastoral day—working in the open fields in the morning and seeking the shade to rest at noon. Though we began by looking at Eden from the outside, we are now at the center looking around us—"a happy rural seat of various view."[10]

The effect is of a complex lesson in point of view, in which the smallest details—"Ambrosial Fruit," "mazy error"—can be either innocent or guilty, and the overall impression is one of antithetical patterns contending for our attention. Each pattern's fineness and elaboration suggest the opposite of inadvertency, yet taken together they pull the mind in opposite directions: is Eden fresh or stale, visible or invisible, innocent or fallen? The inevitable presence of Milton's art is deliberately exaggerated until no reader can be oblivious to it:

> meanwhile murmuring waters fall
> Down the slope hills, disperst, or in a Lake,
> That to the fringed Bank with Myrtle crown'd,
> Her crystal mirror holds, unite thir streams. (IV,260–63)

The suspect, detachable beauty of "crystal mirror," so flagrant in its suggestions of narcissism, and of art as artifice, could easily have been avoided and *would* clearly have been so by a poet less eager than Milton to make the reader aware of the limitations of his medium. Yet since nature, too, is art (God's art), no sooner has the question of the adequacy of human art been raised than divine art provides our most beautiful glimpse of Eden thus far:

> The Birds thir choir apply; airs, vernal airs,
> Breathing the smell of field and grove, attune
> The trembling leaves, while Universal Pan
> Knit with the Graces and the Hours in dance
> Led on th' Eternal Spring. (IV,264–68)

The lines, so rich they almost defy analysis, rise out of familiar, almost homely elements to a vision of Eden as harmonious song. Yet Milton's Pegasus is nothing but a pun—simultaneous impressions of country breezes and birdsong fused in the word "airs," so that the very landscape seems to dance, first in the "trembling leaves," then in the imagined dance of Pan and his attendants. This, the truest Eden so far, is not a picture but a *song*: Eden not only *contains* songs, it *is* one. Through the imperfect medium of Milton's fallen pastoral, we hear fragmentary strains sung by no human voice: "so, over that art Which you say adds to nature, is an art That nature makes."[11]

Though nothing could be more "natural" and accessible than the synaesthetic ecstasy of seeing the visible universe momentarily transformed by auditory and olfactory harmony into a great song, the means that Milton used to this end are obtrusively artful—first the pun that can seem frivolous, then the obtrusive entry into a Christian landscape of figures from pagan mythology. The marvelous thing is that in this context such duplicities are for once true: Eden has a use even for the imperfections of fallen language and myth. Our minds are given hope that they can "grasp" Milton's imperfect Eden, if only they can learn to use Milton's poem rightly. The sequence of negated myths that follows ("Not that fair field Of Enna," etc.) shows that such use will be difficult.

I have lingered so long over these eighty lines because they both introduce and exemplify the complex, even contradictory point of view that the narrator adopts toward Eden in Books IV and V. The reader, who comes to Book IV alienated by devices of genre, plot, characterization, and point of view from the theme of Milton's poem, is plunged once more into a Satanic perspective by means of Satan's long soliloquy. With so fresh and vivid an insight into Satan's way of seeing, it is not hard to understand why Eden itself, as mediated to us by the narrator, seems tinged with disagreeables and uncertainties; a closer look at the details of Milton's Eden shows us a deliberate pattern of contrary suggestions that causes Eden to flicker like an oxymoron.

These eighty lines are bounded by explicit references to point of view: "now [Satan] views To all delight of human sense expos'd . . . " (IV,205–206); "the Fiend Saw undelighted all delight . . . . " (IV,285–86). We know from his soliloquy that Satan's point of view is itself complex. It is not that he is blind to pleasure, beauty, or joy, but that such sights are painful to him. The narrator's insistence that Satan is not delighted by Eden's delight distinguishes Satan's point of view from ours, yet there is much in Milton's portrait of Eden that does not delight us either.

"Eden" is Hebrew for "pleasure," but it takes a while to learn that true pleasure derives not from a greedy consumption of detachable "beauties," but from adoration of their Creator. The Eden we have seen so far, however, though richly evocative and stirring, is also tinged with ennui, error, and imprecision, as well as by nagging reminders that we cannot really *see* it at all. For when Eden's "airs" lead on the "dance," it is of characters not literally in the poem at all, personifications of mental processes: Eden cannot be "seen" until it is "danced." Insofar as we follow Milton's lead and feel pleasure in Eden not as a place of beauties to be *viewed*, but of processes to be felt and participated in, we leave the self-preoccupied Satanic viewpoint behind and learn what "delight of human sense" means. Of course we repeatedly make the mistake of lapsing into voyeurism, but this very mistake helps us to spot and eventually to transcend that Satanic element in our own point of view.

Satan views Eden as an outsider, a voyeur, seeing but not participating in its pleasures. Adam and Eve, as we shall see, invariably express their view of Eden in terms not of physical objects but of relationships, of which they are always a part. Milton's narrator, and his reader, too, hover between the two points of view, sometimes eyeing Eden greedily, sometimes joining the dance. When we first meet Adam and Eve, for example, we feast on their exteriors. The narrator virtually invites us to gloat over their physical beauty, yet reproves us for doing so:

> Shee as a veil down to the slender waist
> Her unadorned golden tresses wore
> Dishevell'd, but in wanton ringlets wav'd
> As the Vine curls her tendrils, which impli'd
> Subjection, but requir'd with gentle sway,
> And by her yielded, by him best receiv'd,
> Yielded with coy submission, modest pride,
> And sweet reluctant amorous delay.
> Nor those mysterious parts were then conceal'd,
> Then was not guilty shame: dishonest shame
> Of Nature's works, honor dishonorable,
> Sin-bred, how have ye troubl'd all mankind
> With shows instead, mere shows of seeming pure,
> And banisht from man's life his happiest life,
> Simplicity and spotless innocence. (IV,304–18)

The stance here is complex and contradictory, hovering as it does between reproof of "dishonest shame" and the enactment of shame in the
reader's mind. If "Simplicity and spotless innocence" are the narrator's
goal, then why not suppress a few compromising details—"veil," "wanton," "coy," "sweet reluctant amorous delay"; why not imply the "mysterious parts" without mentioning them directly and avoid the querulous,
guilty denunciation of shame that obscures the image of two charming,
naked innocents untouched by thoughts of sin?

The answer is not easy to give or to understand. "Wanton" is a strong
word to use of Eve, since it clearly implies lasciviousness and arouses in
the reader an erotic response that must be restrained. But Adam and Eve
are sensual, more sensual than you and I in fact, since they experience
no repression of desire, no fear of betrayal or punishment, no apathy or
regret. So, in the moment when we first feel that erotic response, we are
experiencing Eden powerfully and truly. Since Adam and Eve are *lovers*,
and the strong passion they feel for one another *is* paradise, Milton's
poem will misrepresent Adam and Eve if he skirts their sexual, sensual
nature. Yet if he suggests this aspect, he will arouse "guilty shame" in his
fallen reader and thereby make Eden appear fallen. Either way he will
falsify; the best he can do is to show that sensual nature, confront the
reader's shame, and then challenge us to transcend it; shame must be
faced and conquered. Milton cannot rest content with "shows of seeming
pure," for a decorously chaste-seeming Eden will only hide the problem,
not solve it. As long as the reader is a passive viewer of Eden, he will
turn each of its pleasures, no matter how expurgated, to its meanest use,
as does Satan. Only when we participate in Eden and join the dance will
we understand and use it properly. Milton undertakes to teach us how to
dance.

The means derive largely from the very simple, elemental forces of
narrative, used with consummate poetic skill. Two human beings have
walked onto Milton's stage, giving us for the first time a dramatized
choice between characters variously like and unlike ourselves. Satan once
seemed essentially "human" to us, but compared to Adam and Eve he
seems far less so. Satan stirred powerful responses in us; now Adam and
Eve begin to do so, too. Satan's mind has been opened to us; we have
seen through his eyes; now we will begin to share Adam and Eve's
thoughts as well. At first the reader's mind is finely balanced between
these two opposing points of view. Adam and Eve are beautiful, even

arousing, but at first they are objects, exotic figures seen from the outside, charming but remote, like us but also unlike:

> So pass'd they naked on, nor shunn'd the sight
> Of God or Angel, for they thought no ill:
> So hand in hand they pass'd, the loveliest pair
> That ever since in love's imbraces met,
> Adam the goodliest man of men since born
> His Sons, the fairest of her Daughters Eve. (IV,319–24)

Seen this close, Adam and Eve are a perplexing mixture of King and Queen, patriarch and matriarch, perfect man and woman on the one hand, and simple pastoral lovers on the other. Even as they sit at supper, simply chewing the "savory pulp" of ambrosial fruits and dipping water with the rinds, Lions, Tigers, Ounces, Pards, and Elephants stage an impromptu entertainment that effortlessly overgoes the spectacle of a Roman imperial banquet. We have difficulty "placing" them: they alternate between seeming remote, small, childish, innocent, and seeming grand, stately, awesome.

Satan's view of them, expressed in a second soliloquy, in its very ambivalence expresses a complexity like our own, at one moment praising them with seeming generosity:

> Not Spirits, yet to heav'nly Spirits bright
> Little inferior; whom my thoughts pursue
> With wonder, and could love, so lively shines
> In them Divine resemblance . . . , (IV,361–64)

and yet at the next moment condescending to them as helpless, vulnerable innocents:

> Ah gentle pair, yee little think how nigh
> Your change approaches, when all these delights
> Will vanish and deliver ye to woe,
> More woe, the more your taste is now of joy. (IV,366–69)

To view Adam and Eve with foreknowledge of their Fall is to see them as Satan does. Satan's view is sophisticated, corrupt, unpleasant. We don't like Satan in this speech; we don't really see, now that we are here in Eden, that "public reason just" (IV,389) requires its ruin, but Satan still

seems the spokesman of an unwelcome truth, certified both by Genesis
and by Milton's epic voice—Adam and Eve are the victims of a quarrel
between supernatural powers. It is the function of Adam and Eve as
speaking characters to help us find innocence within ourselves, to help
us discover not only its beauty but its strength, and thus to reject the
interpretation that sees them as helpless victims.

Speech in Paradise is perceptibly different from speech in the fallen
world: "Adam from the depth of his inexperience is lavishly sententious."[12]
The suspicion must arise in the reader that the first exchange between
Adam and Eve is a contrivance rather like the first scene of many a Shake-
spearean play, where two characters meet on the stage apron to tell each
other what not they but the audience needs to know. And, on the law of
averages at least, it seems a remote coincidence that Satan should hear
from his proposed victims precisely what he seeks: from Adam news of
the forbidden fruit; from Eve, an incident revealing her potential narcissism. That these two speeches strike us as at least faintly strange, remote,
even contrived, is not necessarily a weakness, however. The strangeness
makes us attend to the differences between their minds and ours.

Like the place itself, speech in Paradise is delightful as well as
strange. Adam and Eve are not represented as making small talk, and
they are too much one flesh to have need of debate. Here, as everywhere
in this section of the poem, we hear them rehearsing in words what both
know but have time enough to celebrate by uttering. They speak, that
is, for the pleasure of speaking, bearing witness to the harmonies of Eden
by harmonies of speech that turn their every utterance into something
whole, balanced, perfect of its kind. Without much exaggeration we can
say that Adam and Eve sing rather than speak to each other.

The subject of Adam's first "song" is, however, the forbidden fruit, a
subject upon which we have decided views of our own. "And do they
only stand By Ignorance?" (IV,518–19), asks Satan a moment later; "O fair
foundation laid whereon to build Thir ruin!" (IV,521–22). Our initial view
is apt to be like Satan's: that the forbidden fruit is an Achilles heel, a weak
spot left with an intent that seems not wholly benevolent. Adam, however, regards it is a mark of privilege:

> Sole partner and sole part of all these joys,
> Dearer thyself than all; needs must the Power
> That made us, and for us this ample World

Be infinitely good, and of his good
As liberal and free as infinite,
That rais'd us from the dust and plac't us here
In all this happiness, who at his hand
Have nothing merited, nor can perform
Aught whereof hee hath need, hee who requires
From us no other service than to keep
This one, this easy charge, of all the Trees
In Paradise that bear delicious fruit
So various, not to taste that only Tree
Of Knowledge, planted by the Tree of Life,
So near grows Death to Life, whate'er Death is,
Some dreadful thing no doubt; for well thou know'st
God hath pronounc't it death to taste that Tree,
The only sign of our obedience left
Among so many signs of power and rule
Conferr'd upon us, and Dominion giv'n
Over all other Creatures that possess
Earth, Air, and Sea. (IV,411–32)

These twenty-two lines are one single, compound, complex sentence, describing the goodness of the sentence's subject, "the Power That made us," by citing various bits of seen evidence pointing to an unseen source. And prominent among the marks of God's goodness is what we regard as a curse, but which Adam treats as a blessing—that he is allowed to render some service in return to so great a benefactor. Adam's one regret is that the service is so easy!

Of all the dark spots in the Garden, the forbidden fruit must certainly be for us the darkest. At last mention, it was, in the narrator's words, "our death." Adam therefore enters the poem implicitly taking a point of view toward the entire poem's subject—the Fall of Man—radically different from that which all our previous experience, including the experience of the poem thus far, has prepared us. Our foreknowledge, contrasted with Adam's innocence, frames the speech darkly with dramatic irony, and we look on like adults watching a baby fumble with an electric socket as Adam clumsily explores the word "death": "So near grows Death to Life, whate'er Death is, Some dreadful thing no doubt."

Such innocence invites condescension, yet Adam is not so easy to condescend to. His song in praise of God's goodness is an accomplished one, orchestrating a number of unambiguous blessings into strong evidence for God's goodness:

> Then let us not think hard
> One easy prohibition, who enjoy
> Free leave so large to all things else, and choice
> Unlimited of manifold delights:
> But let us ever praise him, and extol
> His bounty, following our delightful task
> To prune these growing Plants, and tend these Flow'rs,
> Which were it toilsome, yet with thee were sweet. (IV, 432–39)

Adam's "aria" performs a little circle of perfection, beginning and ending at the same point, the fullness of his love for Eve, and including within its cycle a complete diagram of perfect relationships: love between God and mankind is as perfect as Adam's love for Eve; both loves are mirrored in the perfect harmony between man and created nature. In fact, the song implies, all loves are one and the same; pick any facet of their experience, even the task of gardening or the forbidden fruit, and you will find simply one more aspect of this unitary Love. If we don't as yet see things Adam's way—he still seems both strange and naive—we can at least see that from *his* point of view the conclusion follows. We are being introduced to unfallen vision, and its directness, wholeness, and unselfconsciousness are a welcome change from Satan's self-torment. By showing us the wholeness and harmony of all aspects of life in the garden, inner and outer, spiritual, sensual, even sexual, the narrative voice of unfallen Adam is beginning to alter our view of things.

Eve's answering song follows much the same pattern, beginning and ending in an open celebration of her love for Adam, making God's praises her major premise, and yet managing also to challenge the reader's preconceptions by some "compromising" revelations about her own capacity for narcissism. While Eve's "error" in admiring herself was an innocent one and shows that mistakes are both possible and harmless in Eden, the unseen, corrupt audience—Satan and the fallen reader—recognizes in this particular mistake a potential for ruin. Yet in context the incident merely forms one more instance of God's kindness to man:

> there I had fixt
> Mine eyes till now, and pin'd with vain desire,
> Had not a voice thus warn'd me, What thou seest,
> What there thou seest fair Creature is thyself,
> With thee it came and goes; but follow me,
> And I will bring thee where no shadow stays

> Thy coming, and thy soft imbraces, hee
> Whose image thou art, him thou shalt enjoy
> Inseparably thine. . . . (IV,465–73)

God's words draw a distinction that both Eve and the reader need to learn between images that are lifeless "shadows," pictures without substance, and images that, being substantial, can be participated in. Although not without guidance, and even a small struggle, Eve has learned to prefer the living "image" to the lifeless one, but it is not likely that the reader is so quick to do so.

Participation is the key to our proper understanding of the pleasures of Eden, both of the Garden itself and of "The happier Eden" (IV,507) of unfallen connubial love.[13] Satan's pain in Paradise comes from his exclusion—he is a mere onlooker at pleasures he can never again taste. But we too are viewers in Eden, devouring it and Eve with our eyes. We might say that Satan is our surrogate, embodying and dramatizing all the voyeurism latent in our own role as readers:

> half her swelling Breast
> Naked met his under the flowing Gold
> Of her loose tresses hid: hee in delight
> Both of her Beauty and submissive Charms
> Smil'd with superior Love, as Jupiter
> On Juno smiles, when he impregns the Clouds
> That shed May Flowers; and press'd her Matron lip
> With kisses pure; aside the Devil turn'd
> For envy, yet with jealous leer malign
> Ey'd them askance, and to himself thus plain'd.
> Sight hateful, sight tormenting! thus these two
> Imparadis't in one another's arms
> The happier Eden, shall enjoy thir fill
> Of bliss on bliss, while I to Hell am thrust. . . . (IV,495–508)

Eve has two dramatized viewers here: one participating in and hence enjoying her love; the other excluded, a voyeur. Adam, too, sees Eve's naked breast and mysterious parts, yet he neither turns aside nor ogles. He obviously enjoys looking at Eve, but he enjoys perhaps even more listening to her and touching her. While Satan *sees* Eve's breast meeting Adam's, Adam *feels* it, as he feels her kisses pure. Imparadised in her arms, as Satan jealously remarks, Adam tastes pleasure of which looking is only the smallest part.

Whose response is closer to ours, Adam's or Satan's? Doubtless we feel them both, but the poem invites us to discriminate, to follow pleasure and leave pain behind. In this almost obtrusively dramatic tableau is staged an invitation to the reader to cast aside the joyless role of spectator and to join, however clumsily at first, Eden's dance.

When the narrative center of *Paradise Lost* begins to shift from Satan to Adam and Eve, the reader's disorientation is nicely balanced by a sense of relief: here are characters whose point of view he has far fewer scruples against sharing. In terms of style, Milton sets up a Satanic voice that is progressively more hostile and corrupt (see his fist-shaking, stage villain posturing as he temporarily exits: IV,533–35), while Adam and Eve's speeches are progressively more familiar, sane, and beautiful. With each exchange between Eve and Adam we get to know them better, learn better to see as they do, which means that we begin to participate in the pleasures of Eden:

> To whom thus Eve with perfect beauty adorn'd.
> My Author and Disposer, what thou bidd'st
> Unargu'd I obey; so God ordains,
> God is thy Law, thou mine: to know no more
> Is woman's happiest knowledge and her praise.
> With thee conversing I forget all time,
> All seasons and thir change, all please alike.
> Sweet is the breath of morn, her rising sweet,
> With charm of earliest Birds; pleasant the Sun
> When first on this delightful Land he spreads
> His orient Beams, on herb, tree, fruit, and flow'r,
> Glist'ring with dew; fragrant the fertile earth
> After soft showers; and sweet the coming on
> Of grateful Ev'ning mild, then silent Night
> With this her solemn Bird and this fair Moon,
> And these the Gems of Heav'n, her starry train:
> But neither breath of Morn when she ascends
> With charm of earliest Birds, nor rising Sun
> On this delightful land, nor herb, fruit, flow'r,
> Glist'ring with dew, nor fragrance after showers,
> Nor grateful Ev'ning mild, nor silent Night
> With this her solemn Bird, nor walk by Moon,
> Or glittering Star-light without thee is sweet. (IV,634–56)

Eve's love song conveys the circular perfection of life in Eden by imitating it, moving twice through the pleasant variety of a pastoral day. The repetition of every element of that day strikes us as "artless" and naive, yet their negation and the suspense attendant upon a seven-line delay in the predicate, "without thee is sweet," keep the song from being dull or predictable. The effect of the song's structure, like that of its theme of love without hindrance or conflict is of a familiarity that nonetheless surprises, like a long-forgotten memory nudged into consciousness. Eve's song "uses" every sensual pleasure of the Garden to point to a greater but less effable pleasure. "Hierarchy" is an imperfect word to apply to this relationship, since it carries suggestions of external control and imposed authority, but the fact is that for Eve the essence of Eden is her reciprocated love for Adam. All other pleasures derive from and symbolize that love. Hence, in her description of Eden a masculine Sun radiates light and heat to a terrestrial scene conceived as feminine, as we can tell by both images and pronouns. Eve knows how to use God's gifts rightly, and by her speech she teaches us to do so, too.

The emergence of Adam and Eve as speaking characters, aided by Satan's temporary exit, shifts the poem's entire center of gravity toward the unfallen point of view, a shift that we hear in the narrative voice as well. As if Satan's departure had removed a shadow from Eden, the narrator's descriptions have become, even in advance of Eve's love song, more chaste:

> Now came still Ev'ning on, and Twilight gray
> Had in her sober Livery all things clad;
> Silence accompanied, for Beast and Bird,
> They to thir grassy Couch, these to thir Nests
> Were slunk, all but the wakeful Nightingale;
> She all night long her amorous descant sung;
> Silence was pleas'd: now glow'd the Firmament
> With living Sapphires: Hesperus that led
> The starry Host, rode brightest, till the Moon
> Rising in clouded Majesty, at length
> Apparent Queen unveil'd her peerless light,
> And o'er the dark her Silver Mantle threw. (IV,598–609)

"Living Sapphires," to be echoed shortly by Eve's "Gems of Heav'n," are not sapphires at all, but stars, just as the "Silver" of line 609 is not metal but moonlight. We need not worry (as we did in Book IV, ll. 237–38) whether Eden is actually, rather than figuratively, gilded and begemmed. There is plenty of sensuous particularity here, but no troubling associations with lasciviousness or greed, as if these qualities had been purged with Satan, and Eden dressed in "sober Livery." Even stars, as Adam will shortly explain to Eve (IV,660 –88), have various useful functions to fulfill, so that their beauty is not one of barren adornment but is derived from their dual role as agent and symbol of divine benevolence.

Ordinarily the "fallen" or "corrupt" aspects of Milton's Eden—not only the equivocal words and images but details of plot such as Eve's self-admiration or her Satan-induced dream of eating the forbidden fruit—are explained as Milton's ways of "preparing" us for the Fall.[14] Yet if there is one feature of *Paradise Lost* for which we are prepared from the beginning, it is Adam and Eve's Fall. If anything, Milton should be trying to make us forget what we already know, so that when it does occur, the Fall will have for us some of the freshness of shock and loss that it has for them. And in fact when we look at the arrangement of narrative materials in Books IV and V—Eden at first entered by Satan and dominated by his point of view in three long soliloquies; then the gradual emergence of Adam and Eve as speaking characters; and the disappearance of Satan at the end of Book IV—it is clear that the story moves imaginatively in the opposite direction—*away* from the Fall: Satan enters Eden, fails to seduce Eve, and is purged by Gabriel.

This effect of purging is noticeable everywhere. Adam and Eve enter the poem speaking of forbidden fruit and narcissism; as they go on speaking, their conversation turns to less sensitive topics. Again, as when he began in Hell, Milton seems to have put his worst foot forward, but the technique accords perfectly with the nature of his theme and of his audience. Since we come to Eden with double minds, there is no chance of avoiding thoughts inappropriate to the place. Rather, Milton makes us confront such thoughts and recognize their inappropriateness. He gives us, as it were, a choice between two Edens, one fallen and one innocent, and teaches us how to prefer the latter. With Milton's help we discover not only our corruption but our innocent side as well, and we learn to respond with pleasure to innocence: he pulls the paradisal stop in us.

Since Milton has already shown us Eden's crystal mirrors, sapphire founts and golden rinds, dressing the garden in "sober livery" hardly chastens *the place*. Rather, it chastens our minds, by emphasizing that Eden's guilt or innocence is in the eye of the beholder. Because an innocent Eden is won against obstacles, the reader has been involved in its creation, or re-creation. Milton helps us by chastening his natural descriptions (see also the chaste, sensuously particular description of Adam and Eve's bower, IV,689–705), but meanwhile an even greater challenge to our fledgling innocence emerges—the sensuality between Adam and Eve. There could hardly be a greater tonal contrast than that between their innocent, untroubled acceptance of the joys of sex as the proper expression of love, and the narrator's turbulent, combative spirit as he defends those joys:

> Thus at thir shady Lodge arriv'd, both stood,
> Both turn'd, and under op'n Sky ador'd
> The God that made both Sky, Air, Earth and Heav'n
> Which they beheld, the Moon's resplendent Globe
> And starry Pole: Thou also mad'st the Night,
> Maker Omnipotent, and thou the Day,
> Which we in our appointed work imploy'd
> Have finisht happy in our mutual help
> And mutual love, the Crown of all our bliss
> Ordain'd by thee, and this delicious place
> For us too large, where thy abundance wants
> Partakers, and uncropt falls to the ground.
> But thou hast promis'd from us two a Race
> To fill the Earth, who shall with us extol
> Thy goodness infinite, both when we wake,
> And when we seek, as now, thy gift of sleep.
> This said unanimous, and other Rites
> Observing none, but adoration pure
> Which God likes best, into thir inmost bower
> Handed they went; and eas'd the putting off
> These troublesome disguises which wee wear,
> Straight side by side were laid, nor turn'd I ween
> Adam from his fair Spouse, nor Eve the Rites
> Mysterious of connubial Love refus'd:
> Whatever Hypocrites austerely talk
> Of purity and place and innocence,
> Defaming as impure what God declares
> Pure, and commands to some, leaves free to all.
> Our Maker bids increase, who bids abstain
> But our Destroyer, foe to God and Man? (IV,720–49)

In Adam and Eve's prayer, sexual love is seen as simply one more aspect of their perpetual celebration of God. Not only in propagation, but in the pleasure of "mutual love, the Crown of all our bliss," Adam and Eve are following God's will, using his gifts appropriately. God *means* Adam and Eve to be happy, and in thus following his intention they are simultaneously enjoying themselves and praising him. Sexual intercourse, like every other activity in Eden, is prayer, celebration, and song.

The narrator is particularly close to Adam and Eve as they sing their evening prayer, the demarcation between narrative and dramatic voices being especially informal:

> Both turn'd, and under op'n Sky ador'd
> The God that made both Sky, Air, Earth and Heav'n
> Which they beheld, the Moon's resplendent Globe
> And starry Pole: Thou also mad'st the Night. . . . (IV,721–24)

Yet, as they retire, the narrator seems to draw back, clouding the sexual act itself in a haze of negation ("nor" used twice), guesswork ("I ween"), and mystery (in "Rites Mysterious" the adjective balances nicely between fallen and unfallen meanings: "sacred" or "secret"?). As the mysterious rites begin, the narrator's mind, and therefore the reader's mind as well, is focused upon the *differences* between actors and audience: inasmuch as we all wear "troublesome disguises" we are all implicated, even Milton, in the hypocrisy he denounces, and which of us has not turned from his spouse or been refused the rites of connubial love? Yet, by the same token, which of us has not partaken in those rites and gained at least a glimpse, in some moment of self-transcending bliss, of the pleasures of Paradise? Milton's narrator insists here upon our differences from Adam and Eve as a prelude to affirming our similarities, hoping to elicit from us a choice to turn our backs upon fallen pain in order to experience, though only vicariously and momentarily, unfallen bliss. Milton's method is here, as it was earlier in his "tainted" descriptions of Eden, deliberately impure, not skirting but provoking fallen responses in order to teach us how to transcend them.

When it comes, transcendence comes in a song:

> Hail wedded Love, mysterious Law, true source
> Of human offspring, sole propriety
> In Paradise of all things common else.

By thee adulterous lust was driv'n from men
Among the bestial herds to range, by thee
Founded in Reason, Loyal, Just, and Pure,
Relations dear, and all the Charities
Of Father, Son, and Brother first were known.
Far be it, that I should write thee sin or blame,
Or think thee unbefitting holiest place,
Perpetual Fountain of Domestic sweets,
Whose bed is undefil'd and chaste pronounc't,
Present, or past, as Saints and Patriarchs us'd.
Here Love his golden shafts imploys, here lights
His constant Lamp, and waves his purple wings,
Reigns here and revels; not in the bought smile
Of Harlots, loveless, joyless, unindear'd,
Casual fruition, nor in Court Amours,
Mixt Dance, or wanton Mask, or Midnight Ball,
Or Serenate, which the starv'd Lover sings
To his proud fair, best quitted with disdain.
These lull'd by Nightingales imbracing slept,
And on thir naked limbs the flow'ry roof
Show'r'd Roses, which the Morn repair'd. Sleep on,
Blest pair; and O yet happiest if ye seek
No happier state, and know to know no more. (IV,750–75)

No question but this is a fallen epithalamium, full of equivocation (the pun on "propriety"), artifice (the classical Cupid complete with golden shafts and purple wings), and negation (above all the fourfold repetition of the sound "no" in line 775). Images of fallen love preponderate—bestial herds, the bought smile of harlots, the starved lover, to mention only the most vivid—while the countervailing terms make little appeal to the senses ("Founded in Reason, Loyal, Just, and Pure," "Perpetual Fountain of Domestic sweets").

Paradoxically, an argument in favor of wedded love is being offered by a song that paints pictures of what it is *not*. Negative description such as this asks us to sort through images we already have in mind and come up, by process of elimination, with the right one. It assumes that we already know what is being talked about—Milton assumes that if he can describe Adam and Eve preparing to make love, and then help us to exclude certain irrelevant associations (bestial lust, artificial love-play), what is left after the exclusions is what Adam and Eve do. We are asked, that is, to fill in the blank space in Milton's picture not so much with our imaginings as with our own memories and experiences, suitably selected.

The argument of Milton's epithalamium is that licit sexual inter-course between spouses who love each other is pure and holy. When *we* make love under such conditions (and Milton asks us not to blush at the thought) you and I call back the age of gold and taste the pleasures of Eden. And when we remember ourselves doing so, we enter the poem and "become" Adam and Eve. We participate in Milton's poem and thereby abandon the cheerless role of spectators, of voyeurs. *Paradise Lost*, instead of showing us Eden, helps us to find it within ourselves.

We cannot linger over Ithuriel and Zephon's discovery of Satan, "squat like a Toad, close at the ear of Eve" (IV,800) and their humiliating inability to recognize him, nor over his heroic posturing in front of Ga-briel and his final, ignominious flight from Eden. If any reader comes to the end of Book IV (and many obviously do) still wanting to believe that Satan is its hero, such incidents must further deflate our admiration. And if any reader still maintains (as seems to me almost inevitable at this point in the poem) the same skepticism about God's solicitude for Adam and Eve that the narrator expressed earlier—"O for that warning voice"— then the episode gives him another instance of God's care for his crea-tures. God's forethought in hanging the scales of Libra at such a point in the heavenly vault that they would tip over the zenith at the precise moment of Satan's challenge to Gabriel is a concrete example of how everything works according to God's plan.[15]

But God's plan, including his giving Satan permission to tempt Adam and Eve (an attempt that both he and we know in advance will be suc-cessful), is still problematic, though Book IV has changed our view of it somewhat. Satan seems less strong than he once was; Adam and Eve seem much stronger than they at first appeared; and God seems much friendlier and more sensitive to their needs. One by one Milton's story cuts the threads of fatal necessity, making it progressively harder for us to remember that, after all, this couple is destined to fall. As we learn to see through their eyes, we move toward a point of view from which, though we know better, the Fall seems impossible, since obedience to God, even in refraining from eating the forbidden fruit, is a positive plea-sure, the soul of all other pleasures.

The only evil Adam and Eve can do is to disobey God's one com-mand; hence, Eve's Satan-inspired dream asks her to eat the forbidden fruit. When Eve turns away in horror from such "misuse" of God's gifts, she invites us to turn away also. When Adam pronounces innocent her willingness to contemplate evil without approving it, he is also pronouncing our experience of a fallen Eden to be "sinless," provided we don't approve. Milton's Eden gives us a choice: if we look at it rightly, we can look with innocent eyes, as do Adam and Eve in that most perfect expression of the unfallen point of view, the "Morning Hymn" (V, 153–208).

Joseph Summers, in *The Muse's Method*, has given so fine an analysis of the Morning Hymn that if at all possible, the reader of these pages should stop to read his short Chapter III, "Grateful Vicissitude," before continuing. For those who cannot, I provide this summary. Summers quotes the Hymn in full, dividing it into eleven strophes of varying lengths, each ending at one of the Hymn's ten periods, except the first strophe, which ends at the colon in line 159. Thus divided, the Hymn reveals a varied but gradually accelerating rhythm; the whole, and each of its parts, shows us a world in motion. Even the "unspeakable," "invisible" realm of Godhead moves from "above these heavens" to "these thy lowest works," while in every other strophe the creatures of God are pictured as praising him by *movement*. This motion is characteristically circular, since the circle is an image of perfection, yet in the fourth strophe circular motion becomes vertical motion as well:

> "Fall'st" occupies the strongest possible position as the final syllable of the line, the sentence, and the section, and its appearance is made even more dramatic by the pointing and the accented repetition of the conjunctions. In the midst of praise we have approached the chief metaphysical theme of the poem, the Fall. It is true that the course of the sun is regular and rhythmic and, under God's will, inevitable. But the purpose, both theological and aesthetic, of the entire poem is to show how the falls of man and Satan, although not inevitable, become within the light of all time and eternity a part of the divine rhythm.[16]

The Sun's rising and falling, Summers suggests, seconded by the rising and falling of "Mists and Exhalations," and the rise and implicit fall of "birds" in strophe X, prefigures for the reader, though not for the singers, the possibility that even the "fall" of Satan and mankind can be worked into the divine orchestration.

Summers's division of the Hymn into strophes is a brilliant critical device, since it helps the unpracticed eye of the reader to see order in a complex and shifting pattern, but the lines without strophic divisions convey even more strongly the dynamism of the Hymn, which scarcely allows the eye or the mind to alight at any particular place. Instead we get a vision of the universe as almost unmanageably rich and complex, so full of angels, heavenly bodies, terrestrial creatures, elements, and phenomena that we would be quite bewildered, were it not for constant repetition of sentence structure, vocabulary, and imagery. Each sentence, except the first and last, follows the same pattern: an exhortation to praise God. The imagery repeats certain basic motifs: light-dark, rising-falling, circular motion, and song, while the vocabulary is remarkably chaste and elementary, even monosyllabic—Day, Night, Earth, Stars, Sun, Moon, Sphere, Eye, Soul, Orb, dance, Song, Air, Womb, Hill, Lake, Winds, Pines. The word "praise" (in one case "extol") occurs in every strophe except the first and last, which *are* praise.

The effect then is of extreme diversity and yet, paradoxically, of extreme order and simplicity. The created universe, in one sense incomprehensibly complex (who fully comprehends the "mystic Dance" of the planets, or how the elements "in quaternion run Perpetual Circle, multiform"?) is radiantly simple and unified when we perceive that in a multitude of various ways it performs a single activity: praise of God. Everything changes, yet everything remains the same.

Equally remarkable, I believe, is the hymn's striking lack of visual impact. There are pictures, certainly: the Sun paints the fleecy skirts of mist with gold, clouds deck "th' uncolor'd sky," yet most of these pictures are of typical, familiar scenes rendered with little nuance—the sun rises, the moon meets the sun, pines wave, birds ascend. These are scenes so well remembered as to be virtually transparent, one *feels* as much as sees them. We are so near to them that we get no sense of distanced vision; they come and go so rapidly that we get only fleeting glimpses, while other images—the daystar crowning the smiling morning, the circle of elements, the dancing planets—have more impact as ideas than as pictures.

Replacing visual images are those that appeal to other senses, particularly images of sound and kinesthesia. All strophes contain or describe praise, and many make its auditory nature explicit: Angels speak, winds breathe, streams warble, birds sing their praise, as do the singers themselves. Most shockingly, perhaps, the Sun "sounds" and the planets "resound" his praise, perhaps a reference to the "music of the spheres," but also an instance of synaesthesia, where motion and music, the elements of dance, are seen as interchangeable (see "Bear on your wings and in your notes his praise" V,199). Motion itself—rising and falling, circling, crowning, meeting, gliding, walking, treading, creeping—is perhaps the chief sensual appeal of the entire hymn, unless it be musical sound, so that the senses addressed are largely the more "primitive" ones of hearing and touch. Eden in Adam and Eve's vision is dance and song.

The Morning Hymn, rather like an unfallen soliloquy, but sung in unison by Adam and Eve and addressed not to each other but to God, is the most beautiful, hence the truest expression of unfallen human vision in *Paradise Lost*. The early synaesthetic metaphor that transformed Eden's air into music, (IV,264–68) and Eden's movement into dance, the hint in Eve's evening love poem that Edenic experience was best expressed in song, bear fruit in the spacious and moving vision of the visible universe as a dance in praise of its Creator. Satan has been purged from Eden; Eve's innocence has been attested; and the reader, too, has been nudged by the sovereign principle of pleasure toward identifying with an initially strange, but still attractive, point of view. As the poem progresses he has less difficulty in doing so. For when it comes, the Morning Hymn purges from our view of Eden all that is exotic or suspect. Over our heads the heavenly bodies still circle, rise and fall, move in "mystic dance." In our world birds still sing, pines still wave, the beasts and fishes still glide, tread, creep. If we succumb to the beauty of the Hymn, we leave our role as spectators and enter Adam and Eve's world as participants: their world is *our* world, and Paradise is *now*.

"In *Paradise Lost* the Edenic life is radical growth and process," says Barbara Lewalski, "a mode of life steadily increasing in complexity and challenge and difficulty but at the same time and by that very fact, in perfection."[17] But as Adam and Eve grow forward in complexity toward us, we grow backward in innocence toward them. Our point of view is still double, but we have partly recovered what we thought was irrevocably lost. If only at moments, Eden is reborn within us.

4

Unfallen Narration

JOHN MILTON WAS an inspired poet. Over and over in *Paradise Lost* he asserts, with what may be either becoming modesty or colossal pride, that his poem is not entirely his. "Sing Heav'nly Muse," he prays in the epic's opening lines, yet the implication that the muse rather than Milton is the real singer is contradicted when in the same prologue the poet speaks of "*my* advent'rous Song" and asks the muse to "instruct *me*." Who is singing, Milton or the muse?

Further invocations only perpetuate the ambiguity. In the prologue to Book III the poet asks to be shown "things invisible" so that he can "see and tell" about them. This suggests a division of labor: the muse provides the song's materials; Milton sings the song. Yet this impression is altered by the prologue to Book IX, where the slumbering poet receives dictation (l. 23). Which word most accurately describes the muse's role: "show," "instruct," or "dictate"? Even in Book I Milton shifts between "I" and "thou" too often for us to be able to distinguish what is his from what is hers: all is the muse's, yet (paradoxically) all is Milton's.

Even before writing his holy epic, in his earlier career as defender of the Puritan cause against the English monarchy, Milton pictured himself as an inspired prophet through whom God speaks: "When God commands to take the trumpet and blow a dolorous or a jarring blast, it lies not in mans will what he shall say, or what he shall conceal."[1] But God's choice of spokesman is not casual or arbitrary; one must earn the privilege through one's own faith and effort:

> He who would not be frustrate of his hope to write well hereafter in laudable things, ought himselfe to bee a true Poem, that is, a composition, and patterne of the best and honorablest things; not presuming

to sing high praises of heroick men, or famous Cities, unlesse he have
in himselfe the experience and the practice of all that which is praise-
worthy.[2]

Milton's program for becoming a holy poet demanded the utmost personal effort, yet that effort was not in itself enough. "He who would not
be frustrate of his hope to write well" does not mean precisely "he who
would write well," for it implies that a man can deprive but not insure
himself of this attainment. The poet who is himself a true poem has done
what man can do, has prepared himself to be the instrument of God. Now
he must stand and wait for God to send him inspiration.[3]

Milton's claims to divine inspiration in *Paradise Lost* are obviously
meant seriously, yet they raise serious problems. Although his "source"
is the Bible, the story of the Fall of Man in Genesis occupies only a few
pages. To expand that simple tale into an eighty-thousand word epic re-
quired much that was either invented or directly revealed by God. If, as
critics often assume, such additions to sacred narrative as Hell's geog-
raphy, the personification of Sin and Death, Satan's voyage through
Chaos, the Heavenly and Infernal Councils, and the War in Heaven were
supplied by Milton's own imagination, well primed with an extensive
knowledge of profane literature, then how does this square with Milton's
prophetic claims? If, on the other hand, Milton was favored by God with
knowledge of matters hidden from the rest of us, then how does it happen
that so much of his poem is drawn from, or at least agrees with, secular
literature? In showing the four rivers of Hell, to give one small example,
the Divine Spirit reveals to Milton names by which Vergil calls them in
the *Aeneid*. A poem that repeatedly claims to be not invention but Truth,
yet that has such a clear indebtedness to the literary inventions of others,
raises the question of its own validity. Exactly what degree of confidence
can we have in Milton's narrator?

Of course we believe what the epic voice tells us. What alternative
do we have? The great strength of Milton's poem, the seal of his genius
as a poet, is his ability to make us "see," and though he obscurely warns
us to read carefully, his warnings are largely overridden by the immense
mimetic powers of his poem. We read on, alternately ravished and perplexed by our experience of Hell, Heaven, and Eden, but given no explicit warning not to read with naive literalness until, like the muse, Raphael descends from Heaven in Book V.

Like Milton's narrator, Raphael has a story to tell of Heaven, Earth, and Hell, of salvation and damnation, of rising and falling. Having been witness to the events he describes, however, he has no need to invoke divine aid, and as an unfallen, spiritual being he has none of the narrator's doubts and uncertainties. Yet it is he, not the epic voice, who spells out the epistemological problems behind the poem we are reading:

> High matter thou injoin'st me, O prime of men,
> Sad task and hard, for how shall I relate
> To human sense th' invisible exploits
> Of warring Spirits; how without remorse
> The ruin of so many glorious once
> And perfet while they stood; how last unfold
> The secrets of another World, perhaps
> Not lawful to reveal? yet for thy good
> This is dispens't, and what surmounts the reach
> Of human sense, I shall delineate so,
> By lik'ning spiritual to corporal forms,
> As may express them best, though what if Earth
> Be but the shadow of Heav'n, and things therein
> Each to other like, more than on Earth is thought? (V,563–76)

Of the three obstacles to Raphael's story, the most important is that a language suited to the needs of physical beings in a physical universe is not well suited to talking about the invisible exploits of spirits. To overcome this impediment Raphael will liken spiritual to corporal forms, but Adam (and we) must understand that there is a degree of falsification involved.

This "falsification" is what biblical interpreters called "accommodation," an idea I have already referred to in Chapter Two, though not by name.[4] "God," says John Calvin, "by other means invisible . . . clothes himself, so to speak, with the image of the world, in which he would present himself to our contemplation [i.e., in the Bible]. Therefore, as soon as the name of God sounds in our ears, or the thought of him occurs to our minds, let us also clothe him with this most beautiful ornament."[5] Since God portrays himself to human sense in images drawn from the physical world, Raphael (and Milton) need not fear to do so, too. But the doctrine of accommodation demands a careful, self-conscious reader, who can give exactly the right degree and kind of weight to each of the ways of likening spiritual to corporal facts:

If *Jehovah repented that he had created man*, Gen. vi. 6, *and repented because of their groanings*, Judges ii. 18, let us believe that he did repent. But let us not imagine that God's repentance arises from lack of foresight, as man's does, for he has warned us not to think about him in this way: Num. xxiii. 19: *God is not a man that he should lie, nor the son of man that he should repent. . . .* and if God attributes to himself again and again a human shape and form, why should we be afraid of assigning to him something he assigns to himself, provided we believe that what is imperfect and weak in us is, when ascribed to God, utterly perfect and utterly beautiful?[6]

Likening spiritual to corporal forms demands, on the part of the reader, a complicated response of belief-and-disbelief. God does and does not repent; his form is human, yet in a sense that excludes some of the defining attributes of human form. Admittedly these examples are extreme, but they illustrate most strikingly the problems involved in understanding Raphael's story. His words, appealing to human sense, are like a bridge over which we must march our understanding, then turn and watch the bridge destroyed.

But Raphael takes with one hand only to give back with the other: "what if Earth Be but the shadow of Heav'n, and things therein Each to other like, more than on Earth is thought?" (V,574–76). After stressing the differences between Earth and Heaven, and the inadequacy of terrestrial language to express celestial facts or of human minds to grasp them, Raphael tentatively reasserts their connection, his word "shadow" having here the force not merely of a "copy" but of a *foreshadowing*.[7] Man, as Raphael has just told Adam (V,493–500), may in time work his way up in stages from Earth to Heaven. When he does so, he may find that earthly images of Heaven, though incomplete, were essentially true.

Raphael has in effect contradicted himself: first detaching his words from their normal, terrestrial referents, then suggesting that they need not really be so detached. This amounts to saying that the impending story is both true and not true—not true in one sense, true in another. But true in *what* sense? Raphael has given Adam no formula for understanding celestial epic beyond warning him that it will take discernment. The guiding principle of that discernment emerges only gradually, first hinted at in Raphael's obscure reference to secrets "perhaps Not lawful to reveal." The "secrets" revealed to Adam in the course of the angel's visit will include the Father's begetting and exaltation of the Son, the war in Heaven, Abdiel's loyal refusal to join Satan, the expulsion of the rebel angels, the existence of Hell, and the creation of the world. These are revealed, says Raphael, "for thy good," and in Book VII he expands upon what he means:

> to recount Almighty works
> What words or tongue of Seraph can suffice,
> Or heart of man suffice to comprehend?
> Yet what thou canst attain, which best may serve
> To glorify the Maker, and infer
> Thee also happier, shall not be withheld
> Thy hearing, such Commission from above
> I have receiv'd, to answer thy desire
> Of knowledge within bounds; beyond abstain
> To ask, nor let thine own inventions hope
> Things not reveal'd, which th' invisible King,
> Only Omniscient, hath suppress in Night,
> To none communicable in Earth or Heaven:
> Anough is left besides to search and know. (VII, 112–25)

Here the doctrine of accommodation is explained not in terms of means but of ends. "Secrets" are revealed neither to satisfy curiosity nor to enhance Adam's self-esteem but "To glorify the Maker, and infer Thee also happier." Raphael, in other words, is justifying the ways of God to Adam.

Hence Raphael instructs Adam (and us) in how to understand Christian epic. Many things will be represented not as they are but in such a way as will make them conceivable to us. Since human language is approximation, it can always be misunderstood, so the good will of the hearer must make the necessary adjustments. In particular, the hearer must bear in mind that the story is told for "thy good," which means "To glorify the Maker, and infer Thee also happier." When some aspect of the story seems to contradict these principles (as has frequently been our experience of the poem thus far) it must be examined in the light of God's perfect goodness and love of mankind. This is obviously Milton's own procedure: "If Jehovah repented that he had created man . . . let us believe that he did repent. But let us not imagine that God's repentance arises from lack of foresight, as man's does." God's repentance lacks the defining characteristics of what *we* call repentance (surprise, a change of mind) but there it is: God repented.

All of this applies to Milton's poem as a whole, yet it is withheld from us until the angel begins his tale. Raphael's story is a shorter epic within

Paradise Lost, told by a dramatized narrator to a dramatized audience. Since much of what Raphael has to tell is as new to us as it is to Adam, it would be foolish to claim that for us as readers the interest lies not in what is told but solely in *how* it is told and how received. For long stretches of Raphael's tale we are as absorbed in it as is Adam. But repeatedly we are reminded of the presence of a second story—Adam's instruction by the angel—underlying and paralleling the first. While the angel fills in blank spaces in our knowledge of events prior to the beginning of the plot proper, that plot itself is advancing almost imperceptibly, as Adam masters one lesson and goes on to the next. The effect is at least an intermittent increase in our self-consciousness as readers.

By virtue of Raphael's own comments on the accommodated method and didactic purpose of his poem, we come to Books V–VIII as more sophisticated readers than we were in the previous four-and-one-half books. By virtue of knowledge we have but Adam as yet does not—both the fact of man's impending fall and the events and characters of Books I–III—we are also superior to Adam in knowledge and insight. Our mood is relaxed, contemplative. Some surprises await us, but by and large our sense of being in control is far greater than before. In a variety of ways, Milton will be taking us backstage to show us how his poem is put together, how it works.

Stories are told not merely for the pleasure of the telling but also for their impact on an audience. When God orders Raphael: "Go therefore, half this day as friend with friend Converse with Adam" (V,229–30), he has a purpose in mind beyond friendly conversation:

> such discourse bring on,
> As may advise him of his happy state,
> Happiness in his power left free to will,
> Left to his own free Will, his Will though free,
> Yet mutable; whence warn him to beware
> He swerve not too secure: tell him withal
> His danger, and from whom, what enemy
> Late fall'n himself from Heaven, is plotting now
> The fall of others from like state of bliss. (V,233–41)

"Advise him," "warn him," "tell him," all underline the didactic function of Raphael's impending tale. Yet it is the mimetic aspect that attracts our

attention first. At the promise of a genuine epic battle, after the failed
conflicts of Satan with Death in Book II and Satan with Gabriel in Book
IV, our minds hover between wary memories of earlier abortive conflicts
and the nevertheless considerable atavistic appeal of a championship
fight.

The battle begins promisingly enough, as God sends an army of loyal
angels equal in number to the rebel force to drive Satan out of Heaven.
Spirits who can't die, though they can (and do) feel pain, perform numberless heroic deeds, invent cannon, and pile uprooted mountains on
each other, but the war rages on and on to no conclusion. At the end of
two celestial days the landscape is in need of repair, but no other tangible
result has been achieved or seems likely to be. Milton's sneer at epic
battles in Book IX as "tedious havoc" is nowhere more justly applied than
to his own Book VI.

Spiritual weapons are needed to subdue a spiritual enemy. When
God finally decides to end the interminable tumult, he sends forth
his Son, armed with thunder "such as in thir Souls infix'd Plagues"
(VI,837–38) and with lightning that "of thir wonted vigor left them
drain'd" (VI,851). The pretense that this is a literal rather than a symbolic
struggle is at this point scarcely maintained. After a taste of such fire-
power, the terrified enemy flees toward the wall of Heaven, whence they
throw themselves gladly into the abyss. Raphael's account of the War in
Heaven, if it arouses one more time the expectation of martial deeds,
causes one last disappointment to the reader who thought he knew what
an heroic poem was supposed to be.

But the effect is not one of outright disappointment, for Raphael
prepares us for the anticlimax, beginning in his epistemological preface
a sort of running debate about the kind and degree of truth contained in
his story. First, since a story unfolds in time, Raphael raises the question
of time in Heaven. "On a day," he begins:

> (For Time, though in Eternity, appli'd
> To motion, measures all things durable
> By present, past, and future) on such a day
> As Heav'n's great Year brings forth. . . . (V,580–83)

The parenthetical remark establishes a connection between Heaven and
Earth, yet leaves the connection problematic. If "Heav'n's great Year" is
the one mentioned in Plato's *Timaeus*—the time it takes the sun to move

through the twelve signs of the zodiac back to its starting place—then the Heavenly year is 36,000 earthly years long, and each of their days equals a century of human time. Since there is no certainty even to the notion that Raphael's "great Year" is Plato's, the relationship between human and celestial time is left indeterminate—but with the clear implication that Heavenly scale far exceeds the earthly.

Raphael's manner of narration throughout the War in Heaven accords with the ambiguity of his initial statement on accommodation. Heaven has not only days but variations in light "like Day and Night; . . . though darkness there might well Seem twilight here" (VI,8–12). Angels march to battle in military ranks more perfect than human formations, "for high above the ground Thir march was" (VI,71–72). They wear armor of unspecified material to cover bodies of "Ethereal substance" (VI,330), but though they can be wounded, they cannot die:

> for Spirits that live throughout
> Vital in every part, not as frail man
> In Entrails, Heart or Head, Liver or Reins,
> Cannot but by annihilating die;
> Nor in thir liquid texture mortal wound
> Receive, no more than can the fluid Air:
> All Heart they live, all Head, all Eye, all Ear,
> All Intellect, all Sense, and as they please,
> They Limb themselves, and color, shape or size
> Assume, as likes them best, condense or rare. (VI,344–53)

In these and other places too numerous to mention, Raphael repeatedly raises the question of the commensurability of human language to celestial facts, not to deny the truth of what he is telling but to make us aware that both telling and understanding this story require tact and discernment. This method is unquestionably daring. "Milton's design," grumbles Dr. Johnson, "requires the description of what cannot be described":

> He saw that immateriality supplied no images, and that he could not show angels acting but by instruments of action; he therefore invested them with form and matter. This, being necessary, was therefore defensible; and he should have secured the consistency of his system, by keeping immateriality out of sight, and enticing his reader to drop it from his thoughts. But he has unhappily perplexed his poetry with his philosophy.
>
> . . . . .

> The confusion of spirit and matter which pervades the whole narration of the war of heaven fills it with incongruity; and the book, in which it is related, is, I believe, the favourite of children, and gradually neglected as knowledge is increased.[8]

Though written in its dispraise, this description of Milton's method seems to me remarkably discerning, both of the naive gratifications Book VI offers ("the favourite of children") and of its more sophisticated failures. But Dr. Johnson neglects to mention—perhaps because (in his opinion) it could only serve to make Milton appear more maladroit—the relentless way Raphael's story *exposes* the incongruity of his narration. Where Milton's narrator kept immateriality out of sight in Books I and II, or revealed it with seeming inadvertence, Raphael insists on warning us, repeatedly and emphatically, that he is accommodating.

There is indeed a great deal of incongruity in the story of the War in Heaven, enough to lead Arnold Stein to interpret the whole episode as comic.[9] The best evidence for such a pattern is the fact that God himself jokes about Satan's rebellion, playing a sort of ironic Henry IV to Satan's Hotspur:

> [God] smiling to his only Son thus said.
>   Son, thou in whom my glory I behold
> In full resplendence, Heir of all my might,
> Nearly it now concerns us to be sure
> Of our Omnipotence, and with what Arms
> We mean to hold what anciently we claim
> Of Deity or Empire, such a foe
> Is rising, who intends to erect his Throne
> Equal to ours, throughout the spacious North;
> Nor so content, hath in his thought to try
> In battle, what our Power is, or our right.
> Let us advise, and to this hazard draw
> With speed what force is left, and all imploy
> In our defense, lest unawares we lose
> This our high place, our Sanctuary, our Hill. (V,718–32)

The Father speaks here precisely like an insecure tyrant, playing the role assigned him by Satan; but evident absurdities, like holding "Deity" by "Arms," or "the Eternal eye" (VI,711) losing his godhead "unawares," reveal God's tone as ironic. "Nearly it now concerns us to be sure Of our Omnipotence," he jokes, relying on his audience to perceive that by definition Omnipotence cannot be threatened, much less lost. And in case we miss the joke, the Son mentions and explains it:

> Mighty Father, thou thy foes
> Justly hast in derision, and secure
> Laugh'st at thir vain designs and tumults vain. . . . (V,735–37)

From God's perspective, the War in Heaven is indeed comic, and his levity does obscurely predict the inconclusiveness of that struggle. But as a whole Books V and VI are not funny, at least to a human audience; Raphael tells his story from the point of view not of Omniscience but from that of a human onlooker, for whom the consequences are neither foreordained nor nonexistent. And, despite their laughter at Satan's vain designs, Father and Son go on to play their assigned roles seriously, as if some serious issue were at stake. And indeed it is.

Beneath the pomp and circumstance of the celestial battle, another struggle is silently being waged, one into which by divine *fiat* Omnipotence does not extend. For when Satan rebels against divinity, he takes one-third of the angels with him. A fall occurs, not in the ignominious rout from Heaven at the end of Book VI, but in the "Hoarse murmur" of applause that greets Satan's announcement of rebellion. The issue of keeping or breaking loyalty with God is a solemn one, although not one to be settled by force of arms, and hence is not the fit subject for comedy. Which brings us to the didactic function of Raphael's tale and to the story of Abdiel.

From the standpoint of the poem's doctrine, the existence of Abdiel, who is not in the Bible, is necessary to show that Satan's followers were free either to stand or fall. Like all the others under Satan's command, Abdiel obediently follows his leader to the North. However, once Satan reveals his opposition to God, Abdiel alone demonstrates that Satan's passive audience is free to stand or fall. As Raphael observes later: "firm they might have stood, Yet fell; remember, and fear to transgress" (VI,911–12).

Given this particular arrangement of events, Abdiel is necessary, since he alone proves that the rest of Satan's followers were free not to fall. But let us not forget that Milton might have arranged events differently. Satan might, for instance, have aimed his speech at the entire heavenly host; then every angel might have demonstrated his loyalty to God, or his disloyalty. Abdiel plays his present role in *Paradise Lost* not simply to exonerate God. In his solitary courage he embodies the hero of faith, teaching both Adam and us a lesson.

Abdiel's lesson is that it is possible and necessary for the solitary soul to withstand temptation. Owing allegiance to Satan, he must break that allegiance when it conflicts with his higher allegiance to God. Surrounded by numberless fellows who have chosen error, he must nonetheless stand up for truth:

> So spake the Seraph Abdiel faithful found,
> Among the faithless, faithful only hee;
> Among innumerable false, unmov'd,
> Unshak'n, unseduc'd, unterrifi'd
> His Loyalty he kept, his Love, his Zeal;
> Nor number, nor example with him wrought
> To swerve from truth, or change his constant mind
> Though single. (V, 896–903)

The parallel between Satan's temptation of Abdiel and his impending temptation of Eve are close enough to have provided some guide for her. Like the disguised Satan of Book IX, the rebel angel urges discontent with a position subordinate to another (the angels are to the Son as Eve is to Adam) and encourages them to doubt the truth of what God has told his creatures (V, 853–63). Raphael warns Eve and Adam that Satan speaks "with calumnious Art Of counterfeited truth" (V, 770–71), and Abdiel thrusts home the necessity of humility in the face of Divine decree:

> Shalt thou give Law to God, shalt thou dispute
> With him the points of liberty, who made
> Thee what thou art, and form'd the Pow'rs of Heav'n
> Such as he pleas'd, and circumscrib'd thir being? (V, 822–25)

Both are lessons Eve could usefully have remembered.

Adam, too, could have learned some lessons from Abdiel's example. For instance, that it is neither proper nor necessary to disobey God because others are already doing so. The emphatic solitariness of Abdiel at the moment of temptation, the pressure on him of innumerable companions to follow their example, illustrate that the true servant of God must confront temptation horribly *alone*. Adam, as Milton depicts him in Book IX, is capable of withstanding any temptation but that which Satan sends him: the prospect of solitude and loneliness in Eden, separated by sin

from the only other human being. But the reward of Abdiel's lonely virtue is reunion with God and with a number of his loyal compatriots even
greater than those who fell:

> gladly then he mixt
> Among those friendly Powers who him receiv'd
> With joy and acclamations loud, that one
> That of so many Myriads fall'n, yet one
> Return'd not lost: On to the sacred hill
> They led him high applauded, and present
> Before the seat supreme; from whence a voice
> From midst a Golden Cloud thus mild was heard.
> Servant of God, well done. . . . (VI,21–29)

Adam might also have remembered from Abdiel's story that loyalty to
God is not rewarded with solitude and despair but with loving reunion
with God and with the just.

But of course Adam doesn't want just any companion; he wants *Eve*.
And Eve, when she tempts Adam, is already fallen. It is in fact the seeming finality of Eve's condition that constitutes Adam's true temptation.
And here, too, Abdiel has provided an example Adam might have remembered, when he urges Satan to:

> Cease then this impious rage,
> And tempt not these; but hast'n to appease
> Th' incensed Father, and th' incensed Son,
> While Pardon may be found in time besought. (V,845–48)

Abdiel, that is, does not assume that the effects of sin are irreversible but
urges Satan to seek "Pardon." This is ultimately what Adam and Eve do,
yet Adam might have spared them both much agony had he followed
Abdiel's example from the first, rather than Eve's.

Abdiel's story is, as we might expect, the least ambiguous part of the
entire War in Heaven. In a scene that is practically all dialogue, no angelic narrator intrudes to warn us that he is comparing great things to
small, no apparent absurdity or side remark to a listening Adam reminds
us that the spiritual duel between Satan and Abdiel is being accommodated to our ears. The didactic center of Raphael's account, in other
words, is rendered with an immediateness that the more self-conscious
mimetic portions of the story lack. The figure of the Christian hero stands

out clearly against the murky backdrop of the problematic tussle of celestial soldiers, and the very obscurity of the power struggle in Heaven makes the issue of Abdiel's loyalty to God more clear:

> Servant of God, well done, well hast thou fought
> The better fight, who single hast maintain'd
> Against revolted multitudes the Cause
> Of Truth, in word mightier than they in Arms;
> And for the testimony of Truth hast borne
> Universal reproach, far worse to bear
> Than violence: for this was all thy care
> To stand approv'd in sight of God, though Worlds
> Judg'd thee perverse. . . . (VI,29–37)

But in terms of narrative strategy, the episode of Abdiel is all but swamped by the larger story of the War in Heaven, which properly speaking begins with Abdiel's return to the loyalist camp. The problematic does not yield to the clear in Book VI; rather, the message of Abdiel's inner heroism is garbled by the tedious havoc that follows, as the Father orders his angels to do battle while at the same time decreeing that they shall not overcome Satan by force.

The only discussion of Book VI that makes much sense of its didactic purpose is that of Stanley Fish, who argues that the War in Heaven is a deliberate *non sequitur* to Abdiel's spiritual victory over Satan. Fish observes that, like the rest of the loyal angels, Abdiel tries to obey God's command to "subdue [Satan] By force" (VI,40–41) but shows no slackening or dismay when he cannot do it: "Abdiel is a hero because he keeps loyalty even when his objective eludes him and his assumptions fail the test of experience."[10] When it is generalized to the entire contents of Book VI, this argument becomes a justification of the anticlimax:

> The battle is "reported with such fidelity and at such length" in order to allow the reader time to construct from its thrusts and parries a working definition of heroism and to extend it by analogy to the crisis of the Fall. With Abdiel and Michael and the entire host of loyal angels, the reader experiences the disappointments of the war and learns from their response, in so far as it contrasts with his own, to distinguish between the outward form of a self-glorifying exhibitionism and the true (inner) heroism of obedience.[11]

This interpretation fits the facts of Books V and VI and makes sense out of what before seemed senseless, but it also makes me wonder why the sense eluded readers for so long. Why, if a redefinition of heroism is the "message" of Book VI, did it fail to reach readers before Fish (and not merely modern or agnostic readers, but Christian readers, too, as the example of Dr. Johnson illustrates)? It fails, in the first place, because Raphael, who elsewhere provides elaborate interpretation of the latent didactic content of his story, is silent on the subject of Milton's "working definition of heroism." And this silence is in turn due to the fact that the War in Heaven corresponds to nothing in Adam's unfallen experience. The image of the warfaring Christian undismayed by his own inability to defeat Satan presupposes a world divided, as Heaven is temporarily divided, between good and evil. It lies outside Adam's experience. Not until Eve comes to Adam already fallen and apparently beyond rescue does a situation arise remotely like Abdiel's discovery that his obedience to God does not guarantee him victory over Satan. And of course the foreseen Fall is above all others the secret that Raphael must not reveal. Forbidden to draw parallels between the loyal angels' experience and Adam's future experience, Raphael can only repeat the lesson he started with, the warning to obey God:

> list'n not to his Temptations, warn
> Thy weaker; let it profit thee to have heard
> By terrible Example the reward
> Of disobedience; firm they might have stood,
> Yet fell; remember, and fear to transgress. (VI,908–12)

Raphael's story, teaching by "terrible example," has very little to teach Adam. Warning Adam to obey God is like admonishing you or me to draw breath or like telling a child to eat his dessert—we scarcely have to be told to do what we want to do. As far as Adam is concerned, Raphael's entire mission is accomplished in his first brief warning:

> Son of Heav'n and Earth,
> Attend: That thou art happy, owe to God;
> That thou continu'st such, owe to thyself,
> That is, to thy obedience; therein stand.
> This was that caution giv'n thee; be advis'd.
> God made thee perfet, not immutable. . . . (V,519–24)

Adam needs no warning that eternal misery awaits the disobedient; he obeys from love of God, not fear of punishment. The premise of teaching by example instead of by precept is that when temptation comes, it will seem already familiar. But clearly Adam cannot understand why Satan would choose to resent the Son's exaltation, nor why the other rebel angels would approve Satan's defamation of God. To understand Satan, Adam would himself have had to feel pride, anger, envy, fear, and other emotions of which he knows nothing. Adam has listened attentively and learned what he already knew. But the force of teaching by example, which comes from the ability of the listener to imagine himself in the exemplary situation, is lost on Adam, who can do no other than find Satan and the other fallen angels absolutely inscrutable:

> He with his consorted Eve
> The story heard attentive, and was fill'd
> With admiration, and deep muse to hear
> Of things so high and strange, things to thir thought
> So unimaginable as hate in Heav'n,
> And War so near the Peace of God in bliss
> With such confusion. (VII,50–56)

Not knowing what it is like to fall, Adam can't imagine how others came to fall. He simply accepts it on faith.

But of course Adam, since he is a character in the poem, is not its real audience. Raphael's story is ultimately addressed to us, and it succeeds or fails depending upon how it affects us. Unlike Adam we are familiar with emotions of pride, envy, pain, and anger and are thus better able to imagine "hate in Heaven." But how much, exactly, are we able to understand about Satan's fall? Does envy cause Satan's fall, or is it the product of his fall? Since "Evil into the mind of God or Man May come and go, so unapprov'd, and leave No spot or blame behind" (V,117–19), does Satan fall when he feels an evil emotion, or only when that feeling is consummated in an act of rebellion? And why does Satan feel envy when "other powers as great" do not? From his soliloquies in Book IV we are familiar with Satan's fallen psychology, but his transition from the unfallen to the fallen state is in Raphael's account impenetrably obscure, unilluminated by interior monologue of the sort that accompanies Eve's fall and Adam's. When we hear Satan address his legions, he is already the rhetorical seducer and witty dissembler. Since Milton gives us no help in imagining what it feels like to be Satan in the act of falling, the

Satan of Books V and VI remains a distant, opaque figure, and "hate in Heaven" is nearly as unimaginable to us as it is to Adam.

Nor is Abdiel's virtue more comprehensible than Satan's vice. No more than Satan does Abdiel waver between loyalty to God and loyalty to his commander nor debate with himself what is to be done. We have just learned of his existence when he is declaiming against Satan's blasphemy from the resolved position of unsullied virtue:

> O argument blasphémous, false and proud!
> Words which no ear ever to hear in Heav'n
> Expected, least of all from thee, ingrate,
> In place thyself so high above thy Peers. (V,809–12)

What follows is a debate between Abdiel and Satan about the justice of God's ways, but we get no inkling of the psychological processes that motivate the two disputants. Doubtless it is a mistake to expect psychological insight, since angels do not think like you and me, but this is precisely my point. As far as the examples of Abdiel and Satan touch the human predicament, they do so merely to symbolize a choice open to all of God's sentient creatures: we may choose Abdiel's way, or Satan's.

That Abdiel certainly gets the better of this debate should not obscure the fact that it *is* a debate. Satan loses the argument by answering Abdiel with sneers and threats, but the more irrational Abdiel shows Satan's rebellion to be, the less able we are to understand why it in fact occurred. Spirits, being by nature different from human beings, always end up seeming inscrutable to us.

As everywhere in Raphael's account of Heaven, accommodation fails to annihilate the distance between celestial facts and human minds. Stanley Fish sees this discontinuity between our situation as fallen human beings and that of the unfallen angels but rather glosses it over:

> There are some discrepancies. In the angels' case the limitations imposed on them are arbitrary, as arbitrary as the command not to eat the apple. Fallen man's inability to respond fully to the imperative, on the other hand, is a direct consequence of an earlier failure for which he in the person of Adam, is responsible. And there is some question, both historically and in Milton's own statements, as to whether fallen man is able even to initiate an action of the mind, that is, to believe, without the intervention of grace. In general, however, the analogy holds, especially in terms of the visual image presented, movement simultane-

ously hesitant and assertive, self-confident and dependent, absurd and glorious, erring and right.[12]

To this I would answer that the "visual image presented" is comprehensible but not especially moving. The image of the loyal angels failing to subdue Satan yet remaining faithful, like the images of Satan's envy and Abdiel's zeal, speaks to the mind but not to the emotions. We remain rather distant from the events in Heaven because their connection to our experience is, as Raphael warns us, problematic.

There is a tension in Books V and VI between Raphael's method (the mimesis of a celestial battle) and the message (true conflict is spiritual conflict). Given the nature of the poem we've thus far been reading, there is no longer great surprise in discovering this fact. But circumstances of the telling have changed. The narrator (Raphael) honestly admits the inadequacy of his poem as mimesis and explains the nature of accommodation. His story, moreover, is accommodated not merely to our understandings but to Adam's. Not being the audience directly addressed, we stand a little to the side of Raphael's story, attending not only to what is said, but (under Raphael's guidance) to *how* it is told. Superior in knowledge to Adam, we perceive parallels between his situation and Abdiel's that are hidden from Adam. These multiple indirections and warnings to read carefully are framed by God's foreknowledge of the Fall, which turns Raphael's mission from one of preventing Adam's transgression into one of forestalling a possible excuse:

> let him know,
> Lest wilfully transgressing he pretend
> Surprisal, unadmonisht, unforewarn'd. (V,243–45)

In the "Argument" prefixed to Book V., Milton says: "God *to render Man inexcusable* sends Raphael to admonish him. . . ."

Distanced as we are from Raphael's story by absurdities and contradictions that are rather more manifest than those in previous books, and are in many instances also thoughtfully pointed out by the teller, we are in a better position to learn what was earlier only obscurely hinted at: that seeing "things invisible to human sight" is not an end in itself but is part of the larger process of understanding God's ways. Understanding is superior to seeing, just as faith is superior to understanding; so that the response of Adam is, for an unfallen human being, exactly right—he recognizes that he cannot imagine or understand "hate in Heav'n," but remains unshaken in his love of God. Thus, at the end of Book VI our superiority to Adam actually becomes a liability, as we discover that while we are learning, slowly and painfully, how to understand God's ways, Adam has no need to do so. Adam has no need to justify God's ways, for he loves God already.

It is so difficult to tread the line between "literal" and "figurative" meanings, either in Milton's reading of the Bible or in his poem, that it begins to seem likely that no such line exists. "To Milton," A.C. Dobbins reminds us:

> the point of view presented in *Paradise Lost* was scarcely "theological fiction." *Paradise Lost* is considerably more than a brilliant poetic effort, based upon literary sources, to explain the unexplainable. To Milton, the narrative of Christ's initial "begetting" as the Son of God, the War in Heaven, the begetting of Sin and Death, the construction of the Bridge Across Chaos, the description of Satan's flight from Gabriel were incidents which were as profoundly true as the Book of Revelation itself.[13]

Yet John's Apocalypse is a notoriously murky and confusing text, testifying once again to Raphael's wisdom in warning us not to take Milton's version of it at face value. When we remember that omnipotent God "wrote" not only the text of Revelation but also the "events" that it describes, combining the roles of Prospero and Shakespeare, then it becomes hard to sort out the "truth" from the "fiction," either in the Bible or in *Paradise Lost*.

Ultimately the antithesis is a false one. As I have been saying, in one way or another in every chapter of this book so far, Milton's poem is that ultimate oxymoron, a true fiction: true because (or if) it comes from God, and because, read rightly, it will literally save the reader; fiction not only because God's acts are accommodated to our ears in human language, but because God's acts themselves are expressions of a creative will. Behind the poet John Milton stands a greater Poet, who writes in matter and energy; behind *Paradise Lost* stands a greater poem, Creation itself.

5

True Fiction

The Middle Ages represented the history of the world as
a great poem, which takes on a complete and intelligible
meaning as soon as we know the beginning and the
end.—Etienne Gilson

THE END OF Book VI marks the end of Milton's "classical epic." The
great military climax that comes at or near the end of ancient epic comes
halfway through Milton's, where it is no longer a climax but an anachro-
nistic interruption of a plot that has already moved on to other issues.
Since its results are already known and announced in advance by Raphael, the account of the War in Heaven must pitch its appeal at the
reader's desire for the marvelous, for spectacles overgoing those of other
poems, things unattempted yet in prose or rhyme. But even a naive
reader of Books V and VI can't fail to recognize in Satan's invention of
cannon (attended by a salvo of bad puns), in the uprooting of mountains,
and in the rebels' unceremonious flight toward the wall of Heaven a
movement that mocks heroic battle first by exaggerating, then by belit-
tling it.

Satan has pretty much discredited himself by the time we reach
Book V. He interests us not as the epic hero of Books I and II but as a
poseur and confidence man or as the suffering sinner of the first soliloquy.
His inability to tempt Eve in Book IV and his ignominious flight from
combat with Gabriel leave us wondering less how he managed to lose the
War in Heaven than how he will succeed in causing Man's Fall. If Satan

has actually been degenerating in Books I–V, then we would expect Raphael's flashback to give us an earlier, more admirable Satan, but quite the contrary is the case. Satan is not degenerating, we find, because he *never was* the mighty adversary or badly-treated victim represented in Books I and II. Raphael's story gives us a different understanding of Satan's nature that helps us to see the flaws in our initial view of him. When the attempt to apply epic norms to the true issues of *Paradise Lost* ends in absurdity, it is not merely Satan who looks absurd: the poem's beginning does so too, and so do we for believing it.[1]

Every part of the poem thus far has, in one way or another, questioned its own epic pretensions. In Books I and II the "counterplot" made us subliminally uncomfortable about the scenes we *seemed* to be seeing, the poem we *thought* we were reading; God's sermon in Book III brushed Satan quickly aside in order to launch a disconcerting attack upon man, who had yet to make an appearance in the poem; the scenes set in Eden modulated successfully from the heroic to the pastoral mood, making it hard to imagine how "Man's First Disobedience" was ever to come about by the narrative and poetic processes Milton had set in motion. But the War in Heaven sustains the critique of epic far longer and more overtly than does any previous part of the poem. Raphael's story is hedged round with paradoxes, as is his purpose in telling it. God's own instructions to his messenger suggest a kind of pointlessness to the whole story—perfect as he is, Adam can't be helped to resist the Fall but only to repair its effects afterward. Raphael's warning is accomplished in a few lines; the story which follows tells Adam things he needn't know. Within the story itself, God jokes about what is about to happen, wryly pointing out its absurdity, while the teller questions whether it can be told at all. When he does tell it, he "accommodates" it in such a way that we perceive over and over the way Raphael has to choose his words with regard to his listener's limitations. Small wonder if we conclude, as by and large Milton's modern critics have concluded, that Raphael's mission is "largely a matter of narrative expediency,"[2] and that it is *us*, not Adam, whom the angel has come to instruct. I would only go one step further and suggest that the pretext of Raphael's visit to warn Adam is *perceived* by us as a pretext, that some fraction of our attention is directed away from the events portrayed and toward the fact and method of portrayal. As readers, we are being made self-conscious.

Self-consciousness would seem to be the last thing a poem as speculative as Milton's would want to encourage. The self-conscious reader will ask questions about the status of the story he is reading, especially this question: is Raphael's account (in Milton's terms) fact or fiction? The biblical source for Satan's revolt is the Book of Revelation, a long, obscure, allegorical vision, usually interpreted as a history of celestial events before the Creation, and as a prophecy of Christ's second coming at the end of time.[3] "And there was war in heaven," says the author of Revelation:

> Michael and his angels fought against the dragon; and the dragon fought and his angels, and prevailed not; neither was their place found any more in heaven. And the great dragon was cast out, that old serpent, called the Devil, and Satan, which deceiveth the whole world: he was cast out into the earth, and his angels were cast out with him. (12:7–9)

This, along with references here and there to Satan's fall and to the existence of bad angels (Isaiah 14:12; Luke 8:2 and 10:18; II Peter 2:4) is the sum of the knowledge Milton could regard as certain with respect to Satan's revolt. It is remarkably little, and in *Christian Doctrine* Milton has little to say about the War in Heaven, which enters his discussion only to document his contention that Michael is not Christ:

> There seems to be a leader among the good angels, and he is often called Michael. . . .
> A lot of people are of the opinion that Michael is Christ. But whereas Christ alone vanquished Satan and trod him underfoot, Michael is introduced as leader of the angels and antagonist of the prince of the devils: their respective forces were drawn up in battle array and separated after a fairly even fight.[4]

Here, although Milton is circumspect about ambiguity in biblical matters that "concern us not" (*viz.*, "there *seems* to be a leader. . . . and he *is often called* Michael"), he is positively eager to read the ambiguous phrase "and prevailed not" as applying not simply to "the dragon," but to Michael and his angels as well. For Milton this was the main escatalogical point of the entire conflict—that God alone triumphed over Satan, through the agency of his Son, whose victory at the beginning of time prefigures and guarantees his victory at the end of time. The general military tone of his source in Revelation authorizes Milton's description of a battle in *Paradise Lost*, but scarcely provides the materials for such a description. Hence Raphael's warning that some part of it is invented.

In *Paradise Lost*, too, Milton's treatment of the War in Heaven hovers disconcertingly between claims to truth and warnings of its invention, causing his critics to do so also. "Milton. . ." says Stella Revard, "is pointedly inexact in assigning it time or place or even in determining whether it is real or allegorical."[5] Merritt Hughes, on the other hand, sees it as unmistakably real:

> Milton definitely conceived his celestial battle as representing events which were none the less actual for surmounting the reach of human sense, and . . . he found evidence for their occurrence and models for their likening to corporal forms in the classical accounts of the assaults of the Titans and giants on the gods of Olympus, of which the best example is in Hesiod's *Theogony*.[6]

Hughes's flat assertion that Milton's celestial battle represents actual events is considerably softened, however, by the warning that since these events were unknowable Milton had recourse to Hesiod for a model. The idea that truth must be clothed in fiction in order to become visible is itself a paradox; our awareness of Raphael's "fictionalizing" can hardly fail to make his poem more difficult for the reader, who has to wonder at every point in Raphael's story what is truth and what is "simply poetry."

The problem encompasses the whole middle section of the poem, even the visit of Raphael himself, which as a nonbiblical event must be accounted for by some theory of Milton's narrative strategy. Epic convention, though it recommends interpolated narrative, is not in itself sufficient to explain that strategy. Beginning in Hell in order to enhance his poem's power to implicate his reader in the evil that is his topic, Milton needed some way of eventually straightening his audience out. This of course involved debunking Satan's lies and distortions, but the real problem was not simply to show Satan up but to teach the reader to read with more awareness of the ability of poetry (and of language generally) to misrepresent. So, with respect to us, the purpose of Raphael's mission is twofold: first, to fill the gap between Satan's rebellion and the moment at which Book I opens; second, to tell that story in such a way as to make the reader aware of the fact that the medium through which he sees these events (i.e., language) is not capable of giving a "true" picture without the active collaboration of the receiving mind:

> Good and evill we know in the field of this World grow up together almost inseparably; and the knowledge of good is so involv'd and inter-

woven with the knowledge of evill, and in so many cunning resem-
blances hardly to be discern'd, that those confused seeds which were
impos'd on Psyche as an incessant labour to cull out, and sort asunder,
were not more intermixt.[7]

Milton's argument in *Areopagitica* is that a piece of writing—*any* piece
of writing, even the Bible, and certainly Christian epic—is neither good
nor bad in itself, but as it is used by a reader. To use *Paradise Lost* properly, the reader must understand his role as like that of Psyche, culling
out truth from error, false interpretation from true. And the first step
toward solving the problem is to recognize it.

The thirty-nine line prologue which introduces Book VII is itself a
mimesis of the poet in the process of culling out truth from error. Like
its predecessors in Books I and III, this prologue is preoccupied with
how to name, define, or locate Milton's source of inspiration:

> Descend from Heav'n Urania, by that name
> If rightly thou art call'd, whose Voice divine
> Following, above th' Olympian Hill I soar,
> Above the flight of Pegasean wing.
> The meaning, not the Name I call: for thou
> Nor of the Muses nine, nor on the top
> Of old Olympus dwell'st, but Heav'nly born,
> Before the Hills appear'd, or Fountain flow'd,
> Thou with Eternal Wisdom didst converse,
> Wisdom thy Sister, and with her didst play
> In presence of th' Almighty Father, pleas'd
> With thy Celestial Song. (VII, 1–12)

Previously the narrator called his muse by biblical metaphors—"Spirit,"
"Holy Light"—now he gives her a pagan name, "Urania," which provokes
in him a paroxism of anxiety, lest he name her wrongly: "The meaning,
not the Name I call." Yet names are unavoidable, so he delves beneath
the necessary fiction of a name for the truth it conceals. *His* muse is not
one of the nine who dwelt on Olympus or at Helicon, for she existed long
before mountain or fountain.

The name "Urania" was borrowed from the Greek muse of astronomy and given to "the Christian Muse" by the French Calvinist poet,
Guillaume Du Bartas, in a poem published in 1574.[8] Since by Milton's

time the name had become a commonplace for the muse of divine (as distinguished from secular or pagan) poetry, we might expect him to use it casually as a conventional synonym for "Heavenly Muse." However, such is not the case. Milton's inspiration, like every believing Christian's, comes from God—from His words in the Bible, and from His indwelling spirit that enables us to read the words correctly. To call that spirit "Urania," no matter how pious the intent, is to add human invention to divine truth.

Hence Milton uses the name to distinguish himself from Du Bartas. To invent a Christian Muse is to play by the old rules, to obscure the plain truth of God's inspiration with a multitude of vain conceits that pay the homage of imitation to pagan religion. Milton's is the opposite strategy: dallying with the false surmise of secular poetry in order to suggest a deeper meaning, he deliberately plays the conventional role of epic poet badly. He names his muse in order to back off from the name. Inventing an allegory of two sisters playing before the Lord, he intimates that Urania has another name which, unfortunately, he fails to specify, and which generations of scholars have been unable to discover.[9] His allusions to classical myth point to failures of poetic inspiration: like Bellerophon, Milton will "fall" from his winged steed, unless she deigns to return him to Earth; like Orpheus, the poet will be dismembered by the "wild rout" of an unfit audience, unless protected by his "muse."

The prologue is of course a prayer for poetic inspiration and as such is an affirmation of the superlative capacity of the Christian God to inspire poetry, but such facts make it all the more startling that this affirmation should be achieved almost entirely by negation or denial. It is as if the things the poet wished to say lay beyond the power of words to express; as if the muse were unnameable and unknowable except through fiction; as if the danger of presumptuous pride were inexpressible except in the myths of Bellerophon and Orpheus. Yet surely this is not altogether true. Milton can dispense with the fiction of a muse entirely; he can refer to the Divine Spirit directly (as he did in Book I) as his source of inspiration; he can admit to the possibility of Christian pride (the deadliest sin) implicit in his project of singing of "things invisible;" and he can dispense with all the trifling fictions and vain imaginings that pad his prayer out to thirty-nine lines. Yet by the same logic he ought to purge his poem of all purely secular conventions and pagan fictions, to omit not only epic question (*in medias res* beginning, similes imitating Homer's and Vergil's, military heroism, and every other trapping of secular epic) but also every embellishment, heightening, or ordering of a revelation that comes to us already perfect from the hand of God in the Bible.

He *could* do so, but in so doing he would deny the possibility of Christian poetry and the need (which he feels deeply) of Christians *for* poetry. Instead he adopts a more complex position: poets are purveyors of fiction, liars who may nonetheless point us toward the truth. Under the hypothesis that Milton's inspiration proceeds from God, all of his lies point toward truth; his visions of Hell, Heaven, and Eden, all literally "fabrications" (interpretations of holy writ eked out with invention), will ultimately help to justify God's ways, hence are "true" in a higher sense. But if the poet is not writing under divine guidance, then it is all merely a pack of lies, and he is simply a fallen human being who has never left the ground:

> Standing on Earth, not rapt above the Pole,
> More safe I Sing with mortal voice, unchang'd
> To hoarse or mute, though fall'n on evil days,
> On evil days though fall'n, and evil tongues;
> In darkness and with dangers compast round,
> And solitude; yet not alone, while thou
> Vist'st my slumbers Nightly. . . . (VII,23–29)

What guarantees that these nocturnal visits are not mere "empty dreams"? Only the poet's capacity to clothe Truth without disguising her. Hence he keeps undressing her, here and elsewhere in *Paradise Lost*— "The meaning, not the Name I call"—and then dressing her again, so that we will look on her more willingly.

The process of making lies into truth is, I suggest, the meaning that Milton's entire prologue hints at. The prologue is, to coin a term, a "meta-allegory," written to suggest the relationship between poetry and truth. Just as the fictions of Bellerophon and Orpheus were simply "dreams" until the revelation contained in the Old and New Testaments enabled us to see the truth behind them, so every fiction must be read in the light of the one great Truth: salvation through Christ. I am not claiming that *Paradise Lost* is an allegory, although like the Bible it *contains* allegory. Rather, *Paradise Lost* as a mimetic heroic poem based upon classical models is, like allegory, myth, drama, and every other form of fictional representation, true or false according to how it is read. The prologue to Book VII does for pagan myth, for allegory, for the idea of a "muse," and (by implication) for poetry itself, precisely what its predecessor did for "light": in portraying the mind of the poet in the act of grappling with the "truthful" and "erroneous" aspect of each of these fictions, Milton teaches us the kind of mental operations necessary for the reader of his own fiction, *Paradise Lost*.

The inspiration needed by the poet to complete the epic is nicely balanced by the inspiration needed to read it:

> yet not alone, while thou
> Visit'st my slumbers Nightly, or when Morn
> Purples the East: still govern thou my Song,
> Urania, and fit audience find, though few. (VII,28–31)

Without inspiration, the poet is an archetype of fallen man: his inspired song is his salvation, and it comes not simply from himself but from God's spirit within him. Likewise the audience must have the "spirit" to apprehend the meaning. "Fit audience though few" is the touchstone of those who wish to see *Paradise Lost* as elitist art, yet in context, the reference to "fit audience" is a compliment paid to each one of us who has read thus far in a difficult poem and an invitation to imitate the upwardly aspiring poet, rather than the self-debasing Bacchants, who murdered what they could not understand:

> But drive far off the barbarous dissonance
> Of Bacchus and his Revellers, the Race
> Of that wild Rout that tore the Thracian Bard
> In Rhodope, where Woods and Rocks had Ears
> To rapture, till the savage clamor drown'd
> Both Harp and Voice; nor could the Muse defend
> Her Son. (VII,32–38)

Milton's allegory of writing is one of reading as well; he suggests we quell the "wild Rout" within us to become instead the "fit audience" who alone can grasp his meaning. Rhetorically adroit, he places this suggestion at a position in the poem where it is also a compliment ("You're doing well so far, reader. Keep it up!"). Of things unattempted yet in prose or rhyme, perhaps the chief is to make epic lie into Christian truth and thus to create a phoenix among poems, the "true fiction." To do this seemingly impossible feat, Milton will need the help of the true Urania in each of us as well: "So fail not thou, who thee implores: For thou art Heav'nly, shee an empty dream" (VII,38–39).

Besides its dark allegory of fact and fiction, the prologue also reminds us of the fictional status of Milton's poem in a more obvious way, by breaking the frame of Raphael's narration to reveal the face of the poet behind the angelic mask. Raphael's claim to speak truly is after all no better than Milton's claim to divine inspiration: if Milton errs, Raphael necessarily does so, too. The muse who sang of Hell, Heaven, and Paradise is also singing through Raphael's mouth. Yet in displacing authorship onto a dramatized speaker, Milton gains the great advantage of being able to comment on the limits of his own inspiration from the heavenly perspective of a messenger from God. The result is a corrective to the grandiosity and epic pretension of the prologues. "What cause," asks Adam:

> Mov'd the Creator in his holy Rest
> Through all Eternity so late to build
> In Chaos, and the work begun, how soon
> Absolv'd, if unforbid thou mayst unfold
> What wee, not to explore the secrets ask
> Of his Eternal Empire, but the more
> To magnify his works, the more we know. (VII,90–97)

Adam here plays "blind bard" to Raphael as Muse, proposing the epic question for a new, unfallen divine poem. But Adam's heavenly muse answers with a second warning of the limitations placed upon any such revelation. Some of Raphael's words we have already looked at, but they bear repeating:

> This also thy request with caution askt
> Obtain: though to recount Almighty works
> What words or tongue of Seraph can suffice,
> Or heart of man suffice to comprehend?
> Yet what thou canst attain, which best may serve
> To glorify the Maker, and infer
> Thee also happier, shall not be withheld
> Thy hearing, such Commission from above
> I have receiv'd, to answer thy desire
> Of knowledge within bounds; beyond abstain
> To ask, nor let thine own inventions hope
> Things not reveal'd, which th' invisible King,
> Only Omniscient, hath supprest in Night,
> To none communicable in Earth or Heaven:

Anough is left besides to search and know.
But Knowledge is as food, and needs no less
Her Temperance over Appetite, to know
In measure what the mind may well contain,
Oppresses else with Surfeit, and soon turns
Wisdom to Folly, as Nourishment to Wind. (VII,111–30)

The contrast between this "prologue" and those of the epic poet is sharp. An angelic narrator, who presumably can tell us anything we want to know, warns that not only is there much we will never know, but that it is futile even to speculate on such topics, lest poetic afflatus turn to flatulence. This homely metaphor implicitly mocks the epic narrator's dippings and soarings, his boasts of things unattempted and invisible; what he takes for "spirit" may turn out to be mere wind. But of course Raphael is a *mouthpiece* of that soaring narrator, and he is addressing Adam, not us. So the unwelcome suggestion that much of what we've already read in *Paradise Lost* is vain "invention" is distanced for us by the dramatic context, which seems to say that the danger of overstepping the bounds of beneficial knowledge is Adam's, not ours, and that we already know what it is forbidden him to guess: God's foreknowledge of his impending Fall.

The most important fact about Raphael's Hymn to Creation (VII,131–634) is also the most obvious—that it is a paraphrase, or more properly an amplification, of the first chapter of Genesis. No reader native to Western culture, no matter how sheltered his life or secular his education, can fail to have read or heard, probably many times, those famous sentences in which God creates heaven and earth; nor is it easy to imagine a non-Westerner sufficiently educated in the English tongue to read *Paradise Lost* without having been exposed at one time or another to the opening of Genesis. All or virtually all readers of Milton's epic, then, will recognize in Raphael's voice the words of Scripture:

Thus God the Heav'n created, thus the Earth,
Matter unform'd and void: Darkness profound
Cover'd th' Abyss: but on the wat'ry calm
His brooding wings the Spirit of God outspread. . . . (VII,232–35)

Within the frame of Raphael's narration, the incorporation and alteration of divine writ is perfectly appropriate. Raphael is not quoting the as-yet-unwritten books of Moses, but is speaking, rather, from independent knowledge or inspiration. Nor, since Adam is far more intelligent and comprehending an audience than Moses's Israelites, is it inappropriate that he hear a more comprehensive and logical account of Creation than they. The two versions—that of Raphael and that in Genesis—agree, but since *any* version of Creation must be accommodated to the capacities of its hearers, there is no reason why Raphael should not address Adam's erected wit with an ampler and more connected story than what erstwhile Egyptian slaves were capable of following or in need of knowing. As long as we read Raphael's hymn as the address of heavenly messenger to unfallen Adam, we have no problem accepting it as the sort of thing that *ought* to have been said on such an occasion. But as soon as we recognize that this is also *John Milton's* redaction of Genesis, a human poet's attempt to alter and improve upon the sacred scriptures, then the daring of such an attempt is self-evident.

Nothing was more common, of course, than for pious poets to versify the Bible. Like many others, Milton had long been convinced that the Bible contained worthier models of epic, dramatic, and lyric poetry than did Greek and Latin literature, and from time to time he had tried his hand at finding equivalent English verse forms for the Hebrew psalms. The problem was that they did not translate readily as poetry; inevitably one did violence either to the English verse or to the Hebrew sense. At one time Milton hit on the desperate expedient of italicizing all words not in the original, and in glossing debatable translations with the original Hebrew. The impression given by the result is one of scruple rather than of inspiration:

Psalm LXXXIII

1. Be not thou silent *now at length*
     O God hold not thy peace,
   Sit not thou still O God of *strength*,
     We cry and do not cease.
2. For lo thy furious foes *now* *swell
     And *storm outrageously,   *Jehemajun.
   And they that hate thee *proud and fell*
     Exalt their heads full high.
3. Against thy people they †contrive   †Jagnarimu.
     †Their Plots and Counsels deep,   †Sod.
   *Them to ensnare they chiefly strive   *Jithjagnatsu gnal.
     *Whom thou dost hide and keep.[10]   *Tsephuneca.

At the other extreme from this attempt to keep biblical language intact lay the pedestrian soarings of Du Bartas, who took no particular care to stay close to his source:

> So did Gods Spirit delight it selfe a space
> To move it selfe upon the floting *Masse*:
> No other care th' Almightie's mind possest
> (If care can enter in his sacred brest).
> Or, as a Hen that fain would hatch a Brood
> (Some of her own, some of adoptive blood)
> Sits close thereon, and with her lively heat,
> Of yellow-white bals, doth live birds beget:
> Even in such sort seemed the Spirit Eternall
> To brood upon this Gulf. . . .[11]

Examples like this barnyard image of God as a gigantic brood hen must have taught Milton that poets astride Urania were not exempt from tumbling off. As he acknowledged in the prologue, his task is a supremely difficult one. To versify scripture is to change it. How do we change God's words without making them worse?

The first step, for Milton, is to incorporate all of God's words into his poem. In contrast to Du Bartas's free rendering of Genesis, Milton sticks close to his text, both in word and in word order. The poet, though adding much in the way of detail, incorporates his source in such a way that it is still present, practically verbatim, in the resulting divine poem, like a built-in touchstone. To see how this is done, compare the biblical treatment of the first day of Creation with that of Milton:

Genesis (King James Version)

> In the beginning God created the heaven and the earth.
> And the earth was without form, and void; and darkness was upon the face of the deep. And the Spirit of God moved upon the face of the waters.
> And God said, Let there be light: and there was light.
> And God saw the light, that it was good: and God divided the light from the darkness.
> And God called the light Day, and the darkness he called Night. And the evening and the morning were the first day.

Paradise Lost

> Thus *God the Heav'n created, thus the Earth,*
> Matter *unform'd and void: Darkness* profound

Cover'd th' Abyss: but on the wat'ry calm
His brooding wings *the Spirit of God* outspread,
And vital virtue infus'd, and vital warmth
Throughout the fluid Mass, but downward purg'd
The black tartareous cold Infernal dregs
Adverse to life; then founded, then conglob'd
Like things to like, the rest to several place
Disparted, and between spun out the Air.
And Earth self-balanc't on her Centre hung.
    Let there be Light, said God, and forthwith Light
Ethereal, first of things, quintessence pure
Sprung from the Deep, and from her Native East
To journey through the airy gloom began,
Spher'd in a radiant Cloud, for yet the Sun
Was not; shee in a cloudy Tabernacle
Sojourn'd the while. *God saw the Light was good;*
And light from darkness by the Hemisphere
Divided: Light the Day, and Darkness Night
He nam'd. Thus was the first Day Ev'n and Morn.
                                        (VII, 232–52; my italics)

Here, in the more flexible medium of blank verse, Milton succeeds in doing what he earlier failed to do with the psalms—to fuse English verse and Hebrew sense without damage to either. To heighten the method of fusion I have italicized those words in Milton's text that are identical, or nearly so, to those of his original. Since his source was the Hebrew text, his version is even closer to the biblical version than may appear here, certain differences between the two texts printed above (like "Abyss" for "deep" and "brooded" for "moved,") reflecting not emendation but differences of translators' judgment. Furthermore, where the translators of 1611 rendered the terse, unconnected Hebrew by simple repetition of the conjunction "and," Milton exercised his translator's prerogative to avoid several "and's" by introducing a "but."

The italicized portions of Milton's text are no less authoritative and accurate a version of Creation's first day than the Authorized Version, but there is of course a substantial difference between them in underlying philosophy. The King James version is designedly "primitive" in flavor: its simple vocabulary, its verbal repetition, and above all its ubiquitous "and's" address a naive sensibility, interested more in humble reverence for God's mysterious love and power than in nuanced distinctions or logical and causal sequence. In the English Bible, Creation seems to happen mysteriously, according to principles that are not easily grasped. Milton's treatment, on the other hand, addresses itself to a more sophisticated audience—one who knows the difference between earth and matter, who has "abyss" in its vocabulary as well as "deep," who can wait until the end of a clause for its verb, and who above all wants to understand Creation in terms of seventeenth-century logic and science. Moses's Creation is accommodated to a "primitive," childlike audience; Raphael's is accommodated to a more grown-up audience: Adam—or us.

Milton accordingly interprets and augments his text in the interests of clarity, of logic, and of scientific accuracy. In King James, for example, the creation of heaven and earth seems to pass undescribed: the Spirit of God moves (so far as we can tell) upon the face of the waters *after* their creation, while Milton makes clear by conjunctions and adverbs that the "brooding" *is* the creation, and Genesis's first sentence a summary of what follows.[12] While he preserves not only the biblical words but their order as well, he nonetheless turns a vague, disjointed account into one that makes sense: first there was a flux of unformed matter, without light (the realm of Chaos in Book II); then God gave matter his "vital virtue" and "vital warmth," at which point matter organized itself into Earth, Air, Heaven, and Hell. In the same way, Milton tries to make intelligible the puzzling creation of "Light" without a radiant source by locating light "in a radiant Cloud" until the creation of Sun, Moon, and stars on the fourth day. In the process, the mysterious division of light from darkness is readily explained: since light travels around the Earth even before the Sun is born, half the Earth's sphere is always in darkness.

Usually interpretations of a poem that depend upon its relationship to a particular source are suspect. Even if the relationship is demonstrably there, how aware of it can we expect the reader to be? Watching *Hamlet* does not put us irresistibly in mind of *The Spanish Tragedy*; nor does *Ulysses*, without the help of Stuart Gilbert, remind us very often of the *Odyssey*. However patched together a text may be, it has its own integrity of vision that discourages us from continually applying to it an outlook different from its own. Biblical poetry is an obvious exception to this rule, but even here we are generally better off if we don't compare text and source too closely, something Milton forces us to do, however, by incorporating his source verbatim into the poem. Such a technique not only makes us test the poet's inspiration against that of Moses—are the non-biblical passages as elevated as the biblical?—but reminds us continually of the presence of poetic inspiration as an issue. The poet's source may be human presumption or divine grace, but the fact remains that Scripture has been added to.

From first to last, of course, *Paradise Lost* is an amplification and interpretation of the Bible, but it has heretofore kept its distance from any specific part of the biblical narrative proper. So Milton's amplification and interpretation of the Creation directly confront an issue that has previously been skirted, except in the prologues. In Milton's Hymn to Creation, the relation of poetry to truth is very deliberately being explored, as we see the Holy Bible being turned—almost literally "before our eyes"—into a poem.

The metamorphosis of Genesis into a song or poem is surely one of the most compelling of Milton's reasons for adding to the biblical account a motif not found in the original—in *Paradise Lost*, Creation is accompanied by music:

> Thus was the first Day Ev'n and Morn:
> Nor pass'd uncelebrated, nor unsung
> By the Celestial Choirs, when Orient Light
> Exhaling first from Darkness they beheld;
> Birth-day of Heav'n and Earth; with joy and shout
> The hollow Universal Orb they fill'd,
> And touch'd thir Golden Harps, and hymning prais'd
> God and his works, Creator him they sung,
> Both when first Ev'ning was, and when first Morn. (VII,252–60)

Just as Raphael's many warnings and disclaimers about the accommodated nature of the story he is telling alert us to its "fictional" aspect, so his repeated references to the angelic choruses at Creation emphasize the musical nature of the entire account. Angelic choirs "sung" Creation as it was being accomplished; Raphael sings it to Adam; and through the angel Milton sings it to us. Music attends God's Creation, and there is music in the lines Milton writes to describe it:

> Immediately the Mountains huge appear
> Emergent, and thir broad bare backs upheave
> Into the Clouds, thir tops ascend the Sky:
> So high as heav'd the tumid Hills, so low
> Down sunk a hollow bottom broad and deep. . . . (VII,285–89)

Although there is *some* kind of music in virtually every line of *Paradise Lost*, here sound mirrors and accentuates sense to an unusual degree, calling our attention to the music. The "m" in "Mountains" is reinforced with "m's" in "Immediately" and "Emergent"; "Broad bare backs upheave" carries stress on every syllable, and the obtrusive alliteration heightens the impression of musical organization. The internal rhyme of "Sky . . . high" and "so low" (the latter reinforced by "hollow" in the next line) not only "sing" in themselves, but also pit the "high" sound of long "i" (ī) against the "low" sound of long "o" (ō). As in song, formal patterns of sound "sing" the meanings of the phrases.

In Milton's vision, God's Creation is ruled by two contrasting but complementary qualities: symmetry and variety. Creation occurs by an orderly process of division into opposing qualities: chaos-order, heaven-earth, light-dark, day-night, land-sea, and so on, down to male-female. Symmetry gives Creation its basic form, but variety provides the material abundance of the world and prevents symmetry from being limited and sterile. God makes for man a variety beyond what man needs, in order to delight his senses with difference and change:

> He brought thee into this delicious Grove,
> This Garden, planted with the Trees of God,
> Delectable both to behold and taste;
> And freely all thir pleasant fruit for food
> Gave thee, all sorts are here that all th' Earth yields,
> Variety without end. . . . (VII,537–42)

But symmetry and variety are also the principles of Milton's poetic art, as he explains in his headnote on "why the Poem Rimes not":

> Not without cause therefore some both Italian and Spanish Poets of prime note have rejected Rime both in longer and shorter Works, as have also long since our best English Tragedies, as a thing of itself, to all judicious ears, trivial and of no true musical delight; which consists only in apt Numbers, fit quantity of Syllables, and the sense variously drawn out from one Verse into another. . . .[13]

"Number" and "quantity" refer to the regularities of verse—the rhythm of the line, the sounds of the syllables—but "to vary" is also a Renaissance poetic term, referring to the opposite effect from regularity—the element of surprise, of newness. When God creates the universe in an orderly way (beginning with the most general category, unformed matter, and proceeding by symmetrical division toward greater and greater particularity) and in such a way as to provide his audience with an inexhaustible variety of created things, then he is himself a poet, "singing" a world into being by the power of the inspired "word." The Orphic myth of song causing rocks and trees to dance, though false of Orpheus, is true of God:

> [He] saw that it was good, and said Let th' Earth
> Put forth the verdant Grass, Herb yielding Seed,
> And Fruit Tree yielding Fruit after her kind;
> Whose Seed is in herself upon the Earth.
> He scarce had said, when the bare Earth, till then
> Desert and bare, unsightly, unadorn'd,
> Brought forth the tender Grass, whose verdure clad
> Her Universal Face with pleasant green,
> Then Herbs of every leaf, that sudden flow'r'd
> Op'ning thir various colors, and made gay
> Her bosom smelling sweet: and these scarce blown,
> Forth flourish'd thick the clust'ring Vine, forth crept
> The smelling Gourd, up stood the corny Reed
> Embattl'd in her field: and th' humble Shrub,
> And Bush with frizzl'd hair implicit: last
> Rose as in Dance the stately Trees. . . . (VII,309–24)

The verbs here repay close attention. Vegetation is at first the passive recipient of action: "Earth . . . Brought forth" the grass, which then becomes the subject of the rather sedate verb, "to clad." Soon, though, the plants leave their role of simple adornment, and in the progression "crept . . . stood. . . .Rose" we see them transformed into animate beings, joining in line 324 the dance of created nature that Adam and Eve described in the Morning Hymn. In creating them to music, God causes the trees to dance.

The comparison of Milton's poem to God's world was made by Andrew Marvell at the conclusion of his proem to *Paradise Lost*:

> Thy Verse created like thy Theme sublime,
> In Number, Weight, and Measure, needs not Rime.[14]

In Raphael's Hymn to Creation, Milton reverses the analogy, comparing God's Creation to a vast, sublime poem. The idea is of course a Renaissance commonplace—nature is the art of God—but nowhere to my knowledge has it been used with such a fine awareness of its implications for the truth-fiction problem. Looking at the passages of Genesis that Milton has incorporated into his poem, and then at the increasingly longer passages in which he invents "musical" variations upon biblical themes, we must finally become aware that the entire Hymn is, among other things, a lesson in how to read God's two books—the Bible and the "book of nature." Reading Genesis, Milton's inspired mind adds to God's words those themes, images, and rhythms that bear the stamp of the poet's mind engaged in the task of composing a divine poem. And, in reading Milton's words, our minds duplicate the process, recreating out of bare words, such as "let the earth bring forth grass," a picture of the barren Earth clothing herself in green. The implication is that it was all there already—clust'ring vine and corny reed, pearly shells and jointed armor, clods calving and lions pawing to get free of the earth—all there in the Bible, in Nature, and in our own minds, waiting to be liberated from the spare words of Genesis by the divine spirit in Milton's words. As God created the world, so Milton creates it in his poem, and in striving to be his "fit audience" we create it, too. Through the mediation of Milton's poem, our continuing kinship to God is made evident.

There is, Milton's treatment suggests, a right and a wrong way to understand Raphael's Hymn. Read rightly, the story of the Creation is massive testimony to God's benevolence toward man and of man's direct filial relationship to God. Yet the relationship is a two-sided one, connoting not only kinship but submission. Man, though *like* God, is infinitely God's inferior and holds dominion over the world not by virtue of his own powers but at the pleasure of his Creator. The distance between God and man is still inexpressible "By Numbers that have name" (VIII,114). This disproportion is evident in Genesis, where God is the Artist and man the clay artifact, and equally evident in the Book of Nature, where man is almost lost in the vastness of a created nature that dwarfs his sense of self-esteem.

Since in any retelling of Genesis a possible "negative" response must be expected and allowed for, a great virtue of the interpolated mode of narration is that it includes within Milton's frame a dramatized audience, whose response can objectify for the poem's actual readers some of their own deeper, perhaps inarticulate feelings of estrangement from God. Adam, in answering Raphael's Hymn with some "doubts" he has been feeling, crystallizes and gives voice to ours as well:

something yet of doubt remains,
Which only thy solution can resolve.

When I behold this goodly Frame, this World
Of Heav'n and Earth consisting, and compute
Thir magnitudes, this Earth a spot, a grain,
An Atom, with the Firmament compar'd
And all her number'd Stars, that seem to roll
Spaces incomprehensible (for such
Thir distance argues and thir swift return
Diurnal) merely to officiate light
Round this opacous Earth, this punctual spot,
One day and night; in all thir vast survey
Useless besides; reasoning I oft admire,
How Nature wise and frugal could commit
Such disproportions, with superfluous hand
So many nobler Bodies to create,
Greater so manifold to this one use,
For aught appears, and on thir Orbs impose
Such restless revolution day by day
Repeated, while the sedentary Earth,
That better might with far less compass move,
Serv'd by more noble than herself, attains
Her end without least motion, and receives,
As Tribute such a sumless journey brought
Of incorporeal speed, her warmth and light;
Speed, to describe whose swiftness Number fails. (VIII,13–38)

Adam has, of course, hit upon the most famous crux of seventeenth-century science, the issue of whether the universe is heliocentric or geocentric. Back in 1540 Copernicus had proposed heliocentrism as providing the simpler explanation of celestial motions, and his proposal had slowly been gaining ground against the often ferocious defense of those concerned with the fact that the Bible, starting with the first chapter of Genesis, clearly subscribes to geocentrism.

Milton's poem artfully hovers between the two cosmologies, committing itself irrevocably to neither. Earth is never made the center explicitly, but is described as "downward" from the Sun (III,722). In the Hymn to Creation, Milton, following Genesis, seems to make the Sun circle the Earth (VII,372–73), or so Adam understands Raphael to have said when he questions the arrangement in Book VIII. Yet the Sun is frequently referred to, both by characters and narrator, as the brightest, most imposing body in the created universe, hence, in some sense "central" to it. Clearly Milton has profited from the celestial ambiguity of his age to have his symbolism both ways: he uses heliocentrism as emblem of man's dependence upon God and geocentrism to symbolize the central importance of Man to God's Creation.

But having once established these equations, the poet seems bent on denying them. "Consider first," says Raphael:

> that Great
> Or Bright infers not Excellence: the Earth
> Though, in comparison of Heav'n, so small,
> Nor glistering, may of solid good contain
> More plenty than the Sun that barren shines,
> Whose virtue on itself works no effect,
> But in the fruitful Earth; there first receiv'd
> His beams, unactive else, thir vigor find. (VIII, 90–97)

Since the poem has already celebrated not only Satan but God himself precisely in terms of greatness and brightness, Raphael's answer undermines the very premise of Milton's poem thus far: that spiritual truths can be made visible. He even goes on to attack the theme of his own Hymn to Creation, by denying that God's power and benevolence are necessarily visible in the world he made. For if geocentrism leads us to question rather than to affirm God's wisdom or goodness, then it obviously is not "true," Truth being by definition that which conduces to a love of God:

> This to attain, whether Heav'n move or Earth,
> Imports not, if thou reck'n right. . . . (VIII, 70–71)
> . . . .
>
> What if the Sun
> Be Centre to the World, and other Stars
> By his attractive virtue and their own
> Incited, dance about him various rounds? (VIII, 122–25)
> . . . .
>
> What if that light
> Sent from her through the wide transpicuous air,
> To the terrestrial Moon be as a Star
> Enlight'ning her by Day, as she by Night
> This Earth? (VIII, 140–44)
> . . . .
>
> But whether thus these things, or whether not, (VIII, 159)
> . . . .

Solicit not thy thoughts with matters hid,
Leave them to God above, him serve and fear. (VIII, 167–68)

Adam's question, and the resulting "astronomy lesson," is an explicit instance of what I have been arguing *Paradise Lost* is as a whole: a lesson in the limits of human comprehension. That it should be the astronomical question that Raphael refuses to answer may be a convenience so far as uncertain Milton is concerned, but from the standpoint of the story Raphael's decision is deliberately arbitrary: he knows the answer, but he also knows that Adam has no need to know it. Rather, he wants to teach Adam that faith in God in no way depends upon God's comprehensibility to human minds. To insure Adam's grasp of this point, there must be at least one question that Raphael will not answer.

But Raphael's refusal to answer, although it makes sense within the frame of the story, also reaches off the page to confront us directly as readers. For, as spectators privileged to have seen more of God's universe than Adam himself, we are now being told that what we saw was not necessarily the real thing. "In all conscience," says Howard Schultz:

> [Milton] could not allow Raphael to call the lovely framework of his poem fact; yet as a poet he could not suffer him to call it fiction. The curiosity lecture served all ends with economy by shutting off all discussion. [15]

Well, what is it then, if neither fact nor fiction? Questions not to be answered should never be raised in the first place. Adam's question and Raphael's reply, by causing the cosmology of *Paradise Lost* to flicker before our eyes, scarcely shuts off discussion. Raphael clearly *wants* Adam to ask an unanswerable question so that he can teach him a lesson on the limits of comprehension. But in teaching Adam, Raphael also teaches us; passing judgment on him, on us, and on the cosmological poet as well. Previously, we have taken the cosmology for granted. Now we can't help questioning it, and with it, the poem generally: fact or fiction?

The brilliance of Milton's interpolated narrative is that it creates within the text a model of the poet-reader relationship and allows the reader to talk back vicariously through the personage of Adam. After the War in Heaven, Adam says he can't understand; after the Creation Hymn he asks the "wrong" question. Raphael has warned him that there will be things beyond his grasp, and sure enough Adam demonstrates the truth of this warning. As reader-surrogate Adam prompts us to begin doing consciously what we have been doing unconsciously since the beginning. Through Adam we are now "talking back" to the poem, discovering rather than suppressing our bafflement.

The bond of identification between reader and character is of course far from complete at this point. As we have already seen, Adam and Eve oscillate back and forth between seeming familiar—human beings like ourselves—and seeming like strange exotics, far removed in time and space. Above all, the fact of the Fall intervenes between them and us. Like Adam, we may have our difficulties imagining hate in Heaven, or at least its origins, but hatred itself is real to us, as it cannot be to Adam, and so are swords, shields, cannon, wounds, pain, and anger. That the Son's victory in Heaven prefigures his victory over Satan in the hearts of fallen man is a meaning that unfallen Adam cannot know, but that we can and do. So the uncomprehending Adam who asks the angel to tell him of things nearer to his experience is in part at least a distanced figure, trapped as we are not in a situation that forbids his full understanding of what he has just heard.

But Adam's response to the Creation Hymn is much closer to what ours would be if we were to voice it: awe at the grandeur of God's Creation and an undercurrent of doubt that man is worthy of it. The question he asks is one that Milton's original readers could not answer with any more assurance than does Raphael, and although a twentieth-century reader knows the truth about celestial motions, Adam's *real* question, the puzzle of the disproportion between tiny man and infinite universe, is a problem even more apparent to us that it was to the seventeenth century. At the end of Raphael's Hymn, then, we discover that we are closer to Adam's position than we thought at its beginning. This fact may not seem particularly interesting, however, since Adam is merely the asker of short questions that lead to long answers: little more, that is, than the proposer of chapter headings.

But then, suddenly, the roles of poet and audience are reversed, as Adam takes over the part of narrator and begins to tell the angel *his* story. Nothing so extraordinary there, perhaps; characters in fiction are perpetually swapping stories. What is remarkable is that Adam's story continues Raphael's; the listener has taken over the story and can finish it himself.

Raphael's story has been narrowing in scope as it approaches its au-

dience, and Adam's comprehension has been, in the process, improving.
When the angel reaches events that his listener has himself experienced,
then the two trade positions: Adam becomes the narrator telling a story
that is now cleared of doubt for him, because it arises not from some
Heavenly source of privileged information but from his own experience.
The poem's structure seems to propose a hierarchy of things necessary to
know. The story of war in Heaven is useful, since it explains the existence
of Satan as adversary to God and man, but since it deals with things far
removed from our immediate concerns it is only glanced at in the Bible
and hence remains problematic. The Creation, subject of a few thousand
words in Genesis, touches man's own concerns much more closely, since
it declares his importance to God and his filial relationship to him. Most
important of all, however, is each man's immediate experience of God.
The presence of the spirit within us is the first and hence the essential
aspect of all "knowledge of God." Adam begins his life with this intuitive
knowledge, as does Milton his poem.

Adam is now both narrator and protagonist of his story, giving us the
most immediate view imaginable of events already familiar to us from the
Bible. The effect is almost one of "stepping into" Milton's epic. We enter
Adam's world with Adam, as he experienced it:

> As new wak't from soundest sleep
> Soft on the flow'ry herb I found me laid
> In Balmy Sweat, which with his Beams the Sun
> Soon dri'd, and on the reeking moisture fed.
> Straight toward Heav'n my wond'ring Eyes I turn'd,
> And gaz'd a while the ample Sky, till rais'd
> By quick instinctive motion up I sprung,
> As thitherward endeavoring, and upright
> Stood on my feet; about me round I saw
> Hill, Dale, and shady Woods, and sunny Plains,
> And liquid Lapse of murmuring Streams; by these,
> Creatures that liv'd, and mov'd, and walk'd, or flew,
> Birds on the branches warbling; all things smil'd,
> With fragrance and with joy my heart o'erflow'd.
> Myself I then perus'd, and Limb by Limb
> Survey'd, and sometimes went, and sometimes ran
> With supple joints, as lively vigor led:
> But who I was, or where, or from what cause,
> Knew not; to speak I tri'd, and forthwith spake,
> My Tongue obey'd and readily could name

Whate'er I saw. Thou Sun, said I, fair Light,
And thou enlight'n'd Earth, so fresh and gay,
Ye Hills and Dales, ye Rivers, Woods, and Plains
And ye that live and move, fair Creatures, tell
Tell if ye saw, how came I thus, how here?
Not of myself; by some great Maker then,
In goodness and in power preëminent;
Tell me, how may I know him, how adore,
From whom I have that thus I move and live,
And feel that I am happier than I know. (VIII,253–82)

The contrast between Adam's awakening on Earth and Satan's in Hell, reinforced by details such as the prone position, the turning of eyes, and the apostrophe to the surrounding scenery (Satan: "Is this the Region, this the Soil, the Clime, . . . this the seat That we must change for Heav'n?" [I,242–44]), helps to emphasize Adam's joy at discovering not just himself and his world but also the Maker whose existence his own makes self-evident.

Etymologically, a poet is a maker, too (Greek *poietes*, from *poiein* to make). God the maker is a poet, and Adam in describing his new world begins to "speak" it, too, in a way that evokes memories of his earlier Morning Hymn, though (appropriately for the newly born) it is less organized and complete. Adam's experience is not fiction but fact, as he himself can attest, yet it is expressed in verse, the medium of fiction, and gains thereby in freshness, vividness, and accuracy for us, the audience. God's poetry in making the world for Adam is reflected by Adam's poetry in recreating that world. Unfallen life, Milton's poem suggests, *is* poetry or song.

No sooner has Adam waked to reality than he falls asleep again:

While thus I call'd, and stray'd I knew not whither,
From where I first drew Air, and first beheld
This happy Light, when answer none return'd,
On a green shady Bank profuse of Flow'rs
Pensive I sat me down; there gentle sleep
First found me, and with soft oppression seiz'd
My drowsed sense, untroubl'd, though I thought
I then was passing to my former state
Insensible, and forthwith to dissolve:
When suddenly stood at my Head a dream,
Whose inward apparition gently mov'd

My fancy to believe I yet had being,
And liv'd: One came, methought, of shape Divine,
And said, thy Mansion wants thee, Adam, rise,
First Man, of Men innumerable ordain'd
First Father, call'd by thee I come thy Guide
To the Garden of bliss, thy seat prepar'd.
So saying, by the hand he took me rais'd,
And over Fields and Waters, as in Air
Smooth sliding without step, last led me up
A woody Mountain; whose high top was plain,
A Circuit wide, enclos'd, with goodliest Trees
Planted, with Walks, and Bowers, that what I saw
Of Earth before scarce pleasant seem'd. Each Tree
Load'n with fairest Fruit, that hung to the Eye
Tempting, stirr'd in me sudden appetite
To pluck and eat; whereat I wak'd, and found
Before mine Eyes all real, as the dream
Had lively shadow'd. (VIII,283–311)

Remarkably, Adam sees God and God's two greatest gifts, Eden and Eve, first in dream visions. Dream seems to be a form of mediation between Adam and aspects of reality that are too impressive or overwhelming to be met for the first time directly. Yet having seen God first in his dream, Adam can then see him face-to-face:

                    Here had new begun
My wand'ring, had not hee who was my Guide
Up hither, from among the Trees appear'd,
Presence Divine. (VIII,311–14)

In other words, God-inspired dreams are true dreams; they are not indistinguishable from direct experience—since Adam knows when he sleeps and when he wakes—but are in every way as reliable, as true.

"The Imagination," wrote Keats in a famous letter of 1817, "may be compared to Adam's dream—he awoke and found it truth."[16] Here Keats gives to "the Imagination," a sovereign faculty responsible to no higher entity, a power that Milton invests in dreams *only* if they are God-inspired. Adam's dream, parallel in disturbing ways to Eve's Satan-inspired dream of Book V (ll. 31–93), down to the invitation (muted, in Adam's dream) to pluck and eat the fruits of paradise, is a true dream because it comes from God. The incident iself teaches that God-inspired dreams are true, while the parallels to Eve's earlier dream suggest that not all dreams come from God.

The analogy between Adam's dream and Milton's poem is one last way in which the poet fuses our experience of reading *Paradise Lost* with Adam's experience of Paradise and Milton's own experience of writing the poem—Adam, the blind bard, and the reader of *Paradise Lost* are surrogates for each other; what happens to each happens to all. Urania "Visit'st my slumbers Nightly, or when Morn Purples the East" (VII,29–30), yet she is for all that no mere "empty dream." *Paradise Lost* is true if (or because) it, like Adam's dream, is inspired by God. Milton's dream is now roughly two-thirds over; when it ends, how will we know if it was God-inspired? The test, for Milton, was a simple one: the poem comes from God if we wake to find it true.

6

The Comedy of the Fall

BOOK IX BEGINS with an utter change of mood and tone:

> No more of talk where God or Angel Guest
> With Man, as with his Friend, familiar us'd
> To sit indulgent, and with him partake
> Rural repast, permitting him the while
> Venial discourse unblam'd: I now must change
> Those Notes to Tragic. . . .(IX, 1–6)

When, in his last prologue, Milton's narrator cancels the long-standing
assumption under which we have, despite all obstacles, been reading—
that we have before us an epic poem based upon classical models—he
does so by changing his "notes to tragic." In so doing he invokes a whole
new set of expectations connected with the words "tragic" and "tragedy."
While continuing to pursue the traditionally epic theme of heroism, he
will do so in the mode of tragedy. But the narrator's comments give only
an imperfect idea of what is to come. For Milton's drama of the Fall is as
much comic as it is tragic.

Paradise Lost, although it is a narrative poem, is in many ways close
to drama. Two-thirds of its lines are spoken by dramatized speakers, and
much of what we remember of the poem—the Infernal Council, the dialogue in Heaven, the warring angels, the Fall—are scenes that, although
they could not be acted on a stage, are nonetheless highly dramatic. Miltonists have also by now generally accepted Arthur Barker's hypothesis
that the poem's original ten-book structure shows the influence of the
Italian theoreticians of the "five-act epic," who assimilated to epic genre
Aristotle's norms for tragedy.[1] The poem's blank verse, a flexible and "re-

alistic" medium relative to Spenserian stanzas or even to heroic couplets, was borrowed from Elizabethan drama. And, finally, *Paradise Lost* is superbly "dramatic" in Kenneth Burke's sense of offering a dialectic of opposing viewpoints.

To speak, therefore, of the poem's "tragic" or "comic" aspects is common practice, reflecting recognition of the poem's affinities with drama. But there is one difficulty with these labels, and that is simply knowing which to apply to *Paradise Lost* as a whole. Since the poem tells the story of Man's Fall and the resulting woe, tragedy seems the applicable yardstick, but since the poem ends with Adam's joyful discovery of God's plan of salvation, it bears considerable traces of comedy's happy ending as well. Certain scenes in *Paradise Lost* seem productive of the "pity and terror" Aristotle specified as the tragic effects, but others, like Satan's encounter with Sin and Death in Book II, are much closer to a grisly kind of humor, while still others mix the two effects.

This combination of the tragic and the comic is in turn related to the poem's complex handling of point of view, for although from God's position Satan inspires laughter, from the standpoint of fallen humanity Satan would seem anything but funny. *Paradise Lost* shifts points of view, shows us the universe from various perspectives, and throws contradictory lights upon the same persons and events. Hence it keeps our expectations with regard to the antithetical modes of tragedy and comedy in flux as well. Is Adam weak or strong? Is Satan terrible or ridiculous? Is the Fall fortunate or unfortunate? We aren't certain, and this, along with other uncertainties, is a source of the peculiar power the poem has over its readers.

The tendency of most criticism is to deny such ambiguity, to insist that the poem be either purely comic or purely tragic. Take, for example, Helen Gardner's discussion of the moment when Eve eats the forbidden fruit. The action is, in Gardner's opinion, a trivial one—"a thing in itself indifferent," as Milton himself called it in *Christian Doctrine*—and the poem's own terse description of the deed: "she pluck'd, she eat" (IX,781), is reflective of that same triviality. It is at least possible that Milton meant to mingle tragic and comic effects at this moment in the poem, to show Eve's action from two perspectives: the ease with which God could have been obeyed versus the pity and terror of the consequences of disobedience. But Professor Gardner seems deliberately bent on excluding this moment's comic possibilities when she says:

For seventeen centuries the trivial act of eating the forbidden fruit had gathered to itself a weight of religious feeling and awe. It was the sign and token of man's refusal to fulfil the prime end of his creation: to glorify God and enjoy him forever. The act was so universally signifi- cant that, as I have said, Milton could present it with no elaboration and no attempt to arouse in us any sense of horror. It is enough for him to say "she pluck'd, she eat," and "he scrupl'd not to eat." Relying here on a universal response, Milton could allow to Eve and to Adam nobil- ity of motive, or, as in all tragic acts, a mixture of the noble and the base.[2]

Despite her reference to a supposed "universal response," Professor Gardner is in fact invoking the same "seventeenth-century reader" argu- ment that I have earlier had occasion to dispute. As is usually the case with this argument, it is invoked at precisely the point where textual evidence is weak. There is, of course, plenty of evidence in the poem itself that the results of Eve's disobedience are tragic, yet the curious fact is that, *at the moment of eating*, the poem makes the event look trivial rather than fatal. To guard against an "irrelevant" modern response of laughter at the apparent triviality of this moment in the poem, Professor Gardner asks us to suppose that Milton's intended audience was inca- pable of feeling other than a tragic stock response to Eve's sin.

It is indeed true that supreme moments of tragic feeling in literature are sometimes conveyed in what must almost be called ludicrous lines. Why Othello at the moment of murdering Desdemona should linger over a *double-entendre*—"Put out the light, and then put out the light"—or why Lear's entire mad grief should be expressed in so flat a line as "Pray you undo this button," is not easy to understand, unless it be that the most powerful artistic effects can come from a mingling of moods that are logical opposites. But whatever the source of these lines' tragic power, no one would dream of making an historical argument to support it— their tragic impact is self-evident. I believe that if we are as unconde- scending to Milton as we are to Shakespeare, if we ask first not what effects he "must have intended," but what responses we do in fact feel, then we will often have a juster appreciation of the poem he wrote. With respect to Books IX and X, we will be better able to appreciate how, like Shakespeare, he derives his greatest effects from a mingling of comedy and tragedy.

As with most terms in the literary critic's lexicon, the words "tragedy" and "comedy" are anything but precise. Formal definitions of the two dramatic genres tend to become long and unwieldy and yet fail to describe any single work in either genre with real accuracy. The intuitive definition, though rudimentary, is on the whole the most reliable: tragedy moves us to tears, comedy to laughter; or, what amounts to much the same thing, comedy ends happily, tragedy unhappily. But why should we be moved at all? In either case we seem to identify with a protagonist who faces the difficulties and contradictions in life that we all face, but in a heightened or concentrated form. In tragedy the contradictions are menacing ones that threaten to destroy him and in the end are only resolved by his death. In comedy the protagonist, with great luck and skill, manages to surmount the obstacles in his path and to achieve his goal—often marriage to the right partner.

In fact, then, comic and tragic plots have a great deal in common. *Hamlet*, for example, contains a failed comic plot in the impediments to the Hamlet-Ophelia marriage, while *As You Like It* has a very *Hamlet*-like situation in the usurpation of Duke Senior's throne by his brother Frederick. The two plays (presumably written close together, since they were first performed within a year of each other) and their respective protagonists, are in fact mirror-images of each other. The difference between their two plots is not the world's out-of-jointness, or the obligation to set it right, but the fact that fate (or the playwright) has marked Hamlet to suffer and die, Rosalind to live and marry.

Aside from the fact that fate seems to favor the comic protagonist and oppose his tragic counterpart, the chief difference between comedy and tragedy is a difference in distance. It is more pleasant to identify with a fortunate person than an unfortunate one, so in compensation, in order to insure identification, a tragic hero must be depicted as a noble, virtuous, or extremely gifted person, while the comic hero need be no better than the rest of us. In much comedy—Ben Jonson's, for example—the audience is distant from and superior to all the characters, looking down like God on their exposed vices and follies. In "high" comedy, although we identify with the hero or heroine, we can laugh at him/her, too, a momentary distancing that tragedy cannot afford.

The related questions of point of view and distance are those that must be raised with the story of the Fall as Milton presents it. Adam and Eve as victims of the Serpent lack the heroic stature of tragedy; as fellow-victims, however, we have no superior vantage point from which to laugh. The effects of the Fall are certainly sad, but in the Christian promise of redemption lies a promise that tears will turn to laughter. The Genesis story is really neither tragic nor comic: it is *historic*, rather, purporting to explain why the human condition is as we find it. The Fall is Milton's raw material and will seem tragic or comic depending on how he shows it to us.

In what follows I will dwell on the comic patterns in Milton's treatment of the Fall, since most readers have no difficulty acknowledging its tragic aspect. In the process, however, I may seem to oversimplify or overstate their effect. We do not laugh at the Fall, we may not even smile, but its comic side complicates our view of it.

Book IX begins by denouncing the formal genre of epic as not worthy of the *true* heroic theme—patience and martyrdom—and explicitly changes its notes to tragic for the coming disaster. It then proceeds to show us two dramatic scenes—an angel crawling into a snake's mouth and a family squabble. If the Fall is trivial as well as tragic, then the events leading to it must be laughable as well as fatal.

Satan declines by stages toward the moment when he befouls himself with "bestial slime." At first his self-accusation and self-pity strike almost but not quite the right tragic note:

> O Earth, how like to Heav'n, if not preferr'd
> More justly, Seat worthier of Gods, as built
> With second thoughts, reforming what was old!
> For what God after better worse would build? (IX,99–102)
> . . . .
>
> With what delight could I have walkt thee round,
> If I could joy in aught, sweet interchange
> Of Hill and Valley, Rivers, Woods and Plains,
> Now Land, now Sea, and Shores with Forest crown'd,
> Rocks, Dens, and Caves; but I in none of these
> Find place or refuge. . . . (IX,114–19)

Rocks, dens, and caves? Places of refuge, of course, but also the sort of places we would expect the reptilian eye to notice. Satan the tragic hero is dwindling, in front of our eyes, into Satan the snake.

This metamorphosis has been covertly under way for some time now. The "squat like a toad" simile in Book IV brought him close to the Serpent, who is implicit also in the "venom" (IV,804) Satan was said to be putting into Eve's blood. Long before he finds the Serpent, Satan has been behaving like one: hiding, spying, shunning the light, proceeding by stealth. What makes a passage like the following so ironic, in fact, is that it shows how Satan brings these qualities to the hapless Serpent:

> through each Thicket Dank or Dry,
> Like a black mist low creeping, he held on
> His midnight search, where soonest he might find
> The Serpent: him fast sleeping soon he found
> In Labyrinth of many a round self-roll'd,
> His head the midst, well stor'd with subtle wiles:
> Not yet in horrid Shade or dismal Den,
> Nor nocent yet, but on the grassy Herb
> Fearless unfear'd he slept: in at his Mouth
> The Devil enter'd. . . . (IX,179–88)

This Serpent is harmless, fearless, defenseless, and sleeps in the open at night, while it is Satan who shuns the light, creeps like a black mist (the Serpent, as we will soon learn, moves himself somehow in an upright posture) and who turns the Serpent's "subtlety" to malignant ends.

Since it is Satan himself who brings "serpent-ness" to the innocent reptile, his fastidious revulsion at "incarnating" himself as a snake—"O foul descent" etc.—adds comedy to what is in other ways a tragic moment: "Revenge, at first though sweet, Bitter ere long back on itself recoils" (IX,171–72). His whole soliloquy (IX,99–178) is itself a "siege of contraries," genuinely sad and elegiac as he laments his degenerate state, yet toppling over into comedy as he describes himself as "constrain'd" to become what he so obviously has already chosen to be: Satan doesn't *find* the Serpent, he *is* the Serpent.

But since our view of Satan has been flickering between comic and tragic perspectives at least since his meeting with Sin and Death in Book II, we have had some preparation for this new incongruity in his character. Great villains, one thinks of Iago and Edmund, are able on occasion to make us laugh without becoming thereby less villainous. But what of the tragic hero and heroine? Can Adam and Eve stand being laughed at, too? The consensus seems to be that they cannot, and thus critics blame the marked change of tone (between the sublime exchanges of Books IV and V and the squabble that now ensues) on defects in the source: Genesis omits mention of how Satan found Eve alone, so Milton had to invent a separation. Could he help it if the result seems faintly contrived?

Once we look, however, it is not difficult to see what is comic in this scene, nor does the comedy seem accidental. Eve's crafty persistence in urging her argument against Adam's obvious disapproval ("With thy permission then, and thus forewarn'd" [IX,378]) clashes incongruously with her naiveté about the threat of Satan's malignancy ("nor [do I] much expect A Foe so proud will first the weaker seek" [IX,382–83]). Both lines are funny. Adam's patriarchal sententiousness and authority also collapse suddenly, unexpectedly, into an adolescent diffidence toward his beloved:

> These paths and Bowers doubt not but our joint hands
> Will keep from Wilderness with ease, as wide
> As we need walk, till younger hands ere long
> Assist us: *But* if much converse perhaps
> Thee satiate, to short absence I could yield. (IX,244–48, my italics)
>
> . . . .
>
> Wouldst thou approve thy constancy, approve
> First thy obedience; th' other who can know,
> Not seeing thee attempted, who attest?
> *But* if thou think, trial unsought may find
> Us both securer than thus warn'd thou seem'st,
> Go; for thy stay, not free, absents thee more. (IX,367–72, my italics)

In each of these passages Adam begins by speaking sensibly, if a little pompously, yet at each of the two "but's" I have italicized, he suddenly "swerves" (see l. 359) into a different tone and a different point of view—that of the rejected lover reproaching his darling for wishing to separate. Such swerving is "human" and forgivable, but it is hardly heroic. At such moments Adam seems no better than we. In the scene as a whole, too, Adam's tone degenerates from the serene to the baffled and exasperated, as we can hear most easily in the rhetoric of his addresses to Eve, which begin with the simultaneously ceremonial and intimate "Sole Eve, Associate sole, to me beyond Compare above all living Creatures dear" (IX,227–28) and end with the barely concealed irritation of "O Woman!" (IX,343). With the benefit of foresight we are not simply "involved" in Adam's weakness, though we are that, but we are also looking down from above at his commission of errors that we perceive and he does not.

Now of course quarrels and lovers' misunderstandings are as much the stuff of tragedy as comedy. Sometimes a dispute can be over a weighty issue, as it is between Sophocles's Antigone and Creon, but it need not be. One thinks immediately again of *Othello*, where the occasion of Othello's murderous jealousy is nothing more than a handkerchief.

The triviality of the occasion for Othello's jealousy is reminiscent of the triviality of the occasion for Adam and Eve's parting—the need to garden more effectively—but the compensatory "tragic" aspect of *Othello*, the awful grandeur of its hero's rage, however misguided, is simply missing from this scene of *Paradise Lost*. Such grandeur is supplied only by the narrator, who amplifies (or attempts to amplify) the domestic quarrel we have been watching into an event of tragic proportions:

> O much deceiv'd, much failing, hapless Eve,
> Of thy presum'd return! event perverse!
> Thou never from that hour in Paradise
> Found'st either sweet repast, or sound repose;
> Such ambush hid among sweet Flow'rs and Shades
> Waited with hellish rancor imminent
> To intercept thy way, or send thee back
> Despoil'd of Innocence, of Faith, of Bliss. (IX,404–11)

Of course there is, or should be, a terrible sublimity surrounding so momentous an event as the Fall of Man, and it is not my purpose to deny the fact. But while the narrator is repeatedly assuring us of these tragic implications, the dramatic scenes that the characters enact in front of our eyes seem to tell a different story, one no less compelling or significant. Nor is the issue one of what we would like to read into the passage versus what we know is really there. For reasons we will shortly examine, two perspectives on the same set of events are both present in the poem. They jostle one another in our minds, preventing the "pure" response of either unadulterated laughter or tears.

From this point on until Adam's Fall, the comic moments of Milton's story become almost too frequent to mention, but they all share the same basic feature—they all reduce either Satan, Eve, Adam, or events themselves to small, and hence laughable, dimensions. Satan, for example, is depicted as the beneficiary of almost idiot good luck in finding Eve separated from Adam:

> He sought them both, but wish'd his hap might find
> Eve separate, he wish'd, but not with hope
> Of what so seldom chanc'd, when to his wish,
> Beyond his hope, Eve separate he spies. . . . (IX,421–24)

As he criss-crossed Eden looking first for the Serpent, then for Eve, Satan was implicitly weaving a net. Here the net entraps not only Eve but

Satan, narrator, and reader as well, as the "wish'd . . . hap . . . wish'd
. . . hope . . . wish . . . hope" repetition tangles the verse itself in comic
ineptitude. Satan's mind is a muddle at this moment, as this "inside view"
goes on to suggest:

> Eve separate he spies,
> Veil'd in a Cloud of Fragrance, where she stood,
> Half spi'd, so thick the Roses bushing round
> About her glow'd, oft stooping to support
> Each Flow'r of slender stalk. . . . (IX,424–28)

Satan's eye-rubbing surprise, scarcely daring to believe what he sees, is
conveyed in the images of "Veil'd," and "Half spi'd." The effect is not one
of rapacious Antichrist about to swoop down on his victim but of a comic
bumbler, in control neither of himself nor of events.

A moment later Satan stands transfixed by Eve's beauty and solilo-
quizes one last time:

> Thoughts, whither have ye led me, with what sweet
> Compulsion thus transported to forget
> What hither brought us, hate, not love, nor hope
> Of Paradise for Hell, hope here to taste
> Of pleasure, but all pleasure to destroy,
> Save what is in destroying, other joy
> To me is lost. Then let me not let pass
> Occasion which now smiles, behold alone
> The Woman, opportune to all attempts,
> Her Husband, for I view far round, not nigh,
> Whose higher intellectual more I shun,
> And strength, of courage haughty, and of limb
> Heroic built, though of terrestrial mould,
> Foe not informidable, exempt from wound,
> I not; so much hath Hell debas'd, and pain
> Infeebl'd me, to what I was in Heav'n.
> Shee fair, divinely fair, fit Love for Gods,
> Not terrible, though terror be in Love
> And beauty, not approacht by stronger hate,
> Hate stronger, under show of Love well feign'd,
> The way which to her ruin now I tend. (IX,473–93)

The spectacle of Satan misled by "thoughts" of Eve into being "Stupidly
good" (IX,465) is one that further diminishes our opinion of his mighty, if
malignant, powers. Like Adam in the preceding scene, Satan sounds like

a rejected lover, made impotent by the sight of beauty and cringing away from his rival, whom he now admits he is no match for—"Foe not informidable." But of all the signs of Satan's weakened and distempered mind, none is more immediate or convincing than his last non-sentence, which approaches stream-of-consciousness in its illogical sequence. Lines 489–93 move by antithesis, pivoting around the words "love" and "hate." It seems likely that Satan is trying to say that he *would* feel terror of Eve's loveliness *were he not* motivated by a hate stronger than love; but the exceptional verbal and grammatical ambiguity of the phrase "not approached by stronger hate" (Does "approach" mean "to equal" or "to draw nearer to"? Does the phrase modify "beauty," "Love," "terror," or "Shee"?) makes it equally possible that he is confessing the impotence of hate to overcome the love he feels for Eve. Since no interpretation makes perfect sense of Satan's actual words, we are forced to see the lines as a sort of free association test, in which love reminds Satan of terror, terror of hate, and hate of love again. The important point, though, is that Satan quite loses control of himself, and in contrast to his usual articulateness becomes tongue-tied and redundant here, not only unable to act but even to speak or think coherently. Satan here is not "stupidly good," but just stupid.

Satan may feel terror at Eve's loveliness, but Eve herself seems no more awesome a figure than he is: beautiful, surely, veiled in fragrance, but really herself no more than a frail flower, like those she is ministering to:

> them she upstays
> Gently with Myrtle band, mindless the while,
> Herself, though fairest unsupported Flow'r,
> From her best prop so far, and storm so nigh. (IX,430–33)

"Mindless the while" is the most telling stroke, for though it may literally say no more than that Eve isn't paying attention to what goes on around her, it inevitably suggests that Eve is—well, "mindless." While Satan is thinking undisciplined, contradictory "thoughts," Eve isn't thinking at all. Their anticipated meeting promises to be less tragic than ridiculous. Satan approaches Eve obliquely, moving in the faintly absurd manner of unfallen serpents—"not . . . Prone . . . but on his rear, Circular base of rising folds" (IX,496–98)—at last standing before her with "gentle dumb expression" until at length Eve notices him. Then, with a passing glance at the problem of using the unsuitable "Serpent Tongue" for speech, the poem hastens to their interview.

As the moment of the Fall approaches, we, the audience, continue to be of two minds about it: half involved with Eve in events that we foresee she will soon come to rue bitterly, yet also half detached as well. Satan's rhetoric is hyperbolic, outrageously flattering, aimed at an audience too mindlessly innocent to recognize the sinister, seductive intent behind such overstatement:

> Wonder not, sovran Mistress, if perhaps
> Thou canst, who are sole Wonder . . .
> . . . .
>
> Fairest resemblance of thy Maker fair,
> Thee all things living gaze on, all things thine
> By gift, and thy Celestial Beauty adore
> With ravishment beheld, there best beheld
> Where universally admir'd: but here
> In this enclosure wild, these Beasts among,
> Beholders rude, and shallow to discern
> Half what in thee is fair, one man except,
> Who sees thee? (and what is one?) who shouldst be seen
> A Goddess among Gods, ador'd and serv'd
> By Angels numberless, thy daily Train. (IX,532–48)

We, who have no difficulty perceiving the appeal to narcissism, are sufficiently familiar with flattery to rise above Satan's rhetoric and can look down with mingled sorrow and amusement at Eve's naiveté. Yet what Satan has to say is not really much different from what the narrator has frequently told us about Eve. While recognizing, as Eve does not, the sinister intent behind the words, we have to admit their truth and the power of their expression. We are, in other words, simultaneously in and out of this scene, in part sharing Eve's credulity, in part superior to it. Hence Satan's address evokes both amusement (at the transparent flattery) and respect (at its power to deceive Eve).

To be fair to Eve, it is not the Serpent's flattering words that chiefly fool her—"thy overpraising," as she tells him a little later, "leaves in doubt The virtue of that Fruit" (IX,615–16)—but the mere fact that he is speaking at all. Her first response to Satan stresses the "miracle," the "wonder" of this ability. Eve's awe at the speaking Serpent is really much the same as her earlier awe at God's Creation, but, given our superior knowledge, her credulity now is funny:

> What may this mean? Language of Man pronounc't
> By Tongue of Brute, and human sense exprest? (IX,553–54)

Given Eve's inexperience and the circumstances of her temptation, her response to Satan seems neither perverse nor ominous. The tone is less that of Oedipus's interview with Teiresias, or of Macbeth's with the witches, than that of a thousand jokes where country bumpkin meets city slicker.

If Satan knows how to use grandiloquence to achieve his ends, he is able to use the opposite virtue of humility, too. Much of his persuasiveness, after all, comes not from Eve's inability to detect lies or exaggeration, but from the fact that she is willing to overlook imperfection in a lowly snake. Satan plays upon the Serpent's humble status, uses it to encourage in Eve an exaggerated confidence in her own higher powers of discernment. But to us, who see the speaker behind the mask, the effect is again amusing:

> I was at first as other Beasts that graze
> The trodden Herb, of abject thoughts and low,
> As was my food, nor aught but food discern'd
> Or Sex, and apprehended nothing high:
> Till on a day roving the field, I chanc'd
> A goodly Tree far distant to behold
> Loaden with fruit of fairest colors mixt,
> Ruddy and Gold: I nearer drew to gaze;
> When from the boughs a savory odor blown,
> Grateful to appetite, more pleas'd my sense
> Than smell of sweetest Fennel, or the Teats
> Of Ewe or Goat dropping with Milk at Ev'n,
> Unsuckt of Lamb or Kid, that tend thir play. (IX,571–83)

The Serpent's testifying to his own "lowness," though an effective strategy as far as Eve is concerned, is for us another instance of Satan's involuntary self-condemnation, and one that moreover provokes us to laughter by showing us a Satan absurdly reduced to sucking the teats of goats.

From the deluded position of superiority that Satan has shrewdly encouraged her to take, Eve rebukes him for excessive flattery (IX,615–16), lectures him on the abundance of fruit in Paradise, but ends up nonetheless putting herself in the armless Serpent's hands: "Lead then, said Eve" (IX,631). That such leading is misleading is clear to us from the narrator's comments and comparisons (the Serpent leads "In tangles"; makes "intricate seem straight"; is like a will o' the wisp or fool's fire, "blazing with delusive Light" [IX,632–39]) but not to Eve, who is enjoying the role of "Empress" sufficiently to risk her first pun:

> Serpent, we might have spar'd our coming hither,
> Fruitless to mee, though Fruit be here to excess. . . . (IX,647–48)

It appears that flattery of Eve's intellect has had the effect of putting that intellect to sleep. She scarcely bothers to ask whether it is likely that God has put "magical" fruit in paradise. Satan's words make her out to be a "Goddess humane" whose rights are being infringed upon:

> Indeed? hath God then said that of the Fruit
> Of all these Garden Trees ye shall not eat,
> Yet Lords declar'd of all in Earth or Air? (IX,656–58)

while God's interdiction now makes her seem in her own eyes a child, a hopeless inferior, which no doubt accounts for the childish sing-song in which she now repeats that interdiction, as if it were something learned by rote but not really understood:

> To whom thus Eve yet sinless. Of the Fruit
> Of each Tree in the Garden we may eat,
> But of the Fruit of this fair Tree amidst
> The Garden, God hath said, Ye shall not eat
> Thereof, nor shall ye touch it, lest ye die. (IX,659–63)

Satan meets this objection, made in a manner suggesting the speaker herself would like to see it refuted, by putting on a "New part" and playing orator:

> She scarce had said, though brief, when now more bold
> The Tempter, but with show of Zeal and Love
> To Man, and indignation at his wrong,
> New part puts on, and as to passion mov'd,
> Fluctuates disturb'd, yet comely, and in act
> Rais'd, as of some great matter to begin.

As when of old some Orator renown'd
In Athens or free Rome, where Eloquence
Flourish'd, since mute, to some great cause addrest,
Stood in himself collected, while each part,
Motion, each act won audience ere the tongue,
Sometimes in highth began, as no delay
Of Preface brooking through his Zeal of Right.
So standing, moving, or to highth upgrown
The Tempter all impassion'd thus began. (IX,664–78)

At first glance the image is impressive, but it is, as the narrator warns us, all "show." By dragging in "some Orator renown'd In Athens or free Rome" the poem encourages us to dignify the scene by imagining something like Cicero in front of the Roman Senate, but details like "Fluctuates" (reminding us of serpentine motion) and "tongue" (evoking the earlier puzzle of how Satan spoke with "Serpent tongue") insist that we remember what Eve is really looking at: a parlor trick. From one point of view, looking at certain details and patterns, the moment is impressive indeed. But, as other details insist on reminding us, this point of view is a fraud, a show. Looked at with a colder, more skeptical eye, it really is all terribly (if painfully) funny: golly, a talking snake!

This second, comic perspective is important because it answers the objection, so frequently heard from readers and critics, that Milton makes the Fall seem inevitable and hence fails to substantiate the poem's central contention that Adam and Eve were free to resist temptation. If Book IX moves entirely to a logic of tragic fatality, then it would seem that God, not man, ordained the Fall and must take the blame; Adam and Eve are responsible for their actions only if they were free to choose. Hence the poem mixes perspectives: the tragic, which involves us in Eve's position, makes us see how very hard it was for her to resist such a tempter and implicates us in her disobedience (when she falls, we fall); and the comic, which distances us from Eve, makes us see how easy it would have been to resist, had she known what we know, had she not judged by appearances.

Despite its transparent flattery and recognizable lies, Satan's speech is impressive. Once Eve has swallowed the story (remember that she has no experience, except in Raphael's story, of "guile") that he is as he appears—a beast made human by eating the forbidden fruit—then the rest seems to follow inevitably: the fruit is magic; eating it does not entail death; and God's interdiction cannot be taken at face value. To the degree that we identify with Eve, feel the force of each argument and her lack of preparation to deal with deceit, it seems inevitable that she should fall. Looking with a colder eye, however, we see a different picture. Either God is tricking her or the Serpent is: why does she choose to believe beast over Creator?

Tragedy places us inside the fatal action, feeling the full force of Eve's situation, but thereby no more able than she to see the way out. Comedy places us above the action, perceiving her mistakes, but unable to recognize our own mistakes in them. Only a mingling of the two perspectives, contradictory though they are, will give us the effect the poem needs: the feeling that Eve is both justified and deluded, that the Fall is both fortunate and unfortunate. Hence Eve's speech of self-temptation (IX,745–79) has a measure of dignity, showing a mastery of Satan's arts of rhetoric and logic, yet is absurd in the way she uses these subtleties to ensnare herself:

> What fear I then, rather what know to fear
> Under this ignorance of Good and Evil,
> Of God or Death, of Law or Penalty? (IX,773–75)

Her behavior after eating is, of course, an even blacker comedy. She sings a parody Morning Hymn to the tree: "henceforth my early care, Not without Song, each Morning, and due praise Shall tend thee" (IX,799–801), bows to the Tree with "low Reverence" (IX,835), and, after weighing the merits of keeping the powers of the fruit secret from Adam and thereby gaining the upper hand of him ("for inferior who is free?" [IX,825]), decides that on the whole it will be safer to share her crime with Adam, lest "Death ensue" (IX,827), a marvelously impersonal way of saying that she is going to risk her lover's life:

> So dear I love him, that with him all deaths
> I could endure, without him live no life. (IX,832–33)

If this is love, what need of hatred? The first effects of sin are shocking indeed, but they persist in having a black-comedic side to them, as in Eve's echo of the reptilian hiss in her greeting to Adam:

> Hast thou not wonder'd, Adam, at my stay?
> Thee I have *misst*. . . . (IX,856–57; my italics)

The scene of Adam's temptation has a different impact from that of Eve. For one thing Adam is not tempted by a wily adder but by his own wife; for another, he is "not deceiv'd," as Eve was, by promises of the magical properties of the fruit. There is less levity in Adam's Fall than in Eve's; the stakes are higher; and the scene more nearly approaches the tragic than any other in Book IX. The image of Adam dropping the garland he had made for Eve is genuinely pathetic:

> horror chill
> Ran through his veins, and all his joints relax'd;
> From his slack hand the Garland wreath'd for Eve
> Down dropp'd, and all the faded Roses shed. . . . (IX,890–93)

Although we might wish that Adam would display less chill in his veins and more *sang-froid*, we cannot help but be deeply involved in his moving interior monologue, in which he chooses Eve over God:

> O fairest of Creation, last and best
> Of all God's Works, Creature in whom excell'd
> Whatever can to sight or thought be form'd,
> Holy, divine, good, amiable, or sweet!
> How art thou lost, how on a sudden lost,
> Defac't, deflow'r'd, and now to Death devote?
> Rather how hast thou yielded to transgress
> The strict forbiddance, how to violate
> The sacred Fruit forbidd'n! some cursed fraud
> Of Enemy hath beguil'd thee, yet unknown,
> And mee with thee hath ruin'd, for with thee
> Certain my resolution is to Die;
> How can I live without thee, how forgo
> Thy sweet Converse and Love so dearly join'd,
> To live again in these wild Woods forlorn?
> Should God create another Eve, and I
> Another Rib afford, yet loss of thee
> Would never from my heart; no no, I feel
> The Link of Nature draw me: Flesh of Flesh,
> Bone of my Bone thou art, and from thy State
> Mine never shall be parted, bliss or woe. (IX,896–916)

Surely there are false notes, even here. If we look carefully enough we will notice the egocentrism of the speech: a preoccupation with how Eve's disobedience will effect Adam and a commensurate silence on how to help Eve. For if Adam, instead of asking "how can I keep from being separated from Eve?" had asked "how can I best intercede on her behalf before God?" then he would not so rashly have joined her in disobedience. Even before consummating the Fall by eating the fruit, Adam has provisionally adopted a fallen perspective, redefining love as possession, Eden's pleasant park as "wild woods," and God as adversary rather than ally.

The situation in which Adam finds himself is not what it appears to be, either to him or to us. Overcome by his sense of dependency on Eve, Adam doesn't think clearly, and overcome by the movingly tragic circumstances of his plight and the seeming nobility of his speech, it is really impossible for us to remain aloof from and skeptical of Adam's decision to join Eve in sin. Which raises—in even more acute form than before—a problem we have already touched on: if the poem makes it *seem* that the Fall was inevitable (whatever the true facts), hasn't it betrayed its own doctrine, enunciated by both God and the narrator, that Man's Fall is Man's fault, because Adam and Eve freely *chose* to fall?

Again, doctrine and poetry are at odds in *Paradise Lost*. Which does the reader believe? Can he entirely believe, or entirely disbelieve, either one? I don't think he can. To argue, as Stanley Fish does, that Milton left it to the reader to see through the illusion of tragic inevitability seems insufficient:

> Empson would reply [to the claim that Adam should have found alternatives to eating the fruit], 'The poem somehow does not encourage us to think of an alternative plan', and Milton would say in return: true, the poem does not encourage you to think of an alternative plan, just as the situation (as it seems to be) does not encourage Adam to think of an alternative plan; but I require you to think of one yourself, drawing encouragement from an inner resource which prevails against the claims of a dramatically persuasive moment, even if the moment is one I have provided; and God requires the same of Adam.[3]

Here again, Fish invokes a prior commitment on the part of the reader to do work that the poet himself should have done and has, in fact, done. We needn't speculate on what "Milton would say," when Milton *has* said at many points in the poem that Adam and Eve were free to stand or fall. What Fish is trying to explain is why, when we get to the Fall itself, there is so little dramatic evidence of that freedom. Fish argues that the poet

expects us to disbelieve his poem at this point, but how do we know *what*
the poet "expects of us" except on the evidence of the poem itself?

The answer is under our noses. We needn't invoke history or biography to solve a problem that the text itself is designed to render insoluble. At points God has insisted on Man's freedom, so we know that,
for this poem at least, this doctrine has the status of Truth, while the
same poem also demonstrates how impossible (not simply difficult) it is
to read about Man's Fall and to remember that Truth. The two perspectives are irreconcilable, yet we as readers must maintain them both. But
lest, under the pressure of the poetry, we abandon all awareness of the
divine perspective on events, Milton has provided an undertone of incongruity even to the mimesis of Adam's Fall. Milton *shows* us not only a
tragic Adam unable to resist temptation but a comic Adam *choosing* to
fall.

The initial incongruity in Adam's Fall is the discrepancy between
what he first says to himself and what he then says to Eve. Having just
heard Adam's inner thoughts, we can't help but recognize the falsity both
of substance and tone in the (mere) "Words" he turns to Eve. He begins
in the posturing "heroic" tone that the poem has taught us to distrust:

> Bold deed thou hast presum'd, advent'rous Eve,
> And peril great provok't, who thus hath dar'd
> Had it been only coveting to Eye
> That sacred Fruit, sacred to abstinence,
> Much more to taste it under ban to touch.
> But past who can recall, or done undo?
> Not God Omnipotent, nor Fate. . . . (IX,921–27)

Such a tone encourages exaggeration and distortion; Eve's foolishness is
disguised as "boldness," and God begins to share his Omnipotence with
a mysterious deity called "Fate." Such small dishonesties lead next to
outright lies, as Adam questions God's promise of death as the punishment for disobedience. Since, in his interior monologue, Adam was certain that Eve would die, we have no trouble hearing the dishonesty of his
arguments to her that "Perhaps thou shalt not Die" (IX,928).

Such lies and distortions clash unpleasantly with the "noble" ending
of Adam's speech to Eve, which, certified as sincere by its repetition of
thoughts that Adam has just spoken to himself, successfully strikes the
note of heroic, doomed love:

> However I with thee have fixt my Lot,
> Certain to undergo like doom; if Death
> Consort with thee, Death is to me as Life;
> So forcible within my heart I feel
> The Bond of Nature draw me to my own,
> My own in thee, for what thou art is mine;
> Our State cannot be sever'd, we are one,
> One Flesh; to lose thee were to lose myself. (IX, 952–59)

We get two views of Adam from his own words: Adam the comic role-player versus Adam the tragic lover. Doubtless the latter is the more immediately impressive, but our sympathy is qualified not only by Eve's counterpoint of foolish and dishonest words, and by the narrator's sour but rather subdued comments, but most of all by a shocking change of tone in Adam's own words after he eats:

> Eve, now I see thou art exact of taste,
> And elegant, of Sapience no small part,
> Since to each meaning savor we apply,
> And Palate call judicious. . . . (IX, 1017–20)

Adam here casuistically equates knowledge or wisdom with tasting and cements the connection with English puns on "taste" and "judicious palate," as well as Latin puns on "Sapience" and "savor" (from the verb *sapio*, meaning originally "to taste," and by extension "to be discerning").

Adam's paltry display of wit here is blackly comic, not merely because it evokes Satan's word play in Book VI, or because it demonstrates how little he has attained the "Divinity" (IX, 1010) he drunkenly believes the fruit has conferred, but most of all because it reveals a new stance toward the relation of language to truth: anything can be made "true" by finding the right words, Adam implies; it's all just a game. But Adam goes on to make an unintended *double-entendre* that consummates his deformation of truth with grisly humor:

> if such pleasure be
> In things to us forbidden, it might be wish'd,
> For this one Tree had been forbidden ten. (IX, 1024–26)

"Soon enough," the reader is obliged to mutter, "soon enough." And his closing words to Eve—"never did thy Beauty . . . so *inflame* my sense With *ardor* to enjoy thee" (IX, 1029–31; my italics)—again show Adam as unwittingly betrayed by words into making the same point that the narrator has just made: "in Lust they burn" (IX,1015).

The contradictions in Adam's words—silent vs. spoken, pre- vs. post-Fall, conscious vs. unintended meanings—are reinforced by contraditions in his behavior. Heroic love deteriorates to a frantic sexual gluttony ("they thir fill of Love and Love's disport Took largely" [IX,1042–43]), then to shame, and finally to bickering and reproach. We are forced to recognize that Adam's heroic stance, at first so impressive, was no less "show" than his other lies, although unlike them it fooled him and us as well as Eve. So the action that Adam took to keep himself and Eve together ends in a bitter quarrel, and so the comedy of the Fall is complete: half *Liebestod*, half farce.

7

The Curse

Surely though we place Hell under the Earth, the
Devils walk and purlue is about it: Men speake
too popularly who place it in those flaming moun-
taines, which to grosser apprehensions represent
Hell. The heart of man is the place the devill
dwells in; I feel sometimes a hell within my selfe,
Lucifer keeps his court in my brest, *Legion* is re-
vived in me.
—Sir Thomas Browne, *Religio Medici*

A FALL THAT projects opposite concepts is bound to be difficult for the
reader to assimilate. The mind wants to see one stable picture, not a
flicker between contradictory images. We want to say (with Gardner) that
Eve's fall is tragic not comic, or (with Fish) that Adam's fall is freely chosen as opposed to being determined; furthermore, our natural tendency
is to suppress evidence to the contrary or to become angry when we
cannot. Adam kept his temper when Raphael fixed his story of war in
Heaven in the shadowy region between truth and error; nor did he lose
it even when the angel refused outright to settle the ambiguity of celestial
motions; but postlapsarian readers are not generally so forbearing. Our
refuge is less apt to be in resignation than in anger or inattention.

In truth it must be admitted that, unlike Raphael, Milton's narrator
ignores rather than discloses inconsistencies in the poem's treatment of
the Fall. Perhaps Milton expects the "fit reader" to see incongruities by
himself, but it is more likely that he expects us to *feel* without quite
seeing them. For no portion of *Paradise Lost* is so exclusively mimetic,

so aimed at making the reader forget that he is seeing not reality itself but a version of it, than Book IX. Tragic or comic, the Fall is the critical event at which the reader has been aimed since the poem's opening lines, and all of the intervening complications, backtrackings, and delays have only further whetted our anticipation of that decisive moment. Nor, when at last it comes, does the Fall disappoint our expectation of high drama, joining the naive gratifications of spectacle, not excluding pornography, to the more sophisticated pleasures of artful rhetoric and inner spiritual conflict. Cold baths of comedy, as I have argued, do help us to keep some distance from events that otherwise might consume us utterly with their ardor, but there is no denying that we are "involved" with the events in Book IX to a greater extent than at any earlier place in the poem.

By the end of Book IX Adam and Eve are both totally "human" in the fallen sense, hence like ourselves—or ourselves writ large; for like Satan they have learned the art of hyperbolic language and showy gesture, the operatic self-dramatization of great literary characters. The curve of disobedience has been downward to bickering and disharmony, but their story is not yet finished, and we want above all to hear the rest of it. But Milton frustrates this desire by delaying the dénouement of the story of man's first disobedience for over seven hundred lines while he returns us to the poem's "cosmic frame."

Between readings of *Paradise Lost* I manage to forget the existence of this formidable interruption in the story of Adam and Eve's Fall and regeneration, and with each rereading I confess I feel renewed resentment at being asked to attend to events in Heaven and Hell when it is events on Earth that interest me now. The movement of Milton's epic has been consistently away from the superhuman and metaphysical toward the human and concrete. In the prologue to Book VII the Muse descended to Earth, and she has never left since. Meanwhile, the drama on Earth has reached so intense a pitch that a return in Book X to "things invisible to mortal sight" seems no longer a privilege but an unwelcome distraction from the true business of the poem. Why does Milton reintroduce the cosmic frame in this elaborate fashion?

Exigencies of plot alone cannot account for it. Surely the reaction of Heaven to Man's Fall is essential to Milton's story, but that reaction is dramatized most effectively in the judgment scene in Eden. Whatever else we need to know beyond what Adam and Eve experience could be summarized by the narrator in a dozen lines. What Milton gains from again widening his canvas to include Heaven and Hell is a shift in perspective, a second point of view on the events we have just witnessed in Book IX.

The shift to the cosmic frame inevitably distances us from Adam and Eve's plight. Heaven is concerned over what happens to mankind, but there is a limit beyond which Eternity cannot go in sympathy for time-bound creatures:

> Soon as th' unwelcome news
> From Earth arriv'd at Heaven Gate, displeas'd
> All were who heard, dim sadness did not spare
> That time Celestial visages, yet mixt
> With pity, violated not thir bliss. (X, 21–25)

In comparison with earlier scenes set in Heaven, this one positively brims with fellow-feeling and solicitude. God's repetition of his plan to ransom mankind from Satanic captivity this time stresses his concern for man rather than his preoccupation with his own "Glory." But there is nonetheless the old, familiar note of divine self-justification, which suggests once again that God is man's adversary rather than his ally:

> I told ye then he [Satan] should prevail and speed
> On his bad Errand, Man should be seduc't
> And flatter'd out of all, believing lies
> Against his Maker; no Decree of mine
> Concurring to necessitate his Fall,
> Or touch with lightest moment of impulse
> His free Will, to her own inclining left
> In even scale. (X, 40–47)

There is, finally, the curse to be pronounced on fallen mankind, in keeping with God's high decree: "Of the tree of the knowledge of good and evil, thou shalt not eat of it: for in the day that thou eatest thereof thou shalt surely die." God, we know, has a plan to rescue man from the full effects of his Fall, but this plan is abstract and its benefits remote; the curse is concrete, immediate:

> fall'n he is, and now
> What rests, but that the mortal Sentence pass
> On his transgression. Death denounc't that day,
> Which he presumes already vain and void,
> Because not yet inflicted, as he fear'd,

By some immediate stroke; but soon shall find
Forbearance no acquittance ere day end. (X,47–53)

From the perspective of eternity, a plan that unfolds over millennia may present no difficulties. From any normal human perspective, however, it is bound to seem to reduce individual human fate and human aspirations to minuscule porportions. The shift back to a cosmic perspective is humiliating. It shows how small Adam and Eve really are, how circumscribed is their sense of themselves and of their destiny.

The paradoxes of God's curse have already begun to emerge. They continue to ramify in the next scene, where it becomes clear how thoroughly Adam and Eve have cursed *themselves*, in advance of any divine punishment. God (significantly in the person of the Son, not the Father) comes "from wrath more cool . . . the mild Judge and Intercessor both" (X,95–96), but, knowing themselves and what they have done, Adam and Eve hide as if from hot ire:

> the voice of God they heard
> Now walking in the Garden, by soft winds
> Brought to thir Ears, while day declin'd, they heard,
> And from his presence hid themselves among
> The thickest Trees, both Man and Wife. . . . (X,97–101)

When God calls them they come forth like guilty children, the evidence of their distempered minds smeared like jam on their faces:

> [Adam] came, and with him Eve, more loath, though first
> To offend, discount'nanc't both, and discompos'd;
> Love was not in thir looks, either to God
> Or to each other, but apparent guilt,
> And shame, and perturbation, and despair,
> Anger, and obstinacy, and hate, and guile. (X, 109–14)

None of this is God's doing; it is the logical result, rather, of turning their backs on God's love. The act of disobedience is itself the curse Adam and Eve must suffer.

Clearly, punishment for sin is first of all self-punishment. If he wanted them to suffer, God would only have had to leave Adam and Eve alone in their altered paradise; even without Satan's help they would have turned it into a Hell on Earth. But there remains God's judgment: Adam

and Eve still expect to hear their death-sentence; and despite the promises we have heard of God's "mercy," we know that a curse will be pronounced. First comes the Serpent:

> Because thou hast done this, thou art accurst
> Above all Cattle, each Beast of the Field;
> Upon thy Belly groveling thou shalt go,
> And dust shalt eat all the days of thy Life.
> Between Thee and the Woman I will put
> Enmity, and between thine and her Seed;
> Her Seed shall bruise thy head, thou bruise his heel. (X, 175–81)

So far as Adam and Eve know, Eve was tempted by a Serpent; Genesis
itself contains no hint that it was really Satan in disguise. But we know,
and the narrator reminds us explicitly, that this sentence is being pronounced upon the real tempter: "God at last To Satan first in sin his doom
appli'd, Though in mysterious terms, judg'd as then best" (X, 171–73).
This "Oracle" speaks obscurely, but he is prophesying the victory of
Christ over Satan (X,182–92). Adam and Eve do not know all this, but
even so the promise that their seed will bruise the Serpent's head clashes
strangely with the earlier promise that they would die on the "day" that
they ate the fruit.

Next comes Eve's punishment:

> Thy sorrow I will greatly multiply
> By thy Conception; Children thou shalt bring
> In sorrow forth, and to thy Husband's will
> Thine shall submit, hee over thee shall rule. (X,193–96)

Cursed to order in a newly disordered world, cursed above all to fecun-
dity, Eve has already been promised that her "seed" will ultimately
bruise the Serpent's head. Though she does not know it yet, her children
will be not only her sorrow's cause, but eventually its cure as well.

And Adam is last:

> Because thou hast heark'n'd to the voice of thy Wife,
> And eaten of the Tree concerning which
> I charg'd thee, saying: Thou shalt not eat thereof,
> Curs'd is the ground for thy sake, thou in sorrow
> Shalt eat thereof all the days of thy Life;
> Thorns also and Thistles it shall bring thee forth
> Unbid, and thou shalt eat th' Herb of the Field,

In the sweat of thy Face shalt thou eat Bread,
Till thou return unto the ground, for thou
Out of the ground wast taken, know thy Birth,
For dust thou art, and shall to dust return. (X,198–208)

Cursed to agriculture and hence to civilization, Adam is doomed to wear
a far heavier yoke than he did before the Fall. But again, as in Eve's case,
the cause of sorrow lies not in God's will but in Adam's will, perverted
before God's curse is pronounced. Fallen as he is, Adam *needs*, as a con-
straint on his erratic nature, the yoke of toil God promises him: as he will
soon discover, it is a blessing, not a curse.

For the reader, at least, these apparent "curses" are not entirely disguised. It is the last curse that troubles us: "dust thou art, and shall to
dust return." That death, too, is a blessing, is God's final secret, hidden
both from Adam and from us. But as visible token of the goodwill concealed within his curses, the destined Seed clothes his own first parents'
nakedness with skins, and their "inward nakedness" with "his Robe of
righteousness" (X,222), as a sign that although they have sinned alone,
for repentance they will have help.

Situations, states of affairs in *Paradise Lost*, have a bewildering way
of changing into their opposites: Adam's "love" for Eve, as demonstrated
in eating the fruit, has turned into something like hatred, while the "distance and distaste" (IX,9) announced for God in the narrator's last prologue comes now to look more like love. By putting his cosmic frame
around events in Eden, Milton offers us antithetical views of God's
curse—Adam and Eve's, which projects their own self-hatred and rage
onto their Judge, versus a broader and more knowing view that shows
the curse to be a blessing in disguise. Again, as with the overlapping
tragic and comic patterns of Book IX, the two points of view are in conflict. Which do we believe? For the first time in the poem, the "cosmic"
perspective on events seems not simply truer but possibly more attractive to human readers than the degraded perspective of the poem's only
human characters. But then Milton reverses his field once again by rein-
voking the two least attractive and at the same time most transparently
"fictional" characters in the poem, those sinister buffoons, Sin and Death.

Sensing a change about to take place on Earth, Sin and Death abandon their watch at the portals of Hell and begin building a bridge be-

tween it and the outer sphere of the created universe. Milton's narrator
compares the feat to God's creation of the world:

> Both from out Hell Gates into the waste
> Wide Anarchy of Chaos damp and dark
> Flew diverse, and with Power (thir Power was great)
> Hovering upon the Waters. (X,282–85)

Perhaps there is irony here, but it is hidden deep, as the narrator *seems*
to be comparing their power to God's. There on the world's outmost shell
they meet Satan returning to Hell with the happy news of Man's Fall.
The unholy trinity rejoices, and Sin sings a parody Morning Hymn, giving Satan credit for the bridge Sin and Death have built:

> O Parent, these are thy magnific deeds,
> Thy Trophies, which thou view'st as not thine own,
> Thou art thir Author and prime Architect:
> For I no sooner in my Heart divin'd,
> My Heart, which by a secret harmony
> Still moves with thine, join'd in connexion sweet,
> That thou on Earth hadst prosper'd, which thy looks
> Now also evidence, but straight I felt
> Though distant from thee Worlds between, yet felt
> That I must after thee with this thy Son;
> Such fatal consequence unites us three:
> Hell could no longer hold us in her bounds,
> Nor this unvoyageable Gulf obscure
> Detain from following thy illustrious track.
> Thou hast achiev'd our liberty, confin'd
> Within Hell Gates till now, thou us impow'r'd
> To fortify thus far, and overlay
> With this portentous Bridge the dark Abyss.
> Thine now is all this World, thy virtue hath won
> What thy hands builded not, thy Wisdom gain'd
> With odds what War hath lost, and fully aveng'd
> Our foil in Heav'n; here thou shalt Monarch reign,
> There didst not; there let him still Victor sway,
> As Battle hath adjudged, from this new World
> Retiring, by his own doom alienated,
> And henceforth Monarchy with thee divide
> Of all things, parted by th' Empyreal bounds,
> His Quadrature, from thy Orbicular World,
> Or try thee now more dang'rous to his Throne. (X,354–82)

In Sin's vision Satan has become what he has so often wished to be—
Prince of Darkness, absolute monarch of an empire fully as vast as
God's own.

Now of course the diligent reader can supply from his memory
words to refute Sin's boast. In his second speech of the Heavenly Council
scene in Book III, the Son had prophesied that:

> I through the ample Air in Triumph high
> Shall lead Hell Captive maugre Hell, and show
> The powers of darkness bound. (III,254–56)

And the Father had sealed the prophecy with his authority:

> thou shalt judge
> Bad men and Angels, they arraign'd shall sink
> Beneath thy Sentence; Hell, her numbers full,
> Thenceforth shall be for ever shut. (III,330–33)

Less explicit undertones and reminders of the futility of Satan's aspirations are scattered the length and breadth of *Paradise Lost*. But again,
this is futility *sub specie aeternitatis*, and though Christians had by Milton's day been momentarily expecting Christ's victory and triumph for
the past sixteen-plus centuries, they had discovered no timetable that
would accurately predict his arrival. Meanwhile we *do* live in a fallen
world; the rule of Satan *is* strong; and apocalyptic fervor must be balanced, as Milton discovered in twenty years of futile service to the
doomed Puritan Republic, with Christian resignation.

The drift of this scene is to counter the reassurance of the preceding
one. It makes Death, the final term of God's curse, loathsomely concrete,
reminding us of the doom we are under as a result of Adam's sin. Here is
the causeway between Hell and Earth, promising frequent unhappy commerce between the two. Here are Sin and Death, only too able, as we
know, to carry out their mission of torture and killing against mankind.
And here lastly is Satan, exulting over the easy terms of the sentence
passed by God on him, and of its indefinite postponement: "Not instant,
but of future time" (X,345). Read mimetically, taken at face value, this
encounter among Satan, Sin, and Death gives the reader ample grounds
for worry that God's plan is one that takes the appalling sufferings of

humanity, from Adam and Eve down to the present day, with remarkable equanimity.

But the allegorical nature of Sin and Death as characters gives us a second and rather different set of possibilities to contend with. For if these two don't "really" exist "out there" in the world Milton is apparently bent on portraying with historical accuracy, then neither does their bridge, or their meeting with Satan, or the words Sin speaks to him. Of course there is "essential" truth in the scene: sin and death really do exist, as phenomena if not as persons, and mankind is really subject to their effects. But if, as I think is the case, we are apt to shake our heads a little at the baroque excesses of Milton's inventions, at their comic book appearance and bombastic speech, then we've taken the first step toward the skeptical stance Raphael urged on Adam before he sang *his* divine poem, which, as it happens, is also the stance the narrator took toward the words of God's curse. Words, as Raphael explained, and the pictures poets make out of them, are fundamentally ambiguous. Since no poet can guarantee that his reader will understand correctly, his wisest strategy is to make the reader aware that he, too, along with the poet, is the poem's "author."

As is becoming gradually clearer in Book X, events and characters *within* the frame of the poem evoke and criticize the reader's relationship *to* the poem. In particular, Satan and Adam become surrogate "readers" of God's curse, and Satan's stance is, as we might expect, exemplary of how *not* to read God's words, or Milton's. As he boasts to Hell's assembled legions, he has ruined Adam:

> Him by fraud I have seduc'd
> From his Creator, and the more to increase
> Your wonder, with an Apple; he thereat
> Offended, worth your laughter, hath giv'n up
> Both his beloved Man and all his World,
> To Sin and Death a prey, and so to us,
> Without our hazard, labor, or alarm,
> To range in, and to dwell, and over Man
> To rule, as over all he should have rul'd.
> True is, mee also he hath judg'd, or rather
> Mee not, but the brute Serpent in whose shape
> Man I deceiv'd: that which to mee belongs,
> Is enmity, which he will put between
> Mee and Mankind; I am to bruise his heel;

His Seed, when is not set, shall bruise my head:
A World who would not purchase with a bruise,
Or much more grievous pain? Ye have th' account
Of my performance: What remains, ye Gods,
But up and enter now into full bliss. (X,485–503)

Satan is the paradigm of the literal-minded reader of Genesis: Adam and
Eve were seduced "with an Apple"; God, "Offended" by their disobedience, has "giv'n up" man to Satan and has sentenced "the brute Serpent,"
while Satan's punishment is to be perfunctory: "A World who would not
purchase with a bruise?"

Milton and his fellow Reformation Christians had discovered in their
unremitting efforts to precisely understand God's words that no passage
of Scripture is capable of only one interpretation. In the face of language's
fundamental ambiguity, Milton and his coreligionists developed the doctrine of the "inner light"—that guidance God sends to worthy souls to
help them separate the true interpretation from the false ones. Satan, as
archetype of the soul deprived of inner light, is notoriously unable to
understand God's words. Nor is the curse easy to understand, since it
conceals symbolic meanings behind apparently straightforward, concrete
words—"Serpent" means "Satan," "bruise" means "defeat." Not surpris-
ingly, Satan misunderstands the curse, and we, Milton's readers, are in a
position to see why. First, of course, he has not been privy to Heavenly
conversations that we have overheard; but second, and even more important, he is unable to understand God's continuing love for his fallen
creatures, which turns the apparent curse into a hidden blessing. From
the reader's point of view, Satan's misinterpretation of God's words is an
object lesson in the folly of forgetting the spirit of continuing love for
mankind from which they emanate.

But the immediate results of such folly are unexpectedly concrete
and frightening. Satan's self-congratulatory interpretation of God's curse
is greeted by "A dismal universal hiss" (X,508), as his followers turn into
the serpents they have just been told God cursed in their stead. Satan,
too, feels a sudden change at work in him:

His Visage drawn he felt to sharp and spare,
His Arms clung to his Ribs, his Legs entwining
Each other, till supplanted down he fell
A monstrous Serpent on his Belly prone,

> Reluctant, but in vain: a greater power
> Now rul'd him, punisht in the shape he sinn'd,
> According to his doom. . . . (X,511–17)

Soon Hell is a riot of tangled serpentine forms, for which Milton ransacks mythology for names and comparisons, all joining in the dismal hiss of celebration.

God causes a grove of trees to grow nearby, with fruit like that which tempted Eve, and inspires in the transformed devils an unbearable thirst and hunger, which, though they fear some new punishment, they cannot help but try to assuage by climbing the trees and eating the fruit:

> they fondly thinking to allay
> Thir appetite with gust, instead of Fruit
> Chew'd bitter Ashes, which th' offended taste
> With spattering noise rejected: oft they assay'd,
> Hunger and thirst constraining, drugg'd as oft,
> With hatefullest disrelish writh'd thir jaws
> With soot and cinders fill'd; so oft they fell
> Into the same illusion, not as Man
> Whom they triumph'd, once lapst. (X,564–72)

This scene of snaky metamorphosis is surely intended to show the unhappy consequences of misunderstanding God's words. By divine fiat Satan experiences the literal fulfillment of God's curse: "upon thy belly shalt thou go, and dust shalt thou eat all the days of thy life." Those who insist on taking God's words literally, this scene strongly suggests, will suffer the doom of having them applied literally: "for the letter killeth," as St. Paul says, "but the spirit giveth life." The fruits of Satan's illusory victory turn to real ashes in his mouth, demonstrating at once his own futility and God's power to frustrate all Satan's plans.

It may be that Milton expected human readers, who have just been subjected to a lengthy account of how suffering and death were brought into the world at the instigation of Satan, to rejoice now at his humiliation, but I confess that my reaction to this scene is closer to terror than joy. We have, of course, been given an object lesson in how to read, or how not to read, God's words, but we have also been shown how God punishes his enemies. The picture is not reassuring.

Since leaving Hell with Satan in Book II, we have been brought to see how true is his admission that: "myself am Hell," and how little God has to do with causing Satan's sufferings, beyond allowing him the free-

dom to choose the estrangement from God that is their cause and substance. But Satan's metamorphosis in Book X is not self-inflicted; however just, it is a punishment imposed upon him by a punitive deity. As
Helen Gardner puts it:

> We cannot say: "This is how God appears to Satan who has chosen to
> cut himself off from Light and Love and so sees only Fire and Wrath."
> This is how God appears to us, as far as Satan is concerned: implacable,
> vengeful, and deriding.[1]

But Gardner does not go far enough. This is not merely how God "appears," but how he *is*, and not merely to Satan, but to each one of us
insofar as we are sinners. And Milton makes us *feel* God's wrath: look at
the lines describing Satan's face shrinking and his legs entwining as he
changes into a snake; look at the lines describing the serpents chewing
soot and cinders. Milton forces us to undergo this debasement with them;
he makes us experience the torments of the damned. No other scene in
Paradise Lost comes closer to confirming the popular conception of Milton as the Puritan preacher of hellfire and brimstone than does this account of God's ghastly joke on Satan, Satan's followers, and (we must
assume) in time on the legions of damned human souls. When Milton's
God punishes Satan, the reader participates in the feeling of being pun-
ished. No other scene does more to revive our distrust of a vindictive
deity.

Instead of trying to explain away the horror of this scene, I think it
is necessary to acknowledge it. God shows different faces to the repentant
and the unrepentant sinner. Each of us since Adam's Fall bears a likeness
to Satan—that is what "fallen" means—hence none of us is beyond feeling
fear of God's vengeance, even when its immediate object is Satan. The
seriousness of the choice between God and Satan is clear, and the consequences of choosing Satan have been made graphic and concrete. Milton knows he cannot scare his readers into Heaven, but neither will he
conceal the nature of the choice he is asking them to make. One of God's
faces is terrible and frightening, as Adam and Eve knew when they tried
to hide from him, and as we are reminded now.

In fact, the whole world begins to look frightening. While Hell is
busy eating soot and ashes, back on Earth Sin and Death are planning an
even less appealing menu, the mother adjuring her famished son to begin
with the appetizers until she can properly stuff and dress the main
course:

> Thou therefore on these Herbs, and Fruits, and Flow'rs
> Feed first, on each Beast next, and Fish, and Fowl,
> No homely morsels, and whatever thing
> The Scythe of Time mows down, devour unspar'd,
> Till I in Man residing through the Race,
> His thoughts, his looks, words, actions all infect,
> And season him thy last and sweetest prey. (X,603–609)

Even before their arrival, the narrator tells us, their influence has been felt (X,586–87), and as he lies despairing on the ground Adam looks out on the visible evidence of his sin:

> Discord first
> Daughter of Sin, among th' irrational,
> Death introduc'd through fierce antipathy:
> Beast now with Beast gan war, and Fowl with Fowl,
> And Fish with Fish; to graze the Herb all leaving,
> Devour'd each other; nor stood much in awe
> Of Man, but fled him, or with count'nance grim
> Glar'd on him passing. . . . (X,707–14)

This transformation is not entirely Adam's doing, however. Milton's narrator does not scruple to remind us that, like Sin and Death, God, too, has been at work sowing discord in Eden. God bids the Sun alter its ecliptic to produce extremes of summer heat and winter cold (or, since Milton continues to remind us of the ambiguity of celestial motions, if the universe is heliocentric, angels tip the Earth's axis to produce the same effect). The other heavenly bodies are given malign astrological influences; winds are taught to blow storm and drought, famine and plague. God in fact takes responsibility not only for these changes, but for Sin and Death themselves, who, he says, are his agents:

> See with what heat these Dogs of Hell advance
> To waste and havoc yonder World, which I
> So fair and good created, and had still
> Kept in that state, had not the folly of Man
> Let in these wasteful Furies, who impute
> Folly to mee, so doth the Prince of Hell
> And his Adherents, that with so much ease
> I suffer them to enter and possess
> A place so heav'nly, and conniving seem
> To gratify my scornful Enemies,
> That laugh, as if transported with some fit

Of Passion, I to them had quitted all,
At random yielded up to their misrule;
And know not that I call'd and drew them thither
My Hell-hounds, to lick up the draff and filth
Which man's polluting Sin with taint hath shed
On what was pure, till cramm'd and gorg'd, nigh burst
With suckt and glutted offal, at one sling
Of thy victorious Arm, well-pleasing Son,
Both Sin, and Death, and yawning Grave at last
Through Chaos hurl'd, obstruct the mouth of Hell
For ever, and seal up his ravenous Jaws.
Then Heav'n and Earth renew'd shall be made pure
To sanctity that shall receive no stain:
Till then the Curse pronouc't on both precedes. (X,616–40)

Again, as when in Book V he jokingly put on the role of insecure monarch, God is having a celestial laugh at those who believe they can frustrate his purposes. Those readers hardy or exalted enough to join in God's
laughter may do so. I find it raises the hair on the back of my neck.

In the end the extended cosmic interlude of Book X is neither simply
reassuring nor entirely frightening. The Judgment Scene, which is its
centerpiece, happily frustrates our expectation of a vindictive Curse to
show us instead a kindly disposed deity, but the exact details of his kindness remain vague, and, in the case of the sentence of mortality, entirely
obscure. The scene in Hell, while it concludes the sub-plot (begun in
Book I, where we mistook it for the main plot) of the "struggle" between
God and Satan, demonstrates that there never was a real contest, and
thus that the issues between God and Man cannot be blamed on a third
party. God's ways to men are either just or unjust; there can be no more
hiding behind the scapegoat Satan. The first seven hundred lines of Book
X remind us, after Book IX's extended focus on events in Eden, that God
is a player, too, in this cosmic tragicomedy.

But Book X has a second function in Milton's poetic strategy. By
cutting rapidly back and forth between Heavenly, Infernal, and human
points of view, it speeds up (and hence makes more noticeable) a process
that has been taking place throughout *Paradise Lost*. Shifts in perspective, different points of view on the same situations, have of course been
one of the poet's principal narrative devices since the poem began, sometimes heralded with the pomp and circumstance of an epic "prologue,"
but often incorporated into dialogue or introduced with an unobtrusive
narrative "meanwhile."

What Book X does is to speed up the rapidity of shifts between violently differing perspectives upon God's Curse, thereby caricaturing the method of the epic as a whole. A reader cannot help, I believe, feeling acutely uncomfortable as Adam and Eve change from great lovers to guilty children; Sin and Death from buffoons to mighty rulers and then back to hellhounds licking up draff and filth; Satan from serpent to Prince of Darkness to serpent once again. God's face above all flickers intolerably back and forth: harsh, kind, harsh, kind, harsh. . . .

The discomforts of this kaleidoscopic technique must ultimately breed a certain detachment in the reader, a dissatisfaction with the apparent awkwardness with which Milton is handling his unruly plot, and a necessary skepticism toward the conflicting information the poem is feeding him. All of this is utterly destructive of mimesis, the illusion that we are looking not at words, but at a "reality" behind them. When a picture won't "read," the first thing it tells us is that it is . . . well, a picture. Our dissatisfactions with the "words" of Milton's poem encourage in us precisely the stance we need to understand the words of God's curse. As critics have been arguing for years, to read *Paradise Lost* rightly we must read it in the right spirit; but as they often fail to point out, the text itself helps us to achieve the proper mixture of credulity and skepticism necessary to achieve a correct understanding.

The Long interlude of Book X demonstrates that the cosmic perspective will never, by itself, atone man's feelings to the ways of God. Since his own salvation or damnation rests in the hands of each human being, the Fall itself and the words of God's judgment are either blessing or curse depending on how we take them. But no amount of Satanic humiliation or divine laughter can teach us how the human heart discovers God's kindly face in the words of Genesis. For that we need a human perspective and a human example. Milton gives us Adam.

As I have already suggested, Satan and Adam are paired as "readers" of God's words, and the pairing is heightened by physical parallels between them, a similarity that Adam himself will woefully come to recognize. Fallen Adam in Book X begins, as did Satan in Book I, darkling, prostrate, despairing. Like Satan in Book X, Adam meditates on the words of God's curse, but he does so in a spirit of humility rather than pride. Satan in his arrogance was cast down; his "rise" was a bitterly ironic one that ended in chewing soot and ashes. Adam in his "lowness" is raised up. Unlike Satan he comes to recognize that he needs help, and he gets it where he least expects it—from Eve. Just as a false image of "love" brought Adam low, so real love from Eve will start him on his road to regeneration. But first he must touch bottom.

The poem's longest soliloquy is spoken by darkling, prostrate Adam, suffering from the external signs of the Fall, but more especially from the "troubl'd Sea of passion" within himself. His soliloquy resembles Satan's first and longest (IV,32–113) by being an internal debate between two inner "voices," one accusing God and the other defending him (only fallen, "divided" beings—Satan, Adam, Eve—soliloquize in *Paradise Lost*). Like Satan, Adam begins with the cruel contrast between his former and present state—"O miserable of happy!" (X,720)—but unlike Satan he takes the blame himself: "I deserv'd it." (X,726). As he explores his wound, it comes to seem more and more immense, for he quickly discovers that he and his whole world have been ruined by his sin, and (most painfully) generations of human beings yet unborn:

> All that I eat or drink, or shall beget,
> Is propagated curse. O voice once heard
> Delightfully, *Increase and multiply*,
> Now death to hear! for what can I increase
> Or multiply, but curses on my head?
> Who of all Ages to succeed, but feeling
> The evil on him brought by me, will curse
> My Head; Ill fare our Ancestor impure,
> For this we may thank Adam; but his thanks
> Shall be the execration. (X,728–37)

The word "curse" is the leitmotif here: the very blessings of Eden—food, drink, sex, love, and above all the promise of progeny—are transformed into curses with an almost mathematical precision, as if pluses were erased and minuses put in their place.

Adam is experiencing that paradoxical reversal of values Satan complained of earlier: the greater the blessing seemed when unfallen, the greater curse it now appears to be (see IX,119–23). And he uses language evocative of Satan's imagery of recoiling cannon to express this idea ("Revenge, at first though sweet, Bitter ere long back on itself recoils" [IX,171–72]):

> all from mee
> Shall with a fierce reflux on mee redound. . . . (X,738–39)

Existence itself seems now the heaviest curse of all, and Adam questions
the justice of God's creating man only to condemn him to suffering:

> Did I request thee, Maker, from my Clay
> To mould me Man, did I solicit thee
> From darkness to promote me, or here place
> In this delicious Garden? (X,743–46)

Clearly, though a moment before Adam was saying "I deserv'd it," he did
not entirely mean it; the "curse," which is growing by leaps and bounds
as he examines it, is getting harder and harder to bear.

Like Satan, Adam is rebelling against God's will, yet his rebellion
has a different flavor: Adam complains that God created him, but he does
not deny that he was created. Satan in despair was arrogant, but Adam is
humble; he contemplates not revenge but suicide:

> Be it so, for I submit, his doom is fair,
> That dust I am, and shall to dust return:
> O welcome hour whenever! why delays
> His hand to execute what his Decree
> Fix'd on this day? why do I overlive,
> Why am I mockt with death, and length'n'd out
> To deathless pain? How gladly would I meet
> Mortality my sentence, and be Earth
> Insensible, how glad would lay me down
> As in my Mother's lap! There I should rest
> And sleep secure; his dreadful voice no more
> Would Thunder in my ears, no fear of worse
> To mee and to my offspring would torment me
> With cruel expectation. (X,769–82)

The "curse" of death begins to seem a blessing to Adam, but of course a
completely negative one—a cessation, merely, of unendurable pain. Further unpleasant surprises await him.

There is a contradiction that still puzzles Adam. He knows that he is
part spirit and that spirit cannot "return to dust." Yet it was the spirit that
sinned and was cursed with death; if spirit is eternal, what can "death"
mean:

> How can [God] exercise
> Wrath without end on Man whom Death must end?
> Can he make deathless Death? (X,796–98)

The spirit, which by its nature cannot die, by divine decree *must* die! The answer to this "Strange contradiction" can only be that God's curse of "death" does not mean what Adam (and the reader) supposed:

> But say
> That Death be not one stroke, as I suppos'd,
> Bereaving sense, but endless misery
> From this day onward, which I feel begun
> Both in me, and without me, and so last
> To perpetuity; Ay me, that fear
> Comes thund'ring back with dreadful revolution
> On my defenseless head; both Death and I
> Am found Eternal. . . . (X,808–16)

Words, as Adam is discovering, have more than one meaning. A bit of meditation on his own sufferings led him to accept physical death as a blessing in disguise—an end to misery—but like God's word "day," "death" has a second meaning: Adam is *already* "dead," but death proves to be no anaesthetic.

Earlier in his soliloquy Adam foresaw his descendants suffering temporal misery as a consequence of his own sin; now he foresees their *eternal* misery:

> in mee all
> Posterity stands curst: Fair Patrimony
> That I must leave ye, Sons; O were I able
> To waste it all myself, and leave ye none!
> So disinherited how would ye bless
> Me now your Curse! (X,817–22)

Again Adam must face the fact that he is responsible for an entire race's sufferings, but now the stakes have been raised immeasurably, as their suffering appears endless. Adam has discovered Hell.

Unaided, however, he is unable to discover Grace. The logic seems inexorable: a distempered soul must beget distempered souls, who will win no more approval in their Creator's eyes than does their ancestor. Adam has stumbled upon the need for a Redeemer, but without God's help he will never discover that one exists. How could any one finite being bear the crushing load of infinite sin? Adam knows he himself could not:

> first and last
> On mee, mee only, as the source and spring
> Of all corruption, all the blame lights due;
> So might the wrath. Fond wish! couldst thou support
> That burden heavier than the Earth to bear,
> Than all the World much heavier, though divided
> With that bad Woman? (X,831–37)

Ironically, Adam's words echo those we have heard already from the promised Redeemer ("Behold mee then, mee for him, life for life I offer, on mee let thine anger fall" [III,236–37]), but in Adam's mouth the words, though well-meaning, are grandiose; wishing to bear the sins of all humanity, Adam cannot even bear his own, but must try to divide them with "that bad Woman."

Each time Adam thinks he has touched bottom, he discovers there *is* no bottom. He can stare his guilt in the face only for a moment; then his despair becomes so keen he is driven to lay blame elsewhere—on God, on Eve—for sins he has just acknowledged as his own. Thought has done all that thought can do; now it becomes an endless circle, guilt chasing its own tail:

> O Conscience, into what Abyss of fears
> And horrors hast thou driv'n me; out of which
> I find no way, from deep to deeper plung'd! (X,842–44)

As he recognizes, he is powerless to find his own way out. What Adam needs is help. God sends him Eve.

Still outstretched on the cold ground, Adam continues to blame everyone but himself for his misery. Eve takes pity on him, but for return she earns a tirade—"Out of my sight, thou Serpent" (X,867)—which demonstrates how thin and perishable is Adam's self-condemnation. Her mate now rails at her with every unfair misogynistic argument later ages have derived from Genesis. In this orgy of recrimination Adam completely forgets his own role in the Fall; far from bearing the entire race's burden of guilt, as he has just nobly aspired to do, he cannot even bear his own.

But then something wonderful happens. Eve answers hatred with love:

> [Adam] added not, and from her turn'd, but Eve
> Not so repulst, with Tears that ceas'd not flowing,

And tresses all disorder'd, at his feet
Fell humble, and imbracing them, besought
His peace, and thus proceeded in her plaint.
　　Forsake me not thus, Adam, witness Heav'n
What love sincere, and reverence in my heart
I bear thee, and unweeting have offended,
Unhappily deceiv'd; thy suppliant
I beg, and clasp thy knees; bereave me not,
Whereon I live, thy gentle looks, thy aid,
Thy counsel in this uttermost distress,
My only strength and stay: forlorn of thee,
Whither shall I betake me, where subsist? (X,909–22)

Eve provides Adam with a mirror for his own thoughts. Like Adam in his
soliloquy, she proposes to take all the blame for the Fall upon her own
shoulders (X,930–36), and, when Adam shows her how impossible that
would be, she next suggests that they refrain from bringing children into
the fallen world, even if they must kill themselves to do so (X,979–1006).
In each case Eve speaks Adam's own earlier thoughts back to him, but,
coming from her, their flaws are more apparent. Dialogue, the poem
seems to say, is superior to monologue, if for no other reason than that it
lets us examine our own thoughts at a distance.

　　But Eve's role in Adam's spiritual recovery is much greater than that
of a sounding board. When Eve returns Adam's apparent hatred with
love, she gives him everything. She restores his faith in himself; she
teaches him how to love in a fallen world:

　　　She ended weeping, and her lowly plight,
　　Immovable till peace obtain'd from fault
　　Acknowledg'd and deplor'd, in Adam wrought
　　Commiseration; soon his heart relented
　　Towards her, his life so late and sole delight,
　　Now at his feet submissive in distress,
　　Creature so fair his reconcilement seeking,
　　His counsel whom she had displeas'd, his aid;
　　As one disarm'd, his anger all he lost,
　　And thus with peaceful words uprais'd her soon. (X,937–46)

According to Milton, the two sexes were formed by God with slightly
different, but complementary, natures. Just as Adam is Eve's superior in
analytic thinking, so Eve is Adam's superior in feeling and loving. So,
while Adam has been exploring the fallen condition intellectually, Eve

has discovered how the fallen love—with humility, contrition, and for-
giveness born of a wish to be oneself forgiven.

God's wisdom in making mankind double—man and woman—is
demonstrated more clearly here than at any other place in the poem.
Adam and Eve each have half the picture: Adam has discovered that
deeper meanings must be sought beneath the surfaces of God's words,
but Eve has made the equally (or perhaps more) important discovery that
behind "anger and just rebuke" can hide an enduring love. Only Eve's
discovery can help Adam find the *right* interpretation of God's words, for
God's "curse" will appear as a blessing only if read in the light of the
knowledge of his loving kindness toward mankind. Alone, Adam and Eve
are each helpless, like a traveler with half a map. Together they find
the way.

When Eve proposes suicide as a way of preventing the propagation
of God's curse, Adam hears something "more sublime And excellent"
(X,1014–15) than the foolish words themselves. Something—Eve's
love—has renewed his faith in Eve and in himself and has made him
more responsive to hints of hope in God's words. He suddenly remembers one such hint that turns the promise of progeny into a sort of blessing once again:

> Then let us seek
> Some safer resolution, which methinks
> I have in view, calling to mind with heed
> Part of our Sentence, that thy Seed shall bruise
> The Serpent's head; piteous amends, unless
> Be meant, whom I conjecture, our grand Foe
> Satan, who in the Serpent hath contriv'd
> Against us this deceit: to crush his head
> Would be revenge indeed; which will be lost
> By death brought on ourselves, or childless days
> Resolv'd, as thou proposest; so our Foe
> Shall 'scape his punishment ordain'd, and wee
> Instead shall double ours upon our heads.
> No more be mention'd then of violence
> Against ourselves, and wilful barrenness,
> That cuts us off from hope, and savors only
> Rancor and pride, impatience and despite,
> Reluctance against God and his just yoke
> Laid on our Necks. (X,1028–46)

Earlier, Adam's own disordered mind had supplied his mild Judge with a stern countenance and harsh words. Now that Eve has returned love for anger, Adam begins to remember that God, too, showed a loving aspect when he came to judge his creatures:

> Remember with what mild
> And gracious temper he both heard and judg'd
> Without wrath or reviling; wee expected
> Immediate dissolution, which we thought
> Was meant by Death that day, when lo, to thee
> Pains only in Child-bearing were foretold,
> And bringing forth, soon recompens't with joy,
> Fruit of thy Womb: On mee the Curse aslope
> Glanc'd on the ground, with labor I must earn
> My bread; what harm? Idleness had been worse;
> My labor will sustain me; and lest Cold
> Or Heat should injure us, his timely care
> Hath unbesought provided, and his hands
> Cloth'd us unworthy, pitying while he judg'd. (X,1046–59)

Without meaning to, Eve has taught Adam a lesson in love. When she knelt before Adam, her senses and her reason alike must have told her that her pleas would fall on deaf ears, yet her "unreasonable" faith in Adam's enduring love was rewarded. Now Adam sees that what Eve has shown to him, they must both show to God: "How much more, if we pray him, will his ear Be open, and his heart to pity incline. . . ." (X, 1060–61). It would be wrong to say that Adam learns from Eve's *example*, merely. Even unfallen Adam failed to learn from Abdiel's example. Eve gives Adam much more than the *idea* of prayer; she teaches his heart to feel once again the love that makes prayer possible:

> What better can we do, than to the place
> Repairing where he judg'd us, prostrate fall
> Before him reverent, and there confess
> Humbly our faults, and pardon beg, with tears
> Watering the ground, and with our sighs the Air
> Frequenting, sent from hearts contrite, in sign
> Of sorrow unfeign'd, and humiliation meek.
> Undoubtedly he will relent and turn
> From his displeasure; in whose look serene,
> When angry most he seem'd and most severe,
> What else but favor, grace, and mercy shown? (X,1086–96)

Adam has learned—Eve (although she didn't know she knew) has taught him—how to read God's words. And although technically narrator and reader still know more than he about God and God's plans for mankind, Adam knows the *essential* thing, the thing that is so hard for fallen human beings to remember, no matter how often they are told—God is Love.

After so many privileged glimpses of futurity, so many dramatic ironies pointed out by Milton's narrator, we stand essentially on even ground with Adam, our likeness, our brother. His words, his stance, cannot be improved upon, and so the narrator, adopting them as his own, suggests that we do so, too:

> So spake our Father penitent, nor Eve
> Felt less remorse: they forthwith to the place
> Repairing where he judg'd them prostrate fell
> Before him reverent, and both confess'd
> Humbly thir faults, and pardon begg'd, with tears
> Watering the ground, and with thir sighs the Air
> Frequenting, sent from hearts contrite, in sign
> Of sorrow unfeign'd, and humiliation meek. (X, 1097–1104)

This is perhaps the greatest moment of Milton's poem, when the point of view of the hero (we can call Adam that now) merges with the narrator's, and with the reader's as well. Identification with Adam is at this moment complete: Adam, Eve, narrator, reader—One Flesh—kneeling in contrite prayer before their Creator.

8

Salvation through Reading

> There can hardly be a more elementary critical principle
> than the fact that the events of a literary fiction are not
> real but hypothetical events.
> —Northrop Frye, *An Anatomy of Criticism*

> The substance of [Milton's] narrative is truth.
> —Samuel Johnson

READING *PARADISE LOST* is an education (who can doubt it?), given
not only Milton's cannibalizing of earlier literature and his encyclopaedic
interests but also the seriousness of his aim to make his reader understand the universe so as to live his life better. Yet it is a strange education,
reminiscent at times of a slap from a Zen master, at times a silent order
to "think for yourself." Passive, timid, or lazy readers cannot read *Paradise Lost*; unless we grapple with its complexities, uncertainties, silences,
paradoxes, and lies, the poem angers, bores, and finally defeats us. *Paradise Lost* is profoundly, terrifyingly evolutionary, progressive; as we read,
our understanding is subject to continuing revision and repeated annihilation. Milton's poem is an anti-epic, a "self-consuming artifact," a phoenix that burns and rises from its own ashes; for Milton death-and-rebirth
is not only a physics and a metaphysics, but an aesthetics as well.

From the vantage point of Book XI, we may well wonder what, if
anything, remains of our experience of the first ten books. Certainly little
is left of Hell as portrayed in Books I and II; even the narrator's terse and
sour reminders there of a punitive Christian doctrine have been compro-

mised by the blessings lurking behind God's "curses." Milton believed in Hell but knew it to be located in the human heart; Adam prostrate on the ground in Book X is a far more accurate image of estrangement from God than the entertaining, seductive Never-never land of the poem's opening. Heaven, too, was not so much seen as heard in Book III; if not, like Hell, a downright illusion, Heaven was nonetheless baffling and elusive. Much of our education in *Paradise Lost* has been a process of "unlearning," an evocation of sophisticated, unsound images in order to cancel them, a scraping away of layers to get down to the good wood of ignorance, humility, innocence. Lovely as is the "Morning Hymn" of Book V, it is superseded by the prayer of inarticulate contrition that closes Book X, which is certified "more pleasing" by God himself. In Milton's inverted aesthetic, silence is more eloquent than speech, and unheard melodies are sweetest. One loving motion of the human heart is worth more than all philosophy and poetry—including *Paradise Lost*.

Having ended so well with silence—a prayer heard only by the inner ear—why does Milton continue? Because for Milton even ecstasy must yield to instruction. *Paradise Lost* has thus far taught us by trial and error how to read itself. Now it will teach us how to read a greater text: the Bible, or (if you prefer) human history.

The very existence of *Paradise Lost* testifies to Milton's awareness that the reader of the Bible bears a heavy burden of interpretation. The poem itself "reads" the Bible and bears in its every line testimony to the gravity and effort of that enterprise. The scenes in Hell and Heaven, the descriptions of the Garden, the account of the Fall and its aftermath— the entire poem, one way or another—is a patchwork of biblical borrowings pieced out with imagination. The reader of *Paradise Lost* reads a poem that is overtly based upon another text, and in which (especially in the second half) that text is often visibly embedded. He is reading a "reading" of Genesis, and of the Bible generally, and implicitly is being taught how to read it for himself.

We have seen this embedding often enough already. It occurs again near the beginning of Book XI when God explains his reasons for expelling Adam and Eve from Eden. Here is the Genesis passage:

> And the Lord God said, Behold, the man is become as one of us, to know good and evil: and now, lest he put forth his hand, and take also of the tree of life, and eat, and live forever;
> Therefore the Lord God sent him forth from the garden of Eden to till the ground from whence he was taken. (3:22–23)

This account of the expulsion presents interpretive difficulties to someone set on justifying God's ways, since it seems to say that God exiled Adam and Eve out of a jealous fear that they might attain divine immortality by eating from the Tree of Life. Attribution of such independent magical properties to fruit is a limitation on God's omnipotence as inconceivable to Milton as the image of a jealous God is offensive to his sense of God's perfect goodness. He accordingly has God add a quibble that entirely changes the force of the passage:

> O Sons, like one of us Man is become
> To know both Good and Evil, since his taste
> Of that defended Fruit; but let him boast
> His knowledge of Good lost, and Evil got,
> Happier, had it suffic'd him to have known
> Good by itself, and Evil not at all.
> He sorrows now, repents, and prays contrite,
> My motions in him; longer than they move,
> His heart I know, how variable and vain
> Self-left. Lest therefore his now bolder hand
> Reach also of the Tree of Life, and eat,
> And live for ever, *dream at least to live*
> *For ever*, to remove him I decree,
> And send him from the Garden forth to Till
> The Ground whence he was taken, fitter soil. (XI,84–98; my italics)

So amended, God's worry about the Tree of Life is turned into concern for the spiritual regeneration of his two fallen creatures; Adam and Eve are to be exiled for their own good, before they commit another mortal sin by aspiring to divine immortality.

But Milton's version of this passage is not a simple softening of Genesis harshness. His God insists on denouncing human boastfulness, variability and vanity once more before revealing a compassionate motive behind the impending exile from Eden. In other words, Milton doesn't so much replace the Genesis image of a jealous, wrathful deity as he complicates it by setting a second, kindlier image beside it. Interpreting Genesis in such a way as to make a loving deity seem more possible, he then leaves it to his reader to choose between the two: a God of Wrath or a God of Love.

As is so often the case in this poem, Milton's deeper meaning here is only ambiguously suggested by the text and demands the reader's collaboration to establish. To get at his "real" meaning—to get at any fixed meaning at all, actually—we must be energetic interpreters, reading this passage not only in the light of what we know Milton has added to Genesis, but even more in the light of what we have already seen of God's reactions to Man's Fall in Book X. But we must not forget the *fact* of interpretation: the punitive God of Genesis and the forgiving God of Christianity overlay each other in this (and indeed every) part of *Paradise Lost*. To read it at all is to choose between conflicting patterns: to add to, subtract from, alter, and complete the text before us, just as Milton himself does with Genesis.

This is a pattern we have so frequently remarked in earlier chapters that by now we must accept it as a profound truth both about the poem's construction and of our reactions to it. Milton has built *Paradise Lost* out of conflicting themes and perspectives, so that the poem repeatedly seems at war with itself. This continual conflict forces the reader into an active role of participation: in order to make sense of the poem we have to *make* sense, literally. We are the poem's creators; we make its meaning.

It might seem that there never was a poem of which this latter proposition was *less* true than of *Paradise Lost*. As an expansion and often just a paraphrase of Holy Scripture, Milton's poem lays claim to a kind of authority that will not (it seems) permit the reader to read as he chooses. Yet though this claim raises the stakes—reading is, on Milton's terms, nothing less than an instruction in salvation—it does nothing to lighten the burden placed upon the reader, the burden of interpretation. We may not read "just any way at all," we must read the *right* way; but the final authority for its rightness is inside us, in our own consciences as illumined by God's inner light.

This is another way of saying that Christianity is, in Milton's view, a *reader's* religion. And not in Milton's view alone: the Reformation placed extraordinary emphasis upon literacy and upon translations of the Bible into the vernacular, precisely because Protestants felt that one could not really be a Christian until one could *read* God's words. If the Puritan sermon was almost invariably a textual explication of a biblical passage— a lesson in reading the Word of God—this was precisely because the Word of God, while all-important, is not always easy reading. The Bible is a difficult text: long and diffuse, written over millennia by an Author who, though single, chose a multitude of different idioms in which to express himself: Genesis is chronicle; Job is drama; Canticles is love po-

etry; Revelation is, well, revelation. Above all, the Bible speaks of difficult matters—matters hard to understand and hard to accept. Reading
the Bible is Christian heroism of the highest order.

And that heroism applies equally to the reader of *Paradise Lost*, who
is being offered an opportunity not to escape but to confront the most
insoluble problems of his own moral life: how to face his own defects;
how to strive for good in an evil world; how to love a God who allows evil
to exist. The poem's whole design is immoderately ambitious, since it
invites from the reader an act of Christian heroism in every way compa-
rable to the narrator's, Christ's, or Adam's. As Joseph Summers puts it,
Milton:

> was less concerned with his readers' acceptance of his poem, I believe,
> than with their acceptance of life; or, perhaps more accurately, he
> wished the least possible distance between those two acceptances. He
> would not allow the reader, any more than Adam, to accept ignorantly
> or with more than the minimum of mystery.[1]

Here Summers argues, quite rightly, that Milton wrote his epic not to
divert or entertain his reader but to help him discover justice in God's
ways, and thereby to live his life better.

The implications of the word "acceptance" are not, however, quite
right for *Paradise Lost*. The aim of Milton's poem is not to make us
merely "accept" either life as we live it, or as it is portrayed in the Bible,
but to recognize that this life is comic or tragic, bearable or unbearable,
depending on how we interpret it. *Paradise Lost*, the Bible, life itself,
have endless shifting, conflicting patterns. By themselves they can
"mean" anything. There is no definite meaning, and therefore no possibility of acceptance, until a reader interprets them. No one can *make* us
read a certain way (just as no one makes Satan read a certain way, or Eve,
or Adam)—we *choose* to read as we do. All Milton can do is to make us
aware: first, of the fact that we are interpreting; second, of the consequences of how we interpret.

It would not be unfair to describe the entire action of *Paradise Lost*,
from Satan's plotting to Adam's prayer, as a succession of interpretive acts
performed upon signs, verbal and non-verbal, expressive of God's will.
When Satan apostrophizes the Sun or turns with jealous leer malign away
from Adam and Eve's nuptial kisses, when Eve asks of the Serpent's
newly acquired powers of speech: "What may this mean?", and when the

Son asks the Father to "let mee Interpret for him [i.e., fallen man]," they are all interpreting external circumstances for clues to God's will. And the whole poem, of course, represents the epic narrator's attempt to "read" God's will in Scripture and in his own heart. *Paradise Lost* is an epic of reading, a vast attempt to read the Bible, the world, and the human heart, in order to understand and accept God's ways.

The process of choosing between conflicting patterns and completing Milton's meaning has been the reader's role since the beginning. Part of the experience of reading *Paradise Lost* is learning how to read the Bible, the world we live in, and our own souls. Yet the reader of Books I–X may be excused, amid the pressing demands of a complex mimetic fiction, if he misses the clues pointing to his own central role as interpreter. What Books XI–XII add to the reader's experience of Adam and Eve's fall and rise is the dimension of self-consciousness. If the entire poem has been an education in reading, these final books make "learning to read" their explicit subject-matter, and Adam-as-reader becomes a surrogate for Milton's reader.

Book XI brings the view of man as reader, *homo interpretans*, out into the open, where it can become the conscious focus of our attention. The earlier story of Adam the actor, or the acted-upon, becomes (or merges with) the story of Adam the reader, the interpreter of a story that is simultaneously both his and ours. In the end, true action will be redefined as a certain kind of muscular interpretation. Thus the end of Milton's epic becomes a story-within-a-story, in which we can at once focus upon the story itself and on the conditions of its telling.

That interpretation and understanding are the quintessence of Milton's notion of Christian heroism clarifies what has always been obscure about the poem's ending. It is no secret that the last two books of *Paradise Lost* have generally been judged unsatisfactory by readers of the poem. Filled with talk instead of action, they turn the poem's plot into a telegraphic biblical summary and reduce the newly emergent protagonist to a spectator and listener. The verse, too, is often flat and prosaic, avoiding the grandeur of Books I and II, the lushness of Books IV and V, and the dramatic tension of Books IX and X.

Just to state these criticisms, is, of course, to see how appropriate Milton's ending is to the sort of poem he has been writing. From the beginning *Paradise Lost* has aimed at replacing worldly values (such as powerful personality, action-packed plot, and rich rhetorical effect) by humility, inwardness, and a rhetoric of understatement and silence. But though he may have meant to redefine the *kind* of satisfaction we get from epic poetry (and from art generally), Milton surely didn't mean to leave his reader so dissatisfied with the ending of his poem. What kind of satisfaction *is* available from the ending of *Paradise Lost*?

Critical answers to this question can be grouped, roughly but fairly, under two headings: those of "drama," and those of "doctrine." The dramatic approach to Books XI and XII stresses that action has not ceased in these books; it has merely *evolved* a bit. The focus of our interest, it argues, is still on what Adam says and does, Michael's biblical prophecies being of secondary (though not insignificant) interest. "These books," writes F.T. Prince, "are not merely historical or theological statement; they are what is revealed to Adam . . . the imaginative intensity is to be found . . . in the vibration of the story in Adam's reacting consciousness."[2]

It is, however, precisely the "imaginative intensity" of these last books that has been questioned by readers of the poem. The essence of drama—contrast, conflict, change, surprise—is muted in the poem's last two books. The obvious drama of Adam's fall and repentance lies behind us. Adam's continuing inner struggle to accept the angel's lessons of patience and faith is unemphatic, as inner struggles must be, suggested by the poem rather than "dramatized" in the full sense.

The "doctrinal" approach, while it doesn't necessarily deny the dramatic appeal of Adam's reactions to the biblical story, finds Michael's visit chiefly motivated by a wish to educate the reader in Christian doctrine. One of the best pieces of criticism along these lines is by H.R. MacCallum, who, taking issue with C.S. Lewis's description of Michael's story as an "untransmuted lump of futurity," shows it to be a highly patterned scheme of six historical periods, foreshortened as they recede into Adam's future, and linked by typological events and figures that anticipate Christ.[3]

There is merit in MacCallum's intellectual approach to the poem's ending. Great works of literary art often end on a quiet, contemplative note, where the issue of what will happen next is replaced by that of what it all means, a shift that obviously occurs toward the end of *Paradise Lost*. But MacCallum, like others who take the "doctrinal" approach, persistently minimizes the tragic human implications of all the suffering and sin that Michael reveals to Adam, just as he typically reduces Adam's role in the lesson to that of a sounding board. If those who take a "doctrinal" approach to the poem mean to assert a bracing theological optimism in Books XI and XII, or to discern a "fit audience" so drugged with divine foreknowledge that it feels no pain, then they ignore the substantial real audience who, at the end of Milton's poem, feel nothing *but* pain: "theologically the design may be said to work," laments Louis Martz; "poetically it is a disaster."[4]

Both dramatic and doctrinal approaches to the poem, then, have a piece of the answer to the question of the kind of satisfaction Books XI and XII can give, but neither is itself entirely adequate. Clearly there must be both emotional force and intellectual light at the end of Milton's poem, yet the "dramatic" approach runs the risk of trivializing that ending's high seriousness, and the "doctrinal" approach risks emptying it of all intensity. There is no doubt that many readers find the poem's ending both trivial and remote: only if Michael's doctrine strikes us as vitally applicable both to Adam's immediate situation and to our own can that ending function properly as the climax of Milton's great retelling of the story of the Fall of Man.

The fusion of drama and doctrine, of fiction and fact, that Milton devised for the climax of his poem is an invented incident in the life of a real person. Michael's visit to Adam is not biblical, yet by inventing that visit Milton managed to show how the individual human spirit (whether Adam's or ours) is saved by reading the true history of mankind contained *in* the Bible. Books XI and XII depict Adam's Christian salvation. Dramatically we worry about what is to happen to Adam; doctrinally we discover that his true fate (and our own) is a spiritual one. In the mimesis of Adam's salvation Milton has found a "plot" for his story that is simultaneously entirely dramatic and entirely doctrinal, since the whole point of Christian doctrine is not knowledge for its own sake but knowledge as a means to the saving of the individual soul.

The roots of Adam and Eve's salvation, which occurs in Books XI and XII, go as deep as Book III, though they were at the time scarcely visible. When in Book III God promises that "Man . . . shall find grace" (III, 131), I doubt if it occurs to many readers that he may be referring to Adam and Eve, whom we haven't at this point even met as characters. By "Man" God does (on occasion) mean Adam, but its usual reference in Book III is to humanity in general. And it is of humanity—specifically of humanity since the Incarnation—that he seems to be speaking when he describes how fallen men will achieve salvation:

> [They] shall hear me call, and oft be warn'd
> Thir sinful state, and to appease betimes
> Th' incensed Deity while offer'd grace
> Invites; for I will clear thir senses dark,
> What may suffice, and soft'n stony hearts
> To pray, repent, and bring obedience due.
> To Prayer, repentance, and obedience due,
> Though but endeavor'd with sincere intent,
> Mine ear shall not be slow, mine eye not shut. (III,185–93)

Separated as this passage is by some six thousand lines from the end of Book X, it is not surprising that readers miss the fit between God's description of how sinners attain salvation and the facts of Adam and Eve's repentance in Book X.

Once noticed, however, the correspondence is obvious. Praying contritely, Adam and Eve are, if not fully repentant yet, at least sincerely trying to be so. God, for his part, the narrator informs us, has "remov'd The stony from thir hearts" (XI,3–4). When their prayers fly up to Heaven, they lead to a reiterated offer of intercession from the Son, which God elliptically but definitively accepts:

> [Son:] Accept me, and in mee from these receive
> The smell of peace toward Mankind, let him live
> Before thee reconcil'd, at least his days
> Number'd, though sad, till Death, his doom (which I
> To mitigate thus plead, not to reverse)
> To better life shall yield him, where with mee
> All my redeem'd may dwell in joy and bliss,
> Made one with me as I with thee am one.
>   To whom the Father, without Cloud, serene.
> All thy request for Man, accepted Son,
> Obtain, all thy request was my Decree. . . . (XI,37–47)

Here, though again the reference is to "Man," the promise of redemption is extended not merely to the species but specifically (though unemphatically) to Adam and Eve.

God, for his part, emphasizes the justice of their expulsion from Eden, not the mercy of their eventual salvation, which they have yet to

earn. But even his justification of why Adam and Eve must die (because
immortality without happiness would be eternal woe) includes a reitera-
tion of the Son's reference to redemption:

> so Death becomes
> His final remedy, and after Life
> Tri'd in sharp tribulation, and refin'd
> By Faith and faithful works, to second Life,
> Wak't in the renovation of the just,
> Resigns him up with Heav'n and Earth renew'd. (XI,61–66)

Despite its explicit references to salvation, however, this Heavenly
preamble mixes a large measure of gall with its honey, which I suppose is
why the issue of Adam and Eve's redemption has not been noticed by
critics. As so often before in the poem, two stories are being told simultaneously. First, based on the Genesis account, is the story of God's denunciation of humanity's unworthiness to continue living in Eden, in
which their coming expulsion stands both as a punishment and as a way
of preventing their evasion of another punishment. Second, and in flat
contradiction to the first, is the story of God's loving precautions in pro-
tecting Adam and Eve from making a further mistake that might undo
the process of regeneration in which they are presently engaged.

The two stories are mutually exclusive, forcing the reader again into
the role of actively making Milton's meaning by choosing one over the
other. But to this familiar, uncomfortable situation Milton now adds another dimension by making the interpretation of self-contradictory material the explicit subject-matter of his poem. For, in giving Michael his
commission to narrate biblical history to Adam, God not only proposes
the rather shocking exchange of Paradise for a story but makes clear that
Adam's fate now rests on an act of interpretation. God will not impose an
ending to Adam's story upon him; according to how he responds, Adam
will write the ending by himself:

> Michael, this my behest have thou in charge,
> . . . .
>
> Haste thee, and from the Paradise of God
> Without remorse drive out the sinful Pair,
> From hallow'd ground th' unholy, and denounce
> To them and to thir Progeny from thence
> Perpetual banishment. Yet lest they faint

At the sad Sentence rigorously urg'd,
For I behold them soft'nd and with tears
Bewailing thir excess, all terror hide.
If patiently thy bidding they obey,
Dismiss them not disconsolate; reveal
To Adam what shall come in future days,
As I shall thee enlighten, intermix
My Cov'nant in the woman's seed renew'd;
So send them forth, though sorrowing, yet in peace. . . . (XI,99–117)

Two faces of God look out from these lines: one, hostile and angry, orders Michael to "Without remorse drive out the sinful Pair"; the other, solicitous of their fragile peace of mind, asks that it be done gently. But beside demanding some resourceful interpretation to straighten out the apparent contradiction of divine attitudes, God's last speech in *Paradise Lost* is *about* interpretation, too. God is, after all, making the offer of consolation contingent upon a particular *response* from Adam and Eve: "If patiently thy bidding they obey, Dismiss them not disconsolate." Patience is not the only option open to them—anger, despair, and self-pity are other perfectly possible reactions to the news of their expulsion. So the role of listener is not, in God's description, entirely a passive one; rather, it demands an active choice among attitudes.

Those who know Milton's other work will be aware, moreover, that to him "patience" was not the stolid, unimaginative quality we often picture it to be. Patience arms the Jesus of *Paradise Regain'd* with answers to all of Satan's delusive arguments; patience makes Milton's Samson suddenly decide to follow his captors to a Philistine religious festival. It is even a personified "Patience" who answers the rebellious poet of Sonnet XIX with reasons to "stand and wait." For Milton, in other words, patience does not simply consist in stoically *permitting* God's will to be done, but in the very active, unremitting effort to *affirm* God's will with one's own: I am truly patient when I will what God wills. Naturally, since God's will often wears a forbidding aspect, is never entirely knowable, and is constantly unfolding through events, this active patience demands a continual effort of interpretation (what does God want now?) and choice (I want it, too). As with all its important words, however, *Paradise Lost* allows the deeper meanings of patience to unfold gradually in the reader's mind. For the moment the important thing is that God points to the new role of interpretation in the life of fallen man.

Even before they hear Michael's prophecy of the Redeemer, Adam and Eve have intimations of the salvation that awaits them. At the end of Book X, Adam's resolution to pray is attended by an intuition of divine mercy:

> Undoubtedly he will relent and turn
> From his displeasure; in whose look serene,
> When angry most he seem'd and most severe,
> What else but favor, grace, and mercy shown? (X, 1093–96)

And after they pray, that intuition is supported by an enhanced capacity to understand the deeper meanings of the apparent curses in Book X:

> Eve, easily may Faith admit, that all
> The good which we enjoy, from Heav'n descends;
> But that from us aught should ascend to Heav'n
> So prevalent as to concern the mind
> Of God high-blest, or to incline his will,
> Hard to belief may seem; yet this will Prayer,
> Or one short sigh of human breath, up-borne
> Ev'n to the Seat of God. For since I sought
> By Prayer th' offended Deity to appease,
> Kneel'd and before him humbl'd all my heart,
> Methought I saw him placable and mild,
> Bending his ear; persuasion in me grew
> That I was heard with favor; peace return'd
> Home to my Breast, and to my memory
> His promise, that thy Seed shall bruise our Foe;
> Which then not minded in dismay, yet now
> Assures me that the bitterness of death
> Is past, and we shall live. Whence Hail to thee,
> Eve rightly call'd, Mother of all Mankind,
> Mother of all things living, since by thee
> Man is to live, and all things live for Man. (XI, 141–61)

Here Adam reads the change in his own heart as evidence that God has seen and answered his wordless prayer, and in the light of that change he can now interpret God's prophetic words more accurately. Adam is learning to read better, but, as Joseph Summers observes, not yet well enough:

> The ironies are touching. Everything that Adam says is true, but none
> of it is true in the sense which he imagines. The "bitterness of death"

is truly past, but not the fact of death; they will live, but not as Adam thinks. Eve is all the things which Adam says, but she is also more and other. The "Hail" is startling; it embodies both Adam's knowledge and his ignorance of all the centuries which will ensue before the second Eve will be so addressed.[5]

Adam is reading in the right spirit, discerning a kindlier aspect to God's words than he at first suspected, and is thereby better able to see the blessings hidden in apparent curses. But he doesn't yet know enough to read as well as a Christian must; he simply lacks sufficient text. Michael's mission is to "Christianize" Adam: to give him the indispensible text and to instruct him in deeper reading.

Henceforth, reading will be for Adam what it has been for us from the beginning of *Paradise Lost*: an exposure to the manifold paradoxes of a disordered universe, where things are not always what they seem. Michael warns Adam that the story will mix its effects:

> good with bad
> Expect to hear, supernal Grace contending
> With sinfulness of Men. (XI,358–60)

But, as we have often seen in our own reactions to earlier books, preparation is no substitute for experience. Adam is prepared to see his own sinfulness repeated in his progeny, yet he is still not prepared for the violence and brutality of what he sees. The narrator describes the first vision:

> [Abel's] Off'ring soon propitious Fire from Heav'n
> Consum'd with nimble glance, and grateful steam;
> [Cain's] not, for his was not sincere;
> Whereat hee inly rag'd, and as they talk'd,
> Smote him into the Midriff with a stone
> That beat out life; he fell, and deadly pale
> Groan'd out his Soul with gushing blood effus'd. (XI,441–47)

Adam's response to this horrific vision is a mixture of naiveté and discernment:

> O Teacher, some great mischief hath befall'n
> To that meek man, who well had sacrific'd;
> Is Piety thus and pure Devotion paid? (XI,450–52)

To us, the poem's readers, who know well enough what has befallen Abel, (we even know his name, which Adam does not) there is a sad irony in Adam's inadequate phrase "some great mischief." Yet precisely because he doesn't recognize death, Adam sees the telling issue perhaps more clearly than we: is Abel's death consonant with God's justice? Michael, in assuring him that Abel's faith will not go unrewarded (although how it will be so is left obscure) lets slip the fact of death: "though here thou see him die, Rolling in dust and gore" (XI,459–60).

As spectator to a tragedy not his own, Adam could respond in a feeling yet restrained way to the moral issue involved: the apparent triumph of evil over good. Once informed that he is looking at the "death" that he knows awaits him as well, Adam loses all trace of detachment:

> But have I now seen Death? Is this the way
> I must return to native dust? O sight
> Of terror, foul and ugly to behold,
> Horrid to think, how horrible to feel! (XI,462–65)

In Adam's shock at the spectacle of Abel's murder, it is easy to recognize our own feelings toward death, stripped of their customary evasions. But Adam's naiveté also gives us a second perspective on the education he is receiving. It is not merely that we know more than Adam—such has often been the case before—but that what we know measures the distance he must come as a reader. While our feelings are with Adam, our intellect is with Michael. Without exaggeration, the angel's reply is one we ourselves could have spoken:

> Death thou hast seen
> In his first shape on man; but many shapes
> Of Death, and many are the ways that lead
> To his grim Cave, all dismal; yet to sense
> More terrible at th' entrance than within.
> Some, as thou saw'st, by violent stroke shall die,
> By Fire, Flood, Famine, by Intemperance more
> In Meats and Drinks, which on the Earth shall bring
> Diseases dire. . . . (XI,466–74)

Horrified at Abel's grisly fate, Adam has cried out against the excessive cruelty of death. What better time for Michael to reveal the blessing behind God's last and most forbidding curse? As God revealed to his Son

(and to us) back at the beginning of Book XI, death is a "final remedy" to
the sinful condition of mankind:

> I at first with two fair gifts
> Created him endow'd, with Happiness
> And Immortality: that fondly lost,
> This other serv'd but to eternize woe;
> Till I provided Death; so Death becomes
> His final remedy, and after Life
> Tri'd in sharp tribulation, and refin'd
> By Faith and faithful works, to second Life,
> Wak't in the renovation of the just,
> Resigns him up with Heav'n and Earth renew'd. (XI,57–66)

Yet Michael refrains from revealing all this to Adam. The obvious reason
for his silence on this point is that he has not reached the place in his
story when Adam can justly understand and appreciate the concept of
salvation and rebirth through the incarnation and crucifixion of the Son
of God. Before he could understand that, Adam would have to understand the inability of the Jews to keep the Mosaic commandments, an
understanding of which rests in turn on grasping the concept of a Chosen
People, which itself depends on the failure of the Flood to eradicate depravity, and so on back to the moment when Adam first sees brother turn
upon brother.

There is, in other words, a logic deeper than mere chronology in the
unfolding of Michael's story, just as there is a necessary sequence to the
ordering of events in *Paradise Lost* as a whole. By divine arrangement,
events unfold in human history *according to the needs of the reader's
evolving comprehension!* Just as Books I–X brought us from an unsatisfactory to a more satisfactory grasp of "God's ways to men," so Michael provides Adam (and God provides humanity) first with a full look at the
worst, as a necessary first step in his education. Michael's visions are
meant to provoke Adam to question God's justice, so that these most
serious and relevant objections can be answered.

Adam's (and the reader's) faith in God is being put on trial here.
Michael's second vision is the non-biblical one of a hospital, a "Lazar-
house," which Milton describes in a grim parody of epic catalog:

> Convulsions, Epilepsies, fierce Catarrhs,
> Intestine Stone and Ulcer, Colic pangs,

Daemoniac Frenzy, moping Melancholy
And Moon-struck madness, pining Atrophy,
Marasmus, and wide-wasting Pestilence,
Dropsies, and Asthmas, and Joint-racking Rheums. (XI,483–88)

At the end of this horrid spectacle (horrible to hear about, more horrible doubtless to view), it is small wonder if Adam questions God's justice:

Why is life giv'n
To be thus wrested from us? rather why
Obtruded on us thus? who if we knew
What we receive, would either not accept
Life offer'd, or soon beg to lay it down,
Glad to be so dismist in peace. (XI,502–507)

And he goes on to question not only the bare fact of death but the apparently gratuitous deformity and suffering that he has seen attending it. Such questioning is not merely natural or inevitable; it is dramatically and doctrinally essential. God's ways cannot be justified until they are questioned; until Adam has accused God not only of injustice but of downright cruelty, Michael cannot answer the charge without seeming to bring it as well. Michael's answer is one that we still hear today from Christian Scientists, yogis, and students of psychosomatic illness: sickness begins as a spiritual disorder. What Adam has just seen, Michael says, are both images of, and the natural consequences of, choosing evil over good. Disease, says Michael, is only one more form of self-punishment: "I yield it just, said Adam, and submit" (XI,526).

However, having shouldered his responsibility, Adam can ask the next question:

But is there yet no other way, besides
These painful passages, how we may come
To Death, and mix with our connatural dust? (XI,527–29)

Rather than surrendering to despair, Adam's faith has learned by this time to look more closely at an apparently hopeless situation. He cannot as yet imagine an alternative to painful death, yet he persists in hoping that one exists. And Michael rewards him with at least a limited mitigation. A temperate, self-respecting life, he says, will greatly lessen the torments of dying (XI,530–46). This hardly disposes of the problem of

suffering; what, the reader may ask, about diseases that strike the temperate? What about accidents that cripple the careful? What about birth
defects, inherited diseases, insanity? (What about blindness?) Yet there is
a good deal of truth in Michael's answer as well: much even of our physical fate rests in our own hands.

Over-impressed with the manifold possibilities of suffering, Adam
interprets death as a blessing only at the cost of seeing *life* as a curse:

> Henceforth I fly not Death, nor would prolong
> Life much, bent rather how I may be quit
> Fairest and easiest of this cumbrous charge,
> Which I must keep till my appointed day
> Of rend'ring up, and patiently attend
> My dissolution. (XI,547–52)

So, though he invokes patience and, in part, achieves it, he still has not
learned to read death perfectly and must be corrected again:

> Michael repli'd.
> Nor love thy Life, nor hate; but what thou liv'st
> Live well, how long or short permit to Heav'n. (XI,552–54)

No truly satisfactory understanding of death and its attendant sufferings
is possible without knowledge of eternal life, so the question of death is
bracketed for the time being. The bracketing is itself important, however; in remaining content with a partial answer, Adam is demonstrating
a growing mastery of reading's cardinal virtue, patience.

But Michael's tactic is to avoid Adam's newly won strength and to
play to his weaknesses. Since Adam has learned to look closely at apparently hopeless situations, the angel gives him an apparently hopeful one.
The sons of God are seduced by the daughters of men:

> they on the Plain
> Long had not walkt, when from the Tents behold
> A Bevy of fair Women, richly gay
> In Gems and wanton dress; to the Harp they sung
> Soft amorous Ditties, and in dance came on:
> The Men though grave, ey'd them, and let thir eyes
> Rove without rein, till in the amorous Net
> Fast caught, they lik'd, and each his liking chose;
> And now of love they treat till th' Ev'ning Star

Love's Harbinger appear'd; then all in heat
They light the nuptial Torch, and bid invoke
Hymen, then first to marriage Rites invok't;
With Feast and Music all the Tents resound. (XI,580–92)

Armed with the interpretive aid of Milton's style ("wanton dress," "amorous Net," etc.) we have no difficulty seeing through the seeming attractions of this tableau. Adam is not so fortunately placed as we, however. Trusting his eyes overmuch, he interprets poorly:

True opener of mine eyes, prime Angel blest,
Much better seems this Vision, and more hope
Of peaceful days portends, than those two past;
Those were of hate and death, or pain much worse,
Here Nature seems fulfill'd in all her ends. (XI,598–602)

Michael (Adam's "reliable narrator") has to correct Adam not once but twice. "Judge not what is best By pleasure" (XI,603–04), he first warns, and he goes on to unmask the daughters of men as "empty of all good" (XI,616). To which Adam replies by reverting to an earlier misogyny: "still I see the tenor of Man's woe Holds on the same, from Woman to begin" (XI,632–33). But just as God would not let Adam blame his transgression on Eve (Book X), so now Michael ends Adam's attempt to evade responsibility for his own error of judgment: "From Man's effeminate slackness it begins" (XI,634).

Michael has been teaching Adam—or helping him teach himself—how to respond to a story: to perceive his own responsibility for its interpretation and to look for the interpretation consistent with both man's continuing freedom of choice and God's continuing love for his erring creatures. (Michael's very presence is eloquent testimony to this last fact for Adam, as is the existence of the Bible and of *Paradise Lost* for us.) Although up to now Adam's only adequate response to his reading has been to acknowledge the inadequacies of his initial responses, he has been learning his lessons, as his reaction to Michael's next vision makes clear. Michael shows Adam a panorama of what Milton might ironically have called "public life": men killing and being killed, while others gravely plan more of the same. Echoes of the military magnificence of Hell in Book I are distinctly audible in the narrator's description of life on Earth:

With cruel Tournament the Squadrons join;
Where Cattle pastur'd late, now scatter'd lies
With Carcasses and Arms th' ensanguin'd Field
Deserted: Others to a City strong
Lay Siege, encampt; by Battery, Scale, and Mine,
Assaulting; others from the wall defend
With Dart and Jav'lin, Stones and sulphurous Fire;
On each hand slaughter and gigantic deeds. (XI,652–59)

In this scene of vainglorious inhumanity, only one man (Enoch) remembers his duty to God and to his fellow man, speaking "much of Right and Wrong, of Justice, of Religion, Truth And Peace, and Judgment from above" (XI,666–68). Predictably, the violence is turned against him, and he is saved only by divine intervention.

Adam is learning fast. His reaction to this vision, insofar as it concerns man's inhumanity to man, cannot be improved upon by Michael, who can only embroider on what Adam has already said:

[Adam:]   O what are these,
Death's Ministers, not Men, who thus deal Death
Inhumanly to men, and multiply
Ten thousandfold the sin of him who slew
His Brother; for of whom such massacre
Make they but of thir Brethren, men of men? (XI,675–80)

. . . .

[Michael:]
For in those days Might only shall be admir'd,
And Valor and Heroic Virtue call'd;
To overcome in Battle, and subdue
Nations, and bring home spoils with infinite
Man-slaughter, shall be held the highest pitch
Of human Glory, and for Glory done
Of triumph, to be styl'd great Conquerors,
Patrons of Mankind, Gods, and Sons of Gods,
Destroyers rightlier call'd and Plagues of men. (XI,689–97)

On the further matter of Enoch's translation to Heaven, however, Adam needs more instruction: "But who was that Just Man, whom had not Heav'n Rescu'd, had in his Righteousness been lost?" (XI, 681–82). Michael's answer greatly expands his earlier hint that Abel would "Lose no reward" and gives Adam his first inkling of "Salvation":

> hee the sev'nth from thee, whom thou beheld'st
> The only righteous in a World perverse,
> And therefore hated, therefore so beset
> With Foes for daring single to be just,
> And utter odious Truth, that God would come
> To judge them with his Saints: Him the most High
> Rapt in a balmy Cloud with winged Steeds
> Did, as thou saw'st, receive, to walk with God
> High in Salvation and the Climes of bliss,
> Exempt from Death; to show thee what reward
> Awaits the good, the rest what punishment. (XI, 700–10)

As an example of the "one just Man" ("the only righteous in a world perverse") Enoch is the latest embodiment of a favorite Miltonic theme that began with Abdiel's refusal to follow Satan in Book V. Exemplary to Adam of the invincibility of faith, Enoch also prefigures (anticipates) Christ, both in his obedience to God and in his bodily translation to Heaven. Of this last matter Adam is, of course, still ignorant, but rather than encourage him in further questions on the subject, Michael hastens on to the story of Noah.

As Michael mediates the story of Noah to Adam, we get a foretaste of the shift in narrative method between Books XI and XII. That is, Adam is first *shown* the story of the Flood (ll. 712–53); then he is *told* that story again. Moreover, the story is interrupted at the moment when things look bleakest for humanity:

> now the thick'n'd Sky
> Like a dark Ceiling stood; down rush'd the Rain
> Impetuous, and continu'd till the Earth
> No more was seen; the floating Vessel swum
> Uplifted; and secure with beaked prow
> Rode tilting o'er the Waves, all dwellings else
> Flood overwhelm'd, and them with all thir pomp
> Deep under water roll'd; Sea cover'd Sea,
> Sea without shore; and in thir Palaces
> Where luxury late reign'd, Sea-monsters whelp'd
> And stabl'd; of Mankind, so numerous late,
> All left, in one small bottom swum embark't. (X, 742–53)

As if to show his own emotion, the hitherto impersonal narrator turns to address Adam as one would a companion:

How didst thou grieve then, Adam, to behold
The end of all thy Offspring, end so sad,
Depopulation: Thee another Flood,
Of tears and sorrow a Flood thee also drown'd,
And sunk thee as thy Sons; till gently rear'd
By th' Angel, on thy feet thou stood'st at last,
Though comfortless, as when a Father mourns
His Children, all in view destroy'd at once. (XI,754–61)

The narrator's tone suggests an intimacy, even identification, with Adam
that the reader may have difficulty in matching. All of us are survivors of
the Flood, hence apt to be at least a little smug at the spectacle of God
wiping out virtually the whole human race: *we* at least were privileged to
escape. Yet, as the narrator's remarks emphasize, Adam's response to the
deed measures ours and finds it wanting—whatever good has come of it,
the fact itself is utter tragedy, the failure of all human effort and aspiration. Adam's collapse and tears at this failure are therefore in some ways
a "better" response than ours, armed as we are by the tranquilizing foreknowledge that man will survive. Man survives, but not by becoming
better. "I had hope," says Adam:

When violence was ceas't, and War on Earth,
All would have then gone well, peace would have crown'd
With length of happy days the race of man;
But I was far deceiv'd; for now I see
Peace to corrupt no less than War to waste. (XI,779–84)

Adam's observation is as true of the post- as of the antediluvian world, as
Michael's answer demonstrates:

                    Those whom last thou saw'st
In triumph and luxurious wealth, are they
First seen in acts of prowess eminent
And great exploits, but of true virtue void. . . . (XI,787–90)
    .   .   .   .

The conquer'd also, and enslav'd by War
Shall with thir freedom lost all virtue lose
And fear of God, from whom thir piety feign'd
In sharp contést of Battle found no aid
Against invaders; therefore cool'd in zeal
Thenceforth shall practice how to live secure,

Worldly or dissolute, on what thir Lords
Shall leave them to enjoy; for th' Earth shall bear
More than anough, that temperance may be tri'd:
So all shall turn degenerate, all deprav'd,
Justice and Temperance, Truth and Faith forgot;
One man except. . . . (XI,797–808)

The "One man" is Noah (but he could as easily be Christ, who found the
world as degenerate after the Flood as Noah did before it), or he could
be anyone today looking at the human condition. The narrator's momentary identification with Adam suggests that as readers we are no less detached from Michael's story than Adam, that its message of woe is as
applicable to our lives as it is to his.

But this is only half the picture, and Adam's wish that he had lived
ignorant of biblical history (ll. 763–76), though natural enough in the
context of what he has just seen, is premature. His response, "right"
though it is in grieving for a world full of men and women unwilling to
love God, is "wrong" to overlook the fact that one man has escaped that
general fate. In his despair, he assumes that one man cannot survive
where a world has perished. The problem is that Adam is *seeing* this
story, hence missing its inwardness, which is not visible. Michael corrects
that problem by *telling* the story again, this time stressing Noah's godli-
ness. Michael's narrative succeeds in doing what Adam's vision failed to
do: it reveals Noah's outward destiny as a function of his spiritual condition.

Thanks to the narrative method, Michael now can point out that the
Ark was built because Noah was just and therefore deserving of surviving
the general cataclysm (ll. 808–21). Hence, when the angel completes
Adam's vision by showing Noah landing safe on dry land once again,
Adam is no longer in doubt about what that landing means—not just the
bare survival of the occupants of the Ark but a judgment by God that the
human race is worthy of continuing:

Far less I now lament for one whole World
Of wicked Sons destroy'd, than I rejoice
For one Man found so perfet and so just,
That God voutsafes to raise another World
From him, and all his anger to forget. (XI,874–78)

Adam has learned to read the *inwardness* of a biblical event: not merely
what it means as an event in human history (Noah will survive) but what

it means as a sign of God's unfolding will (God resolves to let Noah's worth redeem human depravity). Since he correctly understands God's will, Adam has no great difficulty interpreting even a mute natural phenomenon like the rainbow as a sign of that will. "To Adam," says Stanley Fish:

> the rainbow might have signified any number of things, if he had sought its meaning on the surface or made it the reflection of his own small faith. . . . Instead he *chooses*—there is no other word for it—to see in it the signification a merciful God must have intended.[6]

When we know God's will, we know all we need to know. Michael approves Adam's intuition—"Dext'rously thou aim'st"—and confirms it with proleptic knowledge:

> So willingly doth God remit his Ire,
> Though late repenting him of Man deprav'd,
> Griev'd at his heart, when looking down he saw
> The whole Earth fill'd with violence, and all flesh
> Corrupting each thir way; yet those remov'd,
> Such grace shall one just Man find in his sight,
> That he relents, not to blot out mankind,
> And makes a Cov'nant never to destroy
> The Earth again by flood, nor let the Sea
> Surpass his bounds, nor Rain to drown the World
> With Man therein or Beast; but when he brings
> Over the Earth a Cloud, will therein set
> His triple-color'd Bow, whereon to look
> And call to mind his Cov'nant: Day and Night,
> Seed-time and Harvest, Heat and hoary Frost
> Shall hold thir course, till fire purge all things new,
> Both Heav'n and Earth, wherein the just shall dwell. (XI,884–901)

After a beginning so unpromising that we can scarcely believe he survived it, Adam's course of reading has become a staggering success. From the first, he proved the kind of audience every author hopes to have: fully attentive, entirely serious, totally *involved* in what he saw and heard. This very involvement, though a necessary condition for understanding (Adam had to see that he was watching *his own* story) was also his greatest obstacle, however, for it produced in him such initial discouragement and despair that without the angel's help he might never have read further. Yet each time the evidence of things seen perplexed his faith in God, the angel was there to help him interpret more justly.

Just as significant as what Michael does, however, is what he does not do. He never comments on Adam's emotional or spiritual condition, and he especially never *exhorts* Adam to take a particular attitude toward what he shows him. In each case, after a vision is presented, it is Adam who freely responds to it. Michael's corrections never correct the response but the evidence upon which that response is based; his invariable assumption is that, given the proper information, Adam will respond correctly. Even his apparent rebuke: "Judge not what is best By pleasure" (XI,603–04), corrects not Adam's pleasure but his judgment. Adam's interpretation is not evil or corrupt; it is simply *inaccurate*. It does not, as he thinks, portend "hope Of peaceful days" (XI,599–600). In a fallen world, as Adam learns, appearances can deceive.

Though Michael is there to help Adam over the hurdles, what really sustains Adam is something he has already brought to the biblical lesson—faith in God. This faith Michael could not have given Adam had the latter lacked it; furthermore, without it the angel's lessons would have been meaningless. Michael's answers, at first a convenience in overcoming Adam's naiveté ("have I now seen Death?"), soon become little more than courteous expansions of "wait and see." Do the marriages of the sons of God to the daughters of men portend peaceful days? "Wait and see." Does death await Noah and his little ménage? "Wait and see." In each case, the next vision answers the question asked.

There are, in short, paradoxes surrounding Michael's presence and role in *Paradise Lost*. It has no basis in the Genesis account of Adam and Eve; hence Milton must have added it for a specific purpose. In his marvelously precise calculations of what constitutes divine justice, Milton clearly believed that a regenerate Adam and Eve could not have been justly expelled from Eden without a compensatory revelation of the promised redeemer and the paradise within. Yet that revelation could have taken place offstage and been merely summarized in the text. If Michael and Adam go on at such length in Milton's text, it is because they are saying things we need to hear. Michael's mission is ultimately to *us*.

Yet Michael's visions are familiar scenes from Genesis, with which we are presumably already familiar. No angel need come from Heaven to tell us that Cain slew Abel or that Noah survived a flood. Michael's presence is felt, rather, in his *interpretations* of these visions; he is a fellow "reader" of the visions he mediates to Adam—and a reader of a particular sort. As his "wait and see" strategy shows, Michael knows what lies ahead. While Adam is the Bible's naive reader, who experiences each moment of the human history that it chronicles as the final illumination of the mysteries of God's will, Michael reads with an awareness that what comes on the next page will alter our view of what we have read on this one.

Neither Adam's point of view nor Michael's coincides entirely with the reader's growing response to the visions of human history that the angel provides. In Book XI they represent, rather, the two sides of a dialectical process of reading that takes place inside every reader. Adam raises all of our questions about God's justice: its compatibility with suffering, with death, and with the kind of "anger" that can destroy almost an entire world of human beings. The depth of Adam's feeling for his variously erring and slaughtered progeny is an implicit criticism of our own mistaken belief that what we are witnessing is safely in the past (every instance of vice and suffering that Adam sees is occurring at this moment somewhere in our world as well) and an invitation to abandon our detachment to experience freshly the tragedy of being fallen. But though Adam's naiveté distinguishes his point of view from ours (and we frequently find that we silently have to correct his appraisal of a situation with a foreknowledge similar to Michael's), the angel's serene calm in the face of human misfortune and divine inscrutability is not an attitude that we can entirely adopt or would even wish to adopt.

While Adam reads the Bible front-to-back, we might say that Michael reads it back-to-front. Adam reads as human beings must; Michael does not negate but rather alters and completes Adam's interpretation by reading as God illumines. The complete reading is neither Adam's nor Michael's but our own: the aim of proper reading, the poem implies, is to blend the two voices of human experience in time and divine foreknowledge. Milton's poem provides these voices, but we blend them to make the poem's meaning.

The pause between Books XI and XII signals a change in narrative method. Though Book XI has seemed static and talky to many readers, it is enlivened at least by the vividness of Michael's visual tableaux and by the drama of Adam's variously shocked and elated responses. As we move toward the poem's end, however, one poetic device after another is shut down. With the end of Book XI comes the end also of the "spectacle" of

Adam's visions, at which so sensitive a reader as Joseph Addison complains that Milton is like a painter who finishes half his picture and writes down the other half in words.

Such dissatisfaction is not merely common; it is practically inevitable. Not only do the visions stop, but so does the (at times) lively interchange between Adam and Michael and the pathos of Adam's vicarious suffering for his progeny. Michael's narrating voice becomes a drone, and ennui is a constant threat. Clearly the literary expectations of most readers are frustrated by the poetic manner of Book XII. The question is, if the ending forces us to change our expectations, does this mean that the poem has failed?

The answer to this question is, I believe, "no." To end his brilliantly original poem, Milton had both to arouse and to frustrate conventional expectations of many kinds. Yet Addison's comparison of *Paradise Lost* to a half-finished painting is apt. If Milton completed only half his picture, then, it may well be that he expected his reader to share the work with him. He now wants *us* to supply much of the imagination and judgment previously provided by the poem's "grand style." As if he were handing the paintbrush to us, Milton invites us to participate in the making of his picture; by leaving his canvas so bare and functional, he implies that the old role of spectator will no longer prove very satisfying.

We leave the role of spectator to become a participant in the action of *Paradise Lost* by identifying more closely with Adam. The eighteenth-century critic Jonathan Richardson has said that at the end of *Paradise Lost* we stand on even ground with Adam, unable to look down upon him as our inferior either in knowledge or in virtue. The remark, though just, does not go far enough. In Book XII we *become* Adam and supply, from our own imagination and memory, information about his inner life that the poem itself studiously omits. In Adam's silences we begin to assume the role of respondent to Michael's revelations and to supply an inner life to Adam from our own inner life. The poem's tactic is a daring one, for it demands a considerable effort from the reader. Those who make the effort, however, will be rewarded with ecstasy and enlightenment like Adam's own.

When Michael replaces Adam's visions of biblical history with narration, he brings the reader a step closer to Adam: no longer does Adam see what we merely read about; henceforth we share the same text. Yet our new intimacy with Adam is not heightened by a greater expressiveness on his part. As the "text" of biblical history flattens in Book XII, Adam's responses also become less emphatic. He abandons the adversary role of questioner and doubter and recedes into the background as adjunct narrator or yes-man. We might say that—for a while, at least—Adam's most striking contribution to his own education is his *silence*. The first instance of this silence is emphasized by the poem itself:

> As one who in his journey bates at Noon,
> Though bent on speed, so here the Arch-Angel paus'd
> Betwixt the world destroy'd and world restor'd,
> If Adam aught perhaps might interpose;
> Then with transition sweet new Speech resumes. (XII,1–5)

These lines were added to the second edition of *Paradise Lost* (1674), when Milton divided the old Book X into the present Books XI and XII. The effect of ending one book and starting the next is to create a perceived pause in the progress of the story. The pause is itself a kind of "silence," in which for a moment the reader's mind is filled with its own thoughts rather than the poem's words. The pause that Milton introduced into the poem at this point invites the reader to recognize the congruence between his own mind and Adam's, both speechless.

But this silence is also one of the obvious blank places on Milton's canvas that we are invited to try painting in. What is on Adam's mind? Both the narrator and Michael mention endings and beginnings; both describe the ways of God to men as finely poised between destruction and restoration. Adam has already noticed this pattern in the story of Noah and has accepted the price humanity must pay for its regeneration: "Far less I now lament for one whole World Of wicked Sons destroy'd, than I rejoice For one Man found so perfet and so just . . . " (XI, 874–876). What can have caused his new, silent amazement but Michael's glancing, almost casual revelation that Noah's Flood prefigures another, even more significant destruction: "till fire purge all things new, Both Heav'n and Earth, wherein the just shall dwell" (XI,900–01). In Noah's physical salvation, Michael allows us to glimpse a future, more definitive Salvation. We see it well enough; does Adam? Does salvation apply to the first as well as to all subsequent sinners? It almost certainly does, as I have already argued. Does Adam glimpse this possibility in a wild surmise that remains for the moment silent? We shall never know for certain, and yet the poem invites us to fill Adam's mind with such thoughts.

The change that Michael now announces—from visual to aural narration—may come as a disappointment to readers like Addison, who like
the poet to do all the work, but Michael represents it as a mark of favor:

> Much thou hast yet to see, but I perceive
> Thy mortal sight to fail; objects divine
> Must needs impair and weary human sense:
> Henceforth what is to come I will relate,
> Thou therefore give due audience, and attend. (XII,8–12)

We are by now familiar enough with the poem's play with the verb "to
see," which paradoxically can mean either a physical act of viewing or a
spiritual act of understanding generally enhanced by the *absence* of
physical sight. Like Gloucester in *King Lear*, Adam "stumbled when he
saw." Left to the mind's eye, he will see Michael's meaning better and, in
case we miss the point, will repeatedly hereafter assert that he "sees"
what the angel is telling him. Like the epic poet, who had to be blinded
in order to sing of things invisible to mortal sight, "Adam's spiritual vision
grows keener as his physical sight declines."[7] But does ours?

Michael does seem at this point to be talking over Adam's head to us
as well. His comment on the change of narrative mode also hints at a new
aesthetic principle for *Paradise Lost* itself, whose normal poetic appeal to
human sense has left its reader weary and too often confused about "objects divine." The reader has, of course, been limited to words since the
beginning; he has never literally *seen* the events of *Paradise Lost* as Adam
saw the six visions of Book XI. Yet the analogy seems a reasonable one to
draw: Michael's shift in narrative method marks a decline in sensuous
vividness for us as well as for Adam; it is at least likely that we are meant
to participate in its good effects as well as he.

As the narrative resumes, however, it is the weariness rather than
the good effect that we most easily perceive. Life after the Flood is
mostly a stale copy of life before the Flood. Noah's progeny preserve for
a while their forebear's uprightness, but they keep a low profile and don't
arouse much enthusiasm in us. The verse doubtless creates much of the
monotony of this passage, but it is also the banality of a life of tilling the
soil and slitting the throats of dumb animals that almost makes us welcome Nimrod's appearance and a return to bloody drama. Yet even here
we are disappointed: Nimrod is not just an evocation of Satan; he is a

threadbare imitation, while his generalized manslaughter lacks the punch even of Cain's rustic fratricide.

The entire passage (XII,13–62) has for us the staleness of *déjà vu*. It tells Adam that life will be very much the same after the Flood as before, and it stirs up in our minds additional memories—the building of Pandaemonium in Book I, the rebellion of Satan in Book V—but this time robbed of their poetic and dramatic heightening. The whole thing seems . . . well, tawdry and futile. Even the Tower of Babel—built with bricks and "black bituminous gurge" (XII,41)—seems to rise no higher than a pile of mud off of this flat plain of words. Like Satan's attempt to rise out of Hell, this act of rebellion is rewarded with the gift of confusion. Human language itself, until then apparently the same tongue as Adam and Eve spoke in the Garden, becomes itself a fallen and defective instrument. Thus Babel stands for us as an emblem of all human enterprise: the failure of man's words no less than of his deeds; the failure of poetry, perhaps even of *Paradise Lost* itself, written by a fallen poet, who aspires to rise to Heaven through his own efforts, in a fallen language for a fallen audience living in an age no better than Nimrod's:

> each to other calls
> Not understood, till hoarse, and all in rage,
> As mockt they storm; great laughter was in Heav'n
> And looking down, to see the hubbub strange
> And hear the din; thus was the building left
> Ridiculous, and the work Confusion nam'd. (XII,57–62)

What are we to make of all this futility and prosy banality? It may be, as many have conjectured, that Milton himself was getting tired of his poem, but the effect is not one of inadvertence, and I rather think that he was trying to make *us* tired of it. The Tower of Babel episode is *adroitly* oppressive, building cacophonous sound up to a roaring crescendo when it suddenly, frighteningly turns into divine laughter: "a hideous gabble rises loud . . . each to other calls . . . hoarse, and all in rage, . . . they storm; great laughter was in Heav'n" (XII, 56 –59). Is it this riot of ugly sound that makes us uncomfortable, or the anxiety that God may be laughing at us and our works, too? Probably it is both.

The Nimrod-Babel passage is the stuff of epic robbed of its art. Heroic action, this passage seems to say, when stripped of its rhetorical and prosodic ornaments, is pretty dull. Good, as portrayed in the uneventful lives of Noah's progeny, is outwardly dull, but so is evil—bloody but predictable, futile, and ridiculous. As readers we can deal with boredom in several ways. We can read rapidly and inattentively, but such a strategy is more an admission of our problem than a solution to it: we won't find what we're looking for up ahead. As we skip along, we will find Adam repeating the lesson Michael has just taught (no man has a right to rule his brothers), and Michael in turn expatiating on it once again. The poem is repeating and re-repeating itself, and all to make a point—"Tyranny must be"—that if not entirely obvious could have been made in some brief or vivid fashion. Yet if we read more slowly, looking for "deeper" meanings, we will be only further demoralized by what we find: good degenerates inevitably into evil; the works of men's hands and words are futile; tyranny is as much an indictment of the subject as of the ruler; God laughs at man's attempts at escape. Even the self-referential aspect of this passage—the banality of epic story, the futility of epic aspirations—counts against the poem we are reading and our motives for reading it. The longer we linger over this part of the poem the worse we will feel.

Adam's indignation at Nimrod (XII, 64–78) is, I suppose, a slight refreshment in this airless atmosphere, but not enough. Doubtless he feels these things sincerely, but he only repeats what Michael has already said (XII, 25–32). And Adam is naive, as Michael goes on to point out, to think that Nimrod is the real source of the problem: a man whose passions rule his reason is already a slave; unable to rule himself, he will inevitably become a subject, and in his external servitude make his inner subjection visible (XII, 83–96). Though we might like to share Adam's innocent indignation, we cannot.

In sum, what the first hundred lines of Book XII do is to perfect the picture of life after the Fall as Hell-on-Earth and to project it through repetition into an indefinite future. They simply add to the murder, disease, lust, hatred, and impiety of Book XI the final touch: *men* make Earth a Hell for themselves and for their fellows; they can't help it. No law or prison or purge will wall the enemy out, for we are the enemy. Like Hell, this vision is hopeless and therefore boring. Never before has Milton's poem left us without choices; now at last we seem deprived of all choice, since tyranny *must* be. Even God is finally bored:

> Thus will this latter, as the former World,
> Still tend from bad to worse, till God at last

Wearied with their iniquities, withdraw
His presence from among them, and avert
His holy Eyes; resolving from thenceforth
To leave them to thir own polluted ways. (XII, 105–10)

Milton seems to be using boredom itself as a way of influencing his reader. At the very least, the ennui of a fallen world can make us yearn for regeneration; at best, it can be dispelled by an active faith that God will not leave mankind in such a wretched state.

Though Adam's response to the Nimrod-Babel passage is not a particularly fresh or illuminating one, it does give us an example of what a spiritually regenerate reader can be expected to glean from so unpromising a tract of biblical revelation. More important than his superfluous (though warm-hearted) indignation against Nimrod, or his naive observation that the men building the tower will run out of food and air (as if these practical obstacles constituted the project's chief foolishness), is Adam's silence on matters that have previously perplexed him. Adam's response merely marks time, manifesting an inner state by words whose chief function is to display not so much faith and hope as a lack of doubt and despair. In the next part of Michael's narration Adam will remain for a long time silent, while we will have to play his role of respondent.

As the angel resumes his story, things have not improved outwardly in the least. Men, who have fallen to worshiping sticks and stones, have degenerated to such a point that even the "imperturbable" Michael breaks out in a very Adam-like (and rather amusing) indignation:

O that men
(Canst thou believe?) should be so stupid grown
While yet the Patriarch liv'd, who scapt the Flood,
As to forsake the living God, and fall
To worship thir own work in Wood and Stone
For Gods! (XII, 115–20)

God's decision to become the god of "one peculiar Nation" (XII, 111), instead of all humanity, should rationally be seen as a further retreat, yet in contrast to what has happened since Noah's Flood it seems genuinely hopeful. Desperate situations call for desperate remedies, and immersed as we are in Hell-on-Earth, we are desperate enough to see hope in God's reviving interest in mankind and to feel a small but reviving interest in Michael's story.

Yet the basis of our interest has shifted from man's activities to God's plans. The verse remains as flat after Abraham's appearance as before; the story remains as dull. With a wealth of good biblical material to pick from, Milton stays as far as he can from normal narrative interest. He skirts, for example, right around the gripping biblical story of how Abraham, in obedience to a divine command, nearly slit the throat of his only son, Isaac. That story would work beautifully as a further example of heroism through faith and would further demonstrate how events in the Old Testament prefigure events in the New (Isaac is a type of Christ). Milton avoids it because it is too interesting; it would distract from what must be the one bright spot in an otherwise dark canvas, the fact of God's emerging plan of redemption.

Doubtless the reader supplies from his own memory much that Michael omits about Abraham, but what the angel harps on obsessively is not Abraham himself but the promise implicit in Abraham's seed:

> This ponder, that all Nations of the Earth
> Shall in his Seed be blessed; by that Seed
> Is meant thy great deliverer, who shall bruise
> The Serpent's head; whereof to thee anon
> Plainlier shall be reveal'd. (XII, 147–51)

In the next two hundred lines, Michael outlines biblical history from Abraham to Jesus in such a way as to make clear that the entire point of a millennium of human existence is to prepare for the appearance of the Seed and for the bruise he will give the Serpent's head. It is on this divine manipulation of human history that our attention is to be riveted from here on.

The story Michael tells shows no improvement in human nature or the human condition. Abraham's progeny injudiciously settle in Egypt, where Pharaoh (a type of Satan) makes them slaves. God must rescue them. Unable to read the "messages" brought him by Moses and Aaron, Pharaoh must be sent more potent "Signs" of God's will: vermine, plague, tempest, famine, and general slaughter of first-born sons. Finally compelled to release the Israelites, Pharaoh yearns (like Satan) for revenge but is covered by the waves of the Red Sea. The Jews linger in the desert and receive the tablets of the Law from Moses; then they enter Canaan.

Action proceeds on two levels here. On the level of human motive, nothing turns out as expected: the Jews enter Egypt as honored guests

only to be enslaved; they are released only to be pursued; attacked but
miraculously rescued; saved but prevented from entering the Promised
Land; given a set of laws that they are unable to obey. The "natural" curve
of events is consistently downward and must continually be reversed by
God, who sends rivers of blood (XII, 176), darkness at noon (XII, 187–88),
a Sun that stands still in Mid-Heaven (XII, 263), and of course the famous
Commandments (XII, 227–35).

The more significant level of action, then, is that of the Divine Will.
But here, too, the logic is at times perplexing: why does God allow his
Chosen People to be enslaved? why must they wander in the desert forty
years? why above all does he give them laws that they cannot obey? Milton's answer becomes clearest in the case of the Commandments:

> God from the Mount of Sinai, whose gray top
> Shall tremble, he descending, will himself
> In Thunder, Lightning and loud Trumpet's sound
> Ordain them Laws; part such as appertain
> To civil Justice, part religious Rites
> Of sacrifice, *informing them, by types*
> *And shadows, of that destin'd Seed to bruise*
> *The Serpent*, by what means he shall achieve
> Mankind's deliverance. (XII, 227–35; my italics)

God's laws, while of course meant to be taken at face value, also have a
deeper meaning that emerges only when one knows the end of the story;
the blood sacrifice of animals prefigures the sacrifice of God's Son on the
Cross. Reading with that foreknowledge, we are able to see patterns in
the story otherwise as invisible to us as to the participants: the deliverance from Egypt as a prefiguration of the deliverance from sin; the wandering in the desert as foreshadowing Jesus's sojourn in the same place;
and, above all, Moses as a type of Christ:

> the voice of God
> To mortal ear is dreadful; they beseech
> That Moses might report to them his will,
> And terror cease; he grants what they besought,
> Instructed that to God is no access
> Without Mediator, whose high Office now
> Moses in figure bears, to introduce
> One greater, of whose day he shall foretell,
> And all the Prophets in thir Age the times
> Of great Messiah shall sing. (XII, 235–44)

Moses, then, like all figures and events in the Old Testament, has two contradictory meanings. At the level of human motive, he is the man who led the Jews out of bondage but not into the Promised Land, who gave the Law but was unable to have it obeyed. But at the level of the Divine Plan he is the unwitting symbol of the man who will achieve for mankind what he, Moses, failed to do. If we read the story at the first level, Moses as a man is impressive but ultimately a failure; at the second level, both his success and failure are signposts pointing toward a great triumph still to come, of which he is himself ignorant. Adam shows signs of perplexity at this self-contradictory story:

> now first I find
> Mine eyes true op'ning, and my heart much eas'd,
> Erewhile perplext with thoughts what would become
> Of mee and all Mankind; but now I see
> His day, in whom all Nations shall be blest,
> Favor unmerited by me, who sought
> Forbidd'n knowledge by forbidd'n means.
> This yet I apprehend not, why to those
> Among whom God will deign to dwell on Earth
> So many and so various Laws are giv'n;
> So many Laws argue so many sins
> Among them; how can God with such reside? (XII,273–84)

God's plan for mankind seems to advance as much through failure as through success, just as an ocean wave advances through water that, though it rises and falls, itself never moves horizontally.

Adam's perplexed question is how God can regard as chosen a people who continually fail him. Michael's answer is a profoundly humiliating one—humiliating to Adam ("Doubt not but that sin Will reign among them, as of thee begot" [XII,285–86]) and by implication to all of us unable to obey the moral laws of Moses (XII,298–99). Even the greatest of men (like Moses) may achieve something utterly different from what they themselves suppose and are characters in a story written by an unseen hand, whose ending they cannot themselves even surmise. The Divine Plan works *in spite* of human nature, turning even our failures and defects to good use:

> So Law appears imperfet, and but giv'n
> With purpose to resign them in full time

Up to a better Cov'nant, disciplin'd
From shadowy Types to Truth, from Flesh to Spirit,
From imposition of strict Laws, to free
Acceptance of large Grace, from servile fear
To filial, works of Law to works of Faith.
And therefore shall not Moses, though of God
Highly belov'd, being but the Minister
Of Law, his people into Canaan lead;
But Joshua whom the Gentiles Jesus call,
His Name and Office bearing, who shall quell
The adversary Serpent, and bring back
Through the world's wilderness long wander'd man
Safe to eternal Paradise of rest. (XII,300–314)

The net result of the Egyptian adventure for God's Chosen People is
nothing more than a return to where they were a century earlier. To
counterbalance the suffering they have endured, they have only one
thing to show, a closer relationship to their God, as symbolized in the Ten
Commandments and in the Ark of the Covenant (XII,251; XII,333). That
relationship does not lead to a lasting improvement in their spiritual or
moral condition, however, and so does not protect them from a repetition
of the same dreary cycle of bondage as before: the Babylonian captivity
(XII,344–47) and the Roman conquest (XII,358) only duplicate the sorry
experience of Egyptian enslavement and hence can be skimmed over by
the poem.

What emerges, in short, from Michael's rapidly accelerating sweep
down the millennia of Old Testament history, is that at the level of human
motive and aspiration, history is a meaningless cycle of degeneration and
defeat. Even among the Chosen People, progress is inevitably downward, except when God intervenes to save the Jews from their newest
predicament and sends them forth again to a new cycle of decline.
Clearly God does not intervene for their sake but because of a Plan he
has in mind, of which they have only a misconception, believing as they
do that the promised Messiah, sprung from the seed of Abraham and the
line of David, will one day make the Jews rulers of the Earth, as in their
day the Egyptians, Babylonians, Persians, Greeks, and Romans have
been.

The only progress being made is at the level of the Divine Plan, and
here the shocking fact is that human history, when it is not a compendium
of negative instances (i.e., the inability of the Jews, even with repeated

divine intercession, to live godly lives), is simply an allegory written by
an unseen hand, whose meaning the participants cannot grasp! Joshua
leads the Jews into Canaan because his *name* prefigures that of Jesus;
Israel is allowed to fall under Roman rule so that "the true Anointed King
Messiah might be born Barr'd of his right" (XII,358–60).

Read in this way, the functional differences between history and fiction disappear. Not only the Bible but the people and events of which it
speaks are "written" by the hand of God for a reader who does not yet
exist; not until they learn the Messiah's name will readers be able to
understand why Moses did not lead the Israelites into the Promised
Land. Salvation lies in interpretation: like *Paradise Lost*, human history
is itself "written" as it is in order to produce a particular effect.

Its effect upon Adam hovers between joy and tears:

> [Michael] ceas'd, discerning Adam with such joy
> Surcharg'd, as had like grief been dew'd in tears,
> Without the vent of words, which these he breath'd. (XII,372–74)

It is common knowledge that in their extremes, the effects of joy and
grief resemble each other closely, perhaps for merely physiological reasons. But the link between Adam's joy and grief implies a meaning beyond physiology. Extreme joy is a product of suddenness—one is surprised by a happy event where none was expected. The attendant grief
comes from a suddenly renewed appreciation of the appalling plight one
has narrowly escaped. Safe on the shores of deliverance, as it were, one
watches in horror as the ghost of oneself recedes down the path to perdition.

This is what I believe happens to Adam. As he says, he has "searcht
in vain" (XII,377) for the answer to the riddle contained in God's curse
on the Serpent. Now he sees the inconceivable solution to an impossible
problem: those apparent opposites, God and man, will merge in woman's
Seed, and thus will a man, Satan's victim, also be Satan's superior and
conqueror:

> Virgin Mother, Hail,
> High in the love of Heav'n, yet from my Loins
> Thou shalt proceed, and from thy Womb the Son
> Of God most High; So God with man unites. (XII,379–83)

The notion of God-man, as contradictory as tears of joy, is harder by far to comprehend; and his victory over Satan will be as paradoxical as his nature. Adam, expecting literal strokes of head and heel, must be disabused by Michael:

> Dream not of thir fight,
> As of a Duel, or the local wounds
> Of head or heel: not therefore joins the Son
> Manhood to Godhead, with more strength to foil
> Thy enemy; nor so is overcome
> Satan, whose fall from Heav'n, a deadlier bruise,
> Disabl'd not to give thee thy death's wound:
> Which hee, who comes thy Savior, shall recure,
> Not by destroying Satan, but his works
> In thee and in thy Seed. (XII,386–95)

Winning his victory through love (not hate), "bruising" Satan by restoring Satan's victims, winning a crown of thorns and a criminal's death, "slain for bringing Life" (XII,414), this Savior's life and death is a system of contradictions that must elicit both tears and joy:

> thy punishment
> He shall endure by coming in the Flesh
> To a reproachful life and cursed death,
> Proclaiming Life to all who shall believe
> In his redemption, and that his obedience
> Imputed becomes theirs by Faith, his merits
> To save them, not thir own, though legal works.
> For this he shall live hated, be blasphem'd,
> Seiz'd on by force, judg'd, and to death condemn'd
> A shameful and accurst, nail'd to the Cross
> By his own Nation, slain for bringing Life;
> But to the Cross he nails thy Enemies,
> The Law that is against thee, and the sins
> Of all mankind, with him there crucifi'd,
> Never to hurt them more who rightly trust
> In this his satisfaction; so he dies,
> But soon revives, Death over him no power
> Shall long usurp; ere the third dawning light
> Return, the Stars of Morn shall see him rise
> Out of his grave, fresh as the dawning light,

Thy ransom paid, which Man from death redeems,
His death for Man. . . . (XII,404–25)

Michael foretells the career of the Messiah, with special attention to his good effects upon "all who shall believe In his redemption," among whom Adam is specifically included: "this God-like act Annuls thy doom, the death thou shouldst have di'd, In sin forever lost from life" (XII, 427–29). The redemption and salvation of which Michael speaks, then, is both general to the race and specific to Adam, who, like each of us, is offered the chance to believe in Jesus Christ and be restored to Paradise: "for then the Earth Shall all be Paradise, far happier place Than this of Eden, and far happier days" (XII,463–65). Not necessarily saved, since his life has only begun, Adam is clearly eligible for salvation: like us, he has a Savior.

Michael pauses to let Adam respond. Adam's response comes with a fervor that demonstrates his own personal involvement in the promise of redemption and his comprehension of the active role that faith must play. In his joy he sees at last (and helps us to see) that the Fall, Original Sin, despite all of its ghastly and tragic effects, is itself a paradox, a happy fault:

> O goodness infinite, goodness immense!
> That all this good of evil shall produce,
> And evil turn to good; more wonderful
> Than that which by creation first brought forth
> Light out of darkness! full of doubt I stand,
> Whether I should repent me now of sin
> By mee done and occasion'd, or rejoice
> Much more, that much more good thereof shall spring,
> To God more glory, more good will to Men
> From God, and over wrath grace shall abound. (XII,469–78)

Adam has good reason for wondering whether he should repent or rejoice at his Fall. Original Sin will be (has been) on the one hand a staggering tragedy. As the summary of biblical history in Books XI and XII makes clear, the mass of humanity before the Incarnation makes no effort to love God and has little to hope from his Son; even after the coming of Jesus most nominal Christians do not seem, in the poem's account, to have attained the requisite faith and love. And what of the millions of souls in Africa, Asia, and America who never even *heard* of their

Redeemer? For the majority of his progeny, Adam's fault remains a mortal stroke that has not only consigned them to live a Hell on Earth but has apparently delivered their immortal souls to everlasting torment.

Yet paradoxically the effects of Original Sin also include the merging of man and God in the person of the Messiah and the promise of the restoration of humanity to a state nearer divinity than that of Adam and Eve before the Fall. Though not in the way Eve anticipated, the final result of eating the forbidden fruit will be, at least for some, a nearer approach to "godhead" than the state of innocence offered. Moreover, unlike Calvin, Milton did not believe that individual souls are foredoomed by God to salvation or perdition; as the poem makes clear, the choice between these two destinies rests with each of us. In making that choice, each of us, starting with Adam, writes the end of his own story. For us, as for Adam, the story of man's Fall and redemption is either tragic or comic depending on *how we respond to it.*

Adam now understands that Satan's bruise and mankind's victory will not be manifested initially by outward triumph but in internal difference. And so, as in the case of the rainbow that ended Book XI, he anticipates the next chapter of the story: won't those who follow the Messiah be persecuted as he was himself? "Be sure they will, said th' Angel" (XII, 485). We have already recognized in Milton's description of pre-Christian history the same world that we know. We have had, since Christ's coming, our own Pharaohs and Nimrods, our own wars, famines, pestilences, and deaths of every description: "so shall the World go on," as Michael now puts it, "To good malignant, to bad men benign, Under her own weight groaning" (XII,537–39). But Michael now dwells on the trials of faith to which believers will be subjected, as epitomized in the corruption of the Church itself, which, like all earthly institutions, *must* become corrupt. Michael's last warning is against the Church as an institution that tries to deprive the individual believer of the freedom to listen to God's voice directly within himself and to interpret God's will by the lights of his own faith and reason:

> Then shall they seek to avail themselves of names,
> Places and titles, and with these to join
> Secular power, though feigning still to act
> By spiritual, to themselves appropriating
> The Spirit of God, promis'd alike and giv'n
> To all Believers; and from that pretense,

> Spiritual Laws by carnal power shall force
> On every conscience; Laws which none shall find
> Left them inroll'd, or what the Spirit within
> Shall on the heart engrave. What will they then
> But force the Spirit of Grace itself, and bind
> His consort Liberty; what, but unbuild
> His living Temples, built by Faith to stand,
> Thir own Faith not another's: for on Earth
> Who against Faith and Conscience can be heard
> Infallible? (XII,515–30)

But by the same token, God has arranged for all those who believe in him and in his Son to be inspired by an indwelling faith sufficient to rise above these as above all other obstacles:

> Hee to his own a Comforter will send,
> The promise of the Father, who shall dwell
> His Spirit within them, and the Law of Faith
> Working through love, upon thir hearts shall write,
> To guide them in all truth. . . . (XII,486–90)

Ultimately, after all human souls have been tested in the crucible of the fallen world, the Messiah will return to judge all and to restore the faithful to a new paradise on earth. In the meantime, however, they must seek their paradise within themselves.

Not every question has been answered, as Adam acknowledges in a statement that seems to suggest that we, too, recognize the poem's limitations and inconsistencies as in fact our own:

> Greatly instructed I shall hence depart,
> Greatly in peace of thought, and have my fill
> Of knowledge, what this Vessel can contain;
> Beyond which was my folly to aspire. (XII,557–60)

Milton's visionary poem and Christian epic offers us at its close, in the example of Adam, a clear rejection of the cosmic sweep and heroic grandeur with which it began. First by a series of shocks, then by insensible stages, it has led us to what amounts to a complete reversal of the worldly norms of epic in Adam's exemplary affirmation of humility and obedience to God's will:

Henceforth I learn, that to obey is best,
And love with fear the only God, to walk
As in his presence, ever to observe
His providence, and on him sole depend,
Merciful over all his works. . . . (XII,561–65)

The formulaic expressions—"love with fear the only God," "walk as in his presence"—show that the speaker places clarity even higher than ecstasy as a response to the providential beauty of God's ordering of human destiny. Yet as Adam's valedictory speech these words are not only endowed with the dignity of finality but are also embedded in personal experience of the profoundest sort. Every phrase echoes in our memories as emblematic of some phase of Adam's grueling experience: "to obey is best" evoking the Fall; "love with fear" expressing Adam's supreme difficulty in believing in God's continuing love for his fallen creatures; "ever to observe his providence" evoking the entire series of reversals whereby apparent curses were revealed as actual blessings.

Most of all, this final speech expresses Adam's final comprehension and acceptance of the transformations, the spiritual metamorphoses, out of which the life of fallen but regenerate mankind is built:

with good
Still overcoming evil, and by small
Accomplishing great things, by things deem'd weak
Subverting worldly strong, and worldly wise
By simply meek; that suffering for Truth's sake
Is fortitude to highest victory,
And to the faithful Death the Gate of Life;
Taught this by his example whom I now
Acknowledge my Redeemer ever blest. (XII,565–73)

This speech rings strangely as heroic peroration. Adam strikes no pose, assumes no lofty attitude; he even makes, for so personal a statement, very little reference to himself. We don't *see* Adam so much as see through his eyes; he is not our hero but our alter-ego. The beauty of his speech (and it is beautiful) is the beauty of an elegant solution in mathematics, calling attention not to itself or its author but to the simplicity of the order underlying the complex and knotted surface of things. Adam's formulae—weak > strong; wise < meek; suffering = victory; Death $\rightarrow$

Life—are pronounced with a flatness of tone, an absence of rhetorical heightening, that is itself the most effective rhetoric. Truth, Adam implies, needs no dramatizing to prevail. Yet as the dramatic utterance of a character whose entire life story has been laid before our eyes, the speech is rooted in concrete experience that fleshes out its lean abstraction—not on the page but in our responsive minds.

For though it may be a bit perverse to reduce Adam's great summation of earthly wisdom and Christian heroism to an aesthetics, his valedictory does explain how to read *Paradise Lost* as well as how to live life. That strength, wisdom, suffering, and death are not what they seem but yield to their apparent opposites, is not only the message but the method of Milton's anti-epic. And, as the prologue to Book I obscurely foretold, the image of soaring flight must yield to that of a humble kneeling in prayer, as the humble method of Book XII has done its best to convey.

Michael now pays Adam the sincerest tribute of all by merely echoing and expanding on Adam's preference for meekness over worldly wisdom:

> This having learnt, thou hast attain'd the sum
> Of wisdom; hope no higher, though all the Stars
> Thou knew'st by name, and all th' ethereal Powers,
> All secrets of the deep, all Nature's works,
> Or works of God in Heav'n, Air, Earth, or Sea,
> And all the riches of this World enjoy'dst,
> And all the rule, one Empire. . . . (XII,575–81)

Again the epic sweep and grandeur of earlier portions of the poem itself are devalued here as a kind of "worldly wisdom" that, though not forbidden, are inferior to the lowly wisdom of Adam's final speech. And Michael goes on to conclude that all words have their limitations, that even the wisest and best words must reflect and be reflected by nonverbal reality:

>   only add
> Deeds to thy knowledge answerable, add Faith,
> Add Virtue, Patience, Temperance, add Love,
> By name to come call'd Charity, the soul
> Of all the rest: then wilt thou not be loath
> To leave this Paradise, but shalt possess
> A paradise within thee, happier far. (XII,581–87)

Perhaps the statement is too flat, too prosy to take in all at once. Yet what Michael is affirming is not simply that Eden will one day return—"New Heav'ns, new Earth, Ages of endless date" (XII,549)—but that for the faithful, paradise is *now* and "happier far" than the lost Eden! In the souls of the fallen faithful, paradise is both lost and regained!

If the final goal of the poem is not soaring vision but humble faith, then the lessons learned on the mount of speculation must be tested in the crucible of ordinary, everyday life. Naturally there is reluctance mingled with expectation (what F.T. Prince called the ending's "autumnal mood") as Adam prepares to enter the long tunnel of history in which he will live and die and where he will see many things that will try his faith. The world is the crucible in which he will be tried and purified, yet his progress toward his ultimate salvation will be so slow and so fraught with difficulty that it feels at the moment to be retrograde, a fall rather than a rise. Indeed the verb "descend" is used three times here, as if to make clear that ejection from Eden, though "for the best," remains a humbling and bitter experience. In the long run all will be well, but Adam's life will be a series of short runs, where his own faith and courage will be sorely tested. Comfort is tempered in his mind with apprehension, for although he has attained a state of grace, tomorrow he may lose it.

In Adam's absence, Eve has received a prophetic dream, and she, too, is prepared to leave Eden:

> now lead on;
> In mee is no delay; with thee to go,
> Is to stay here; without thee here to stay,
> Is to go hence unwilling; thou to mee
> Art all things under Heav'n, all places thou,
> Who for my wilful crime art banisht hence.
> This further consolation yet secure
> I carry hence; though all by mee is lost,
> Such favor I unworthy am voutsaf't,
> By mee the Promis'd Seed shall all restore. (XII,614–23)

Like Adam's final speech of submission to God's will, Eve's valedictory suggests "the better fortitude of patience and heroic martyrdom." In a Christian universe, as the example of Christ himself makes clear, true heroism lies in humility and faith. She submits to Adam as he submits to God, and though a modern feminist sensibility must bridle a bit at the way Eve lives vicariously through her husband and children, her situation is not essentially different from Adam's, who must also renounce the pleasant but dangerous illusion that he is still at the center of human history.

Jesus Christ is now the central figure of the human drama, and Adam and Eve are to us rapidly diminishing figures on the far edge of history, headed toward an unknown future. The Bible is sparse in details about their subsequent lives. We know that they lived by tilling the soil; that one of their sons murdered another; that they had other sons, including one named Seth, and presumably daughters as well; and that Adam lived to the ripe age of nine-hundred-and-thirty, and then died. Clearly they lived lives of trial and tribulation, as well as perhaps of triumph and satisfaction. But we really know less about their future, as they leave Eden, than we know about our own. And what we would *most* like to know, about them as about ourselves, is entirely hidden from us: will they be (were they) saved?

Paradise Lost succeeds in putting the reader himself into the story by annihilating, in every way possible, the distance between us and its protagonists. No false heroic posture, no fictional or poetic embellishment, no proleptic vision of a personal happy ending, no didactic lecture intervenes between us and these two human beings who are at once themselves, Adam and Eve, and any man and woman setting out upon lives of risk and possibility. Their story, far from being over, has (we realize belatedly) only begun—which accounts, I think, for the marvelous sense of renewal in the final lines, which close one story only to begin another of far greater scope and possibility, one that is left us to write in our own minds:

> Some natural tears they dropp'd, but wip'd them soon;
> The World was all before them, where to choose
> Thir place of rest, and Providence thir guide:
> They hand in hand with wand'ring steps and slow,
> Through Eden took thir solitary way. (XII,645–49)

Adam and Eve, like all who know about the Redeemer, have the necessary knowledge to achieve salvation; the rest is up to them. But for them, as for us, the next page is blank: they will write their own life stories; they will decide, by the choices they make, whether they are living a gruesome tragedy or a divine comedy. And so will we.

Notes

Introduction: Reading and Criticism

1. Roald Dahl, *James and the Giant Peach* (New York: Knopf, 1961), p. 1.

2. Rudolf Arnheim, *Art and Visual Perception* (Berkeley: University of California Press, 1954; paper, 1965; rev. ed., 1975); Morse Peckham, *Man's Rage for Chaos* (New York: Schocken, 1967; first pub. 1965); E. H. Gombrich, *Art and Illusion* (Princeton: Princeton University Press, 1960; rev. 1961; paper, 1969); Norman Holland, *The Dynamics of Literary Response* (New York: Oxford University Press, 1967), *5 Readers Reading* (New Haven: Yale University Press, 1975); David Bleich, *Readings and Feelings* (Urbana, Ill.: National Council of Teachers of English, 1975), *Subjective Criticism* (Baltimore: Johns Hopkins University Press, 1978); Jonathan Culler, *Structuralist Poetics* (Ithaca: Cornell University Press, 1976); Wolfgang Iser, *The Implied Reader* (Baltimore: Johns Hopkins University Press, 1974), *The Act of Reading* (Baltimore: Johns Hopkins University Press, 1978); Stephen Booth, *An Essay on Shakespeare's Sonnets* (New Haven: Yale University Press, 1968), *Shakespeare's Sonnets: Edited with an Analytic Commentary* (New Haven: Yale University Press, 1977). Stanley Fish's works are cited later in this chapter. A collection of original essays, *The Reader in the Text: Essays in Audience and Interpretation*, ed. Susan Suleiman and Inge Crosman (Princeton: Princeton University Press, 1980), contains essays by R. Crosman, Culler, Holland, Iser, and others.

3. Arnheim, p. 380.

4. Iser, p. 288.

5. John Milton, *Paradise Lost*, in *John Milton: Complete Poems and Major Prose*, ed. Merritt Y. Hughes (New York: Odyssey Press, 1957), Bk. I, ll. 24–26, my italics. All citations from *Paradise Lost* refer to this edition.

6. Stephen Booth, "On the Value of *Hamlet*," in *Reinterpretations of Elizabethan Drama: Selected Papers from the English Institute*, ed. Norman Rabkin (New York: Columbia University Press, 1969), p. 139. To Booth's "understanding" I would add "emotions" and "will."

7. B. Rajan, *Paradise Lost and The Seventeenth Century Reader* (London: Chatto & Windus, 1947), p. 94.

8. In the discussion of historical and ideal readers that follows, I draw on my essay "Some Doubts about 'The Reader of *Paradise Lost*,'" *College English* 37:4 (Dec. 1975), 372–82. Readers interested in an ampler treatment of the subject should consult the essay.

9. Wayne Booth, *The Rhetoric of Fiction* (Chicago: University of Chicago Press, 1961), p.138.

10. Anne Davidson Ferry, *Milton's Epic Voice: The Narrator in Paradise Lost* (Cambridge: Harvard University Press, 1963), pp.22–23.

11. For a treatment of the whole subject of irony, see Wayne Booth, *A Rhetoric of Irony* (Chicago: University of Chicago Press, 1974).

12. Stanley Fish, *Surprised by Sin: The Reader in Paradise Lost* (New York: St. Martin's Press, 1967), p.4.

13. William Kerrigan, *The Prophetic Milton* (Charlottesville: University of Virginia Press, 1974), p.180.

14. Peter Berek, "'Plain' and 'Ornate' Styles and the Structure of *Paradise Lost*," *PMLA* 85 (March 1970), 237.

15. Perhaps for resons like those I have given, Fish abandoned his seventeenth-century reader after publishing *Surprised by Sin*, though he never explicitly renounced him. In "Discovery as Form in *Paradise Lost*" (in *New Essays on Paradise Lost*, ed. Thomas Kranidas [Berkeley: University of California Press, 1969]), he makes no reference to such a reader, who is replaced, in his next book, by a reader who is simply "informed" or "attentive" (*Self-Consuming Artifacts* [Berkeley: University of California Press, 1972]). Nor has he surfaced again in Fish's theoretical articles, beginning with "Literature in the Reader: Affective Stylistics" (*New Literary History*, 2 [Autumn 1970]; reprinted in *Self-Consuming Artifacts*), to which I must acknowledge a large intellectual debt.

16. The further question of whether authorial intention can or should govern reader response is too vexed and tangled an issue to be settled here. E.D. Hirsch has, in *Validity in Interpretation* (New Haven: Yale University Press, 1967) given authorial intention its most cogent and eloquent defense, arguing, for example, that "if the meaning of a text is not the author's, then no interpretation can possibly correspond to *the* meaning of the text, since it can have no determinate or determinable meaning" (p.5). But in fact no generally agreed-upon single meaning exists for *any* literary text, and I doubt that many of us need or want such univocality. Those interested in the issue should read *Validity*, an elegant and utterly lucid book, and consult the bibliographies provided there and in Hirsch's next book, *The Aims of Interpretation* (Chicago: University of Chicago Press, 1976). I have answered Hirsch's argument in "Do Readers Make Meaning?" (in *The Reader in the Text*, see note 2 above): "Any word or text. . . .has 'meaning' only when it is fitted into some larger context. Thus the act of understanding a poet's words by placing them in the context of his intentions is only one of a number of possible ways of understanding them. This way of arriving at their 'meaning' is privileged both by long tradition and by our common interest in authors' minds, but it in no way supersedes or precedes other methods of interpretation which are, equally, contextualizing procedures. . . . 'Authors make meaning' is merely a special case of the more universal truth that readers make meaning."

17. John Milton, *Christian Doctrine*, in *Complete Prose Works of John Milton* (hereafter cited as *Yale Milton*), general editor Don M. Wolfe, Vol. VI, ed. Maurice Kelley (New Haven: Yale University Press, 1973), p.118. All citations of Milton's prose will be from the *Yale Milton*; where available, the page reference will also be given to *John Milton: Complete Poems and Major Prose*, ed. Merritt Y. Hughes (New York: Odyssey Press, 1957).

1. Milton's Great Oxymoron

1. John Milton, *Areopagitica*, in *Yale Milton*, Vol. II, ed. Ernest Sirluck (New Haven: Yale University Press, 1959), pp.514–15; Hughes, p.728.

2. E.R. Curtius, *European Literature and the Latin Middle Ages*, trans. Willard Trask (New York: Harper and Row, 1953), p.462.

3. T.J.B. Spencer, "*Paradise Lost*: The Anti-Epic," in *Approaches to Paradise Lost*, ed. C.A. Patrides (Toronto: University of Toronto Press, 1968), p.98. The Phoenix-like rebirth of epic from its own ashes has occurred once before, according to Brooks Otis, who sees the same process operating in the *Aeneid* that I have described in *Paradise Lost*: "The fact is that the contemporary epic available to Virgil was not so much mature as dead. Dead also was the mythology of Homer and the Greeks. The only available source of poetical imagery had seemingly dried up. Nor could Virgil make a new mythology of his own: no man, whatever his genius, could do that. He therefore did the next best thing: he invented, he transformed, the old epic tradition, the old saga—Homer, in short—and restored them to a new Roman existence. This was the original, the unique achievement of Virgil" ("The Originality of the *Aeneid*," in *Virgil*, ed. D.R. Dudley [London: Routledge and Kegan Paul, 1969], p.65).

4. This point has been memorably argued by Stanley Fish in *Surprised by Sin*, but in terms of a seventeenth-century reader (see Introduction). Since the clash of epic and Christian expectations, the self-contradictions of Milton's narrator, the puzzling nature of good and evil as presented in Book I, are as much there for modern readers as for historic ones, for Christians and non-Christians alike, I can see no need of Fish's historic reader. Milton's long, complex poem is, and has always been, difficult reading, but I think its "fit audience" are those who make the effort of feeling comprehension. Books I and II make the reader feel "fallen" not because he is necessarily a Christian, but because either Milton's poetry makes no sense or we are unable to understand it.

5. Affinities between Milton's narrator and Satan have been most completely traced in William Riggs's *The Christian Poet in Paradise Lost* (Berkeley: University of California Press, 1972), pp.15–45.

6. Geoffrey Hartman, "Milton's Counterplot," in *Milton: Modern Essays in Criticism*, ed. Arthur Barker (New York: Oxford University Press, 1965), pp. 386–97. Although I borrow Hartman's useful term, he and I do not use it in precisely the same way. For Hartman, Milton's counterplot undercuts the Satanic plot of Books I and II with images of God's cool imperturbability and mankind's ultimate safety from Satanic attack, while my view is that a counterplot warns the reader of the "fictivity" of the story he is reading.

7. Arnold Stein, *The Art of Presence: The Poet and Paradise Lost* (Berkeley: University of California Press, 1977), p.77. Stein uses the word "flicker" in much the same way as I, to refer to ways in which Milton's poem makes us doubt the reality or reliability of what it is showing us: "Satan draws up into a self-justifying stand, but the rapid, multiple shifts in reference and the acrobatic twists before the final posture comes right—all done with concentrated seriousness—makes him flicker like an old film."

8. See Fish, pp.23–29.

9. Stein, pp.50–51, remarks on the delusive properties of this passage: "[Milton] pretends that the narrative is a truthful account and not a deliberately

overwrought fiction, a glittering but sinister bubble, a diversion of much ado about very little. . . . What is great even in decline is treated with suitable dignity, though the grandeur is more poetic than substantial, art exerting itself to produce shimmering triumphs in which the hand of the artist alternates between ostentation and invisibility."

10. John Milton, *The Reason of Church Government*, in *Yale Milton*, Vol. I, ed. Don M. Wolfe, pp.817–18; Hughes, p.670.

11. John Milton, *Christian Doctrine*, in *Yale Milton*, Vol. VI, p.133; Hughes, p.905.

12. See Stein, p.88: "the responsible freedom to develop and elaborate where Scripture is silent or brief must nevertheless avoid seeming to improve on the story by telling beautiful lies. At the very least the poet must lie properly, as Homer taught, but the nature of his obligation to his material is more demanding."

2. Light Invisible

1. Joan Webber, "Milton's God," *ELH* 40 (1973), 514.

2. Peter Berek, "'Plain' and 'Ornate' Styles and the Structure of *Paradise Lost*," *PMLA* 85 (March 1970), 237.

3. Marjorie Nicolson, *John Milton: A Reader's Guide to His Poetry* (New York: Noonday, 1963), p.225.

4. John Milton, *Christian Doctrine*, in *Yale Milton*, Vol. VI, p.133; Hughes, p.905. See also John Calvin, *Commentaries on Genesis*, trans. J. King, 2 vols. (Edinburgh, 1847), I. 60 (quoted in J.B. Broadbent, *Some Graver Subject* [London: Chatto & Windus, 1960], pp. 138–39): "As for those who proudly soar above the world to seek God in his unveiled essence, it is impossible but that at length they should entangle themselves in a multitude of absurd figments. For God—by other means invisible—(as we have already said) clothes himself, so to speak, with the image of the world, in which he would present himself to our contemplation [i.e., in the Bible]. Therefore, as soon as the name of God sounds in our ears, or the thought of him occurs to our minds, let us also clothe him with this most beautiful ornament; finally, let the world become our school if we desire rightly to know God."

5. John Peter, *A Critique of Paradise Lost* (New York and London: Columbia University Press/Longmans, 1960), pp.12–13.

6. *Christian Doctrine*, p.227; Hughes, p.941.

7. *Christian Doctrine*, p.176; Hughes, p.919: "It seems, then, that predestination and election are not particular but only general: that is, they belong to all who believe in their hearts and persist in their belief. Peter is not predestined or elected as Peter, or John as John, but each only insofar as he believes and persists in his belief. Thus the general decree of election is individually applicable to each believer, and is firmly established for those who persevere."

8. *Calvin's Commentaries: The Epistles of the Apostle to the Romans and to the Thessalonians*, tr. Ross Mackenzie, ed. D.W. and T.F. Torrance (Edinburgh: Oliver and Boyd, 1961), p.204 (cited in *Christian Doctrine*, p.184).

9. See especially John S. Diekhoff, *Milton's Paradise Lost, A Commentary on the Argument* (New York and London: Columbia University Press/Oxford University Press, 1946); Dennis Burden, *The Logical Epic* (Cambridge: Harvard Uni-

versity Press, 1967); and Gary D. Hamilton, "Milton's Defensive God: A Reappraisal," *Studies in Philology* 69 (1972), 87–100. If early readers found the God of Book III reassuring (we really have no evidence to support or refute this claim), they did so because they were so deeply terrified by the image of an angry God instilled by their education and evoked by Books I and II, that even a doubtful and ambiguous clarification of God's ways was for them an improvement. For such readers, a reduction in terror would leave them where the rest of us are already—worried and perplexed, but calm enough to go on reading.

10. William Empson, *Milton's God*, rev. ed. (London: Chatto & Windus, 1965; first pub. 1961), pp.130–146. Empson is the first, to my knowledge, to talk about God as planning to "abdicate." Though Empson understands that Milton's God is an evolving deity, however, he does not feel that even the eventual abdication of a God of Wrath justifies his ways: "the poem, to be completely foursquare, ought to explain why God had to procure all these falls for his eventual high purpose" (p.145). Joan Webber has more recently tried to answer Empson by a sophisticated version of the Fortunate Fall: "as theologian Milton believed that God's creatures had willed their own downfall. But without contradiction or blame to God, he also understood how unlikely it was that any work of art could be instantaneously and permanently impeccable. God's justification is the creative urge itself, and that is finally what *Paradise Lost* is all about. It is creation, it is sheer love of becoming, despite all the pain and frustration intrinsic to the process, that justifies the ways of God to men" ("Milton's God," p.526). Webber argues, in effect, that to create free beings is to create beings who will sooner or later oppose their will to God's, who in effect *must* fall. Thus there would have to be, in any Creation, a built-in plan of Redemption. To which Empson would doubtless want to inquire if the damned, including Satan, are also going to be saved.

3. Points of View in Paradise

1. John Milton, *Areopagitica*, in *Yale Milton*, Vol. II, p.527; Hughes, p.733.

2. See Wayne Booth, *The Rhetoric of Fiction* (Chicago: University of Chicago Press, 1969), p.152: "We should remind ourselves that many dramatized narrators are never explicitly labeled as narrators at all. In a sense, every speech, every gesture, narrates; most works contain disguised narrators who are used to tell the audience what it needs to know, while seeming merely to act out their roles."

3. John Milton, *Of Reformation Touching Church-Discipline in England*, in *Yale Milton*, Vol. I, p. 566.

4. Andrew Marvell, "The Mower against Gardens," in *The Poems and Letters of Andrew Marvell*, 2nd, ed., ed. H.M. Margoliouth, Vol. I (Oxford: Clarendon Press, 1951), p.40.

5. To get past Uriel, Satan had to praise "The Universal Maker" well enough to fool an angel:

> [He] justly hath driv'n out his Rebel Foes
> To deepest Hell, and to repair that loss
> Created this new happy Race of Men
> To serve him better: wise are all his ways. (III,676–80)

The reader who remembers Satan's fist-shaking vow never to "deify his power" (I,112) and Mammon's distaste for singing "Forc't Halleluiahs" (II,243) must smile at how easily Satan changes his principles to fit the occasion.

6. Frank Kermode, "Adam Unparadised," in *The Living Milton*, ed. Frank Kermode (London: Routledge and Kegan Paul, 1960), p.109.

7. F.R. Leavis, "Reflections on the Milton Controversy," in *A Selection from "Scrutiny,"* ed. F.R. Leavis (Cambridge: Cambridge University Press, 1968), I, 197.

8. Christopher Ricks, *Milton's Grand Style* (Oxford: Oxford University Press, 1963), p.110.

9. C.S. Lewis, *A Preface to Paradise Lost* (Oxford: Oxford University Press, 1942), p.49.

10. Paul Alpers, "The Milton Controversy," in *Harvard English Studies 2: Twentieth-Century Literature in Retrospect*, ed. Reuben A. Brower (Cambridge: Harvard University Press, 1971), p.274.

11. William Shakespeare, *A Winter's Tale*, IV, iv, 90–92. On the whole subject of art, nature, and their complex interrelationships, see Edward W. Tayler's learned and witty *Nature and Art in Renaissance Literature* (New York: Columbia University Press, 1965).

12. Lewis, p.116, quoting Sir Walter Raleigh.

13. I am indebted to Owen Barfield's profound and original book, *Saving the Appearances: A Study in Idolatry* (New York: Harcourt, Brace & World, 1965), not only for the term "participation," but for the whole idea that "primitive" or Edenic thought is charactized by an absence of the dogma of the radical separation of subject and object, spirit and substance, viewer and viewed: "Participation is the extra-sensory relation between man and the phenomena. . . . The existence of phenomena depends on it. Actual participation is therefore as much a fact in our case as in that of primitive man. But we have also seen that we are unaware, whereas the primitive mind is aware of it. This primitive awareness, however, is obviously not the theoretical kind which *we* can still arrive at. . . . The primitive kind of participation is indeed not theoretical at all, inasmuch as it is given in immediate experience" (p.40).

14. See, for example, A. Bartlett Giamatti, *The Earthly Paradise and the Renaissance Epic* (Princeton: Princeton University Press, 1966), pp.299–313. In "Innocence and Experience in Milton's Eden" (in *New Essays on Paradise Lost*, ed. Thomas Kranidas [Berkeley: University of California Press, 1969]), Barbara Kiefer Lewalski has ably answered this view from the point of view of Milton's theme: "Nor, though these effects are important and have been brilliantly analyzed in modern criticism, does Milton depart from the expected only to foreshadow the Fall, to establish dramatic causality for it, and to render the unfallen state more credible by presenting it from fallen man's perspective or with the fallen condition 'potentially' present in it. Rather, these Miltonic novelties are of the essence of the poem's vision, for they effect a redefinition of the State of Innocence which is a very far cry from the stable, serene completeness attributed to that state both in myth and in traditional theology. In *Paradise Lost* the Edenic life is radical growth and process, a mode of life steadily increasing in complexity and challenge and difficulty but at the same time and by that very fact, in perfection" (p.88).

15. That God does not hang the scales there only at the moment of Satan's

challenge is clear from the fact that Satan has already seen Libra in the sky as he descends from Heaven (III,558). Although Milton's God does not improvise, he *seems* to do so here, and the apparent eleventh-hour rescue, combined with the uncertainty suggested in the simile that describes the plowman as fearful lest his grain be ruined (IV,980–85), creates a mood of apprehension about whether or not Eve will succumb to Satan's temptation.

16. Joseph Summers, *The Muse's Method: An Introduction to Paradise Lost* (New York: W.W. Norton, 1968; first pub. 1962), p.80.

17. See note 14 above.

4. Unfallen Narration

1. John Milton, *The Reason of Church-Government*, in *Yale Milton*, Vol. I, p.803; Hughes, p. 666.

2. John Milton, *An Apology for Smectymnuus*, in *Yale Milton*, Vol. I, p.890; Hughes, p.694.

3. On the subject of Milton's view of himself as an inspired poet, see James Holly Hanford, "That Shepherd Who First Taught the Chosen Seed: A Note on Milton's Mosaic Inspiration," *University of Toronto Quarterly*, 8 (1939), 403–19; and William Kerrigan, *The Prophetic Milton* (Charlottesville: University of Virginia Press, 1974).

4. See Chapter Two. On the subject of accommodation in Milton, Roland Mushat Frye's *God, Man, and Satan: Patterns of Christian Thought and Life in 'Paradise Lost,' 'Pilgrim's Progress,' and the Great Theologians* (Princeton: Princeton University Press, 1960) is the best introduction.

5. See Chapter Two, note 4.

6. John Milton, *Christian Doctrine*, in *Yale Milton*, Vol. VI, pp.134–136; Hughes, p.906.

7. See William Madsen, *From Shadowy Types to Truth* (New Haven: Yale University Press, 1968).

8. Samuel Johnson, "Milton," in *Milton Criticism: Selections from Four Centuries*, ed. James Thorpe (New York: Collier, 1969; first pub. 1950), pp. 81–82.

9. Arnold Stein, *Answerable Style: Essays on Paradise Lost* (Seattle: University of Washington Press, 1967; first pub. 1953), pp. 17–37.

10. Stanley Fish, *Surprised by Sin: The Reader in Paradise Lost* (New York: St. Martin's Press, 1967), p.188.

11. Fish, pp.196–97.

12. Fish, pp.197–98.

13. Austin C. Dobbins, *Milton and the Book of Revelation: The Heavenly Cycle* (University, Ala.: University of Alabama Press, 1975), p. 119.

5. True Fiction

1. A look back at Books I and II will show a host of incongruities between what we were told there and Raphael's more authoritative version. Moloch, for example, was advertised as "the strongest and the fiercest Spirit That fought in Heav'n" (II,44–45). Yet Raphael shows him not only bested by Gabriel but in the

unseemly (given that angels cannot die) role of crybaby: "Down clov'n to the waist, with shatter'd Arms And uncouth pain flew bellowing" (VI, 361–62).

2. William G. Riggs, *The Christian Poet in Paradise Lost* (Berkeley: University of California Press, 1972), p. 102.

3. The most thorough attempt to relate *Paradise Lost* to Revelation is Austin C. Dobbins's *Milton and the Book of Revelation: The Heavenly Cycle* (University, Ala.: University of Alabama Press, 1975).

4. John Milton, *Christian Doctrine*, in *Yale Milton*, Vol. VI, p.347; Hughes, p.991.

5. Stella Revard, "The Warring Saints and the Dragon: A Commentary upon Revelation 12:7–9 and Milton's War in Heaven," *Philological Quarterly*, 53:2 (April 1974), 183.

6. Merritt Y. Hughes, *Ten Perspectives on Milton* (New Haven: Yale University Press, 1965), pp. 197–98.

7. John Milton, *Areopagitica*, in *Yale Milton*, Vol. II, p.514; Hughes, p.728.

8. Guillaume Du Bartas, "Uranie," in *La Muse Chrestiene*. A useful recent facsimile edition of *La Muse Chrestiene*, together with the *Divine Weeks* and other works, is *Bartas: His Devine Weekes and Workes*, trans. Joshua Sylvester (Gainesville, Fla.: Scholars' Facsimilies & Reprints, 1965).

9. Merritt Y. Hughes, in his Introduction to *John Milton: Complete Poems and Major Prose* (New York: Odyssey Press, 1957), p.199, suggests "Understanding," while John T. Shawcross, in *The Complete Poetry of John Milton* (New York: Doubleday, rev. ed., 1971), p.387, suggests "Inspiration." They confess they are guessing.

10. Hughes, *John Milton: Complete Poems and Major Prose*, p. 153.

11. Guillaume Du Bartas, *La Sepmaine*, trans. Joshua Sylvester, in Watson Kirkconnell, *The Celestial Cycle* (Toronto: University of Toronto Press, 1952), p.48.

12. *The New English Bible* (New York: Oxford University Press, 1971), p.1., agrees with Milton's view on this point, as well as some others: "In the beginning of Creation, when God made heaven and earth, the earth was without form and void, with darkness over the face of the abyss, and a mighty wind that swept over the surface of the waters. God said, 'Let there be light,' and there was light; and God saw that the light was good, and he separated light from darkness. He called the light day, and the darkness night. So evening came, and morning came, the first day."

13. Hughes, *John Milton: Complete Poems and Major Prose*, p. 210.

14. Andrew Marvell, "On *Paradise Lost*," in Hughes, *John Milton: Complete Poems and Major Prose*, p.210.

15. Howard Schultz, *Milton and Forbidden Knowledge* (New York: Modern Language Association of America, 1955), p. 176.

16. John Keats, Letter to Benjamin Bailey, 22 November 1817, in John Keats, *Selected Poems and Letters*, ed. Douglas Bush (Boston: Houghton Mifflin, 1959), p. 258.

6. The Comedy of the Fall

1. Arthur E. Barker, "Structural Pattern in *Paradise Lost*," in *Philological Quarterly*, 28 (1949), 17–30. Reprinted in *Milton: Modern Essays in Criticism*,

ed. Arthur E. Barker (New York: Oxford University Press, 1965), pp.142–55.

2. Helen Gardner, *A Reading of Paradise Lost* (Oxford: Oxford University Press. 1965), p.91.

3. Stanley Fish, *Surprised by Sin: The Reader in Paradise Lost* (New York: St. Martin's Press, 1967), p.270.

7. The Curse

1. Helen Gardner, *A Reading of Paradise Lost* (Oxford: Oxford University Press, 1965), p. 57.

8. Salvation through Reading

1. Joseph Summers. *The Muse's Method: An Introduction to Paradise Lost* (New York: W.W. Norton, 1968; first pub. 1962), p. 189.

2. F.T. Prince, "On the Last Two Books of *Paradise Lost*," in *Essays and Studies*, n.s. 11 (1958), 41–43.

3. H.R. Maccallum, "Milton and Sacred History: Books XI and XII of *Paradise Lost*," in *Essays in English Literature from the Renaissance to the Victorian Age*, ed. Millar MacLure and F.W. Watt (Toronto: University of Toronto Press, 1964), 149–68.

4. Louis L. Martz, *The Paradise Within: Studies in Vaughan, Traherne, and Milton* (New Haven: Yale University Press, 1964), p.150.

5. Summers, p.192.

6. Stanley Fish, *Surprised by Sin: The Reader in Paradise Lost* (New York: St. Martin's Press, 1967), p.281.

7. Barbara Keifer Lewalski, "Structure and the Symbolism of Vision in Michael's Prophecy, *Paradise Lost*, Books XI–XII," *Philological Quarterly*, 42 (1963), 30.

Bibliography

This list of titles, which contains only a tiny fraction of the published work on Milton and *Paradise Lost*, is meant as an aid for students doing further reading and research.

Bibliographies

Hanford, James Holly and McQueen, William. *Milton*. 2nd. ed. Goldentree Bibliographies in Language and Literature. Arlington Heights, Ill.: AHM Publishers, 1978 (paper).

Huckabay, Calvin. *John Milton: An Annotated Bibliography, 1929–68*. Pittsburgh: Duquesne University Press, 1969 (cloth).

Stevens, David Harrison. *A Reference Guide to Milton from 1800 to the Present Day*. Chicago: University of Chicago Press, 1930 (cloth).

From 1977 consult the listings under "English Literature VII. Seventeenth Century: Milton" in the *MLA International Bibliography*, Vol. I, published annually. Since this list is always one to two years behind current publication, the most recent articles can be found only by looking through files of current periodicals. Some good ones to try are: *PMLA, Milton Quarterly, Milton Studies, ELH: English Literary History, Studies in Philology, Modern Philology, English Literary Renaissance*. Recent book titles can be found under "John Milton" in *Books in Print* (New York: R.R. Bowker, annual) or in publishers' advertisements in *PMLA*.

Editions

Milton, John. *Complete Poems and Major Prose*. Edited by Merritt Y. Hughes. New York: Odyssey Press, 1957 (cloth).

———. *The Complete Poetry of John Milton*. Edited by John T. Shawcross. Garden City, N.Y.: Doubleday, 1971 (paper).

———. *Complete Prose Works of John Milton*. Edited by Don M. Wolfe. 8 vols. New Haven: Yale University Press, 1953–. Vol. 8 still to appear.

———. *Paradise Lost*. Edited by Merritt Hughes. New York: Odyssey Press, 1962 (paper).

———. *Paradise Lost and Selected Poetry and Prose*. Edited by Northrop Frye. New York: Rinehart, 1951 (paper).

———. *The Poetical Works of John Milton*. Vol. I: *Paradise Lost*. Edited by Helen Darbishire. Oxford: Clarendon Press, 1952 (cloth).

———. *The Portable Milton*. Edited by Douglas Bush. New York: Viking Press, 1949 (paper).

———. *The Works of John Milton*. Edited by Frank Allen Patterson. 18 vols. New York: Columbia University Press, 1931–38.

Biographies

Hanford, James Holly. *John Milton, Englishman*. New York: Crown, 1949. Hanford is the best introduction for the novice, beyond the biographical sketches usually contained in the introductions to editions of the poetry.

Masson, David. *The Life of John Milton: Narrated in Connexion with the Political, Ecclesiastical, and Literary History of His Time*. 7 vols. Cambridge and London: Macmillan, 1859–94. (Reprinted in New York: Peter Smith, 1946.) The Masson biography makes lively reading, but at seven volumes is too long for the general reader, and is not up-to-date in the details of Milton's life.

Parker, William Riley. *Milton: A Biography*. 2 vols. Oxford: Clarendon Press, 1968. Parker, who incorporates modern research, is solid, uninspiring reading.

Criticism: Books

Berry, Boyd M. *Process of Speech: Puritan Religious Writing and Paradise Lost*. Baltimore: The Johns Hopkins University Press, 1976.

Brisman, Leslie. *Milton's Poetry of Choice and Its Romantic Heirs*. Ithaca: Cornell University Press, 1973.

Broadbent, J.B. *Some Graver Subject: An Essay on Paradise Lost*. London: Chatto and Windus, 1960.

Burden, Dennis. *The Logical Epic*. Cambridge, Mass.: Harvard University Press, 1967.

Cope, Jackson I. *The Metaphoric Structure of Paradise Lost*. Baltimore: The Johns Hopkins University Press, 1962.

Diekhoff, John S. *Milton's Paradise Lost, A Commentary on the Argument*. New York and London: Columbia University Press/Oxford University Press, 1946.

Dobbins, Austin C. *Milton and the Book of Revelation: The Heavenly Cycle*. University, Ala.: University of Alabama, 1975.

Empson, William. *Milton's God*. London: Chatto and Windus, 1961; rev. ed., 1965.

Evans, John Martin. *Paradise Lost and the Genesis Tradition*. Oxford: Oxford University Press, 1968.

Ferry, Anne Davidson. *Milton's Epic Voice: The Narrator in Paradise Lost*. Cambridge, Mass.: Harvard University Press, 1963.

Fish, Stanley E. *Surprised by Sin: The Reader in Paradise Lost*. New York: St. Martin's Press, 1967.

Frye, Northrop. *The Return of Eden*. Toronto: University of Toronto Press, 1965.

Gardner, Helen. *A Reading of Paradise Lost*. Oxford: Clarendon Press, 1965.

Hughes, Merritt Y. *Ten Perspectives on Milton*. New Haven: Yale University Press, 1965.

Kerrigan, William. *The Prophetic Milton*. Charlottesville: University of Virginia Press, 1974.

Lewis, C.S. *A Preface to Paradise Lost*. London: Oxford University Press, 1942.

Lieb, Michael. *The Dialectics of Creation; Patterns of Birth and Regeneration in Paradise Lost*. Amherst: University of Massachusetts Press, 1970.

MacCaffrey, Isabel Gamble. *Paradise Lost as "Myth."* Cambridge, Mass.: Harvard University Press, 1959.

Madsen, William. *From Shadowy Types to Truth*. New Haven: Yale University Press, 1968.

Martz, Louis L. *The Paradise Within*. New Haven: Yale University Press, 1964.

Nicolson, Marjorie Hope. *John Milton: A Reader's Guide to His Poetry*. New York: Farrar, Straus, 1963.

Peter, John. *A Critique of Paradise Lost*. New York: Columbia University Press, 1960.

Rajan, Balachandra. *Paradise Lost and the Seventeenth Century Reader*. London: Chatto and Windus, 1947.

Raleigh, Sir Walter A. *Milton*. New York: Putnam, 1900.

Richmond, Hugh M. *The Christian Revolutionary: John Milton*. Berkeley: University of California Press, 1974.

Ricks, Christopher. *Milton's Grand Style*. Oxford: Clarendon Press, 1963.

Riggs, William G. *The Christian Poet in Paradise Lost*. Berkeley: University of California Press, 1972.

Saurat, Denis. *Milton: Man and Thinker*. New York: Dial Press, 1925; 2nd. ed. London: Dent, 1944; repr. 1946.

Schultz, Howard. *Milton and Forbidden Knowledge*. New York: Modern Language Association of America, 1955.

Stein, Arnold. *Answerable Style: Essays on Paradise Lost*. Minneapolis: University of Minnesota Press, 1950; repr. Seattle: University of Washington Press, 1967.

————. *The Art of Presence: The Poet and Paradise Lost*. Berkeley: University of California Press, 1977.

Summers, Joseph. *The Muse's Method: An Introduction to Paradise Lost*. Cambridge, Mass.: Harvard University Press, 1962.

Tillyard, E.M.W. *Milton*. London: Chatto and Windus, 1930.

Waldock, A.J.A. *Paradise Lost and Its Critics*. Cambridge: Cambridge University Press, 1947.

Webber, Joan. *Milton and His Epic Tradition*. Seattle: University of Washington Press, 1979.

Wheeler, Thomas. *Paradise Lost and the Modern Reader*. Athens: University of Georgia Press, 1973.

Criticism: Collections of Articles

Barker, Arthur E. (ed.) *Milton: Modern Essays in Criticism*. New York: Oxford University Press, 1965.

Critical Essays on Milton from ELH. Baltimore: The Johns Hopkins University Press, 1969.

Franson, John Karl (ed.). *Milton Reconsidered: Essays in Honor of Arthur E. Barker*. Salzburg: University of Salzburg Press, 1976.

Kermode, Frank (ed.). *The Living Milton*. London: Routledge and Kegan Paul, 1960.

Kranidas, Thomas (ed.). *New Essays on Paradise Lost*. Berkeley: University of California Press, 1969.

Martz, Louis L. *Milton: A Collection of Critical Essays*. Englewood Cliffs, N.J.: Prentice-Hall, 1966.

Patrides, C.A. (ed.) *Approaches to Paradise Lost*. Toronto: University of Toronto Press, 1968.

Simmonds, James (ed.). *Milton Studies*. Pittsburgh: University of Pittsburgh Press, 1969–. *Milton Studies* is an annual clothbound volume, containing original articles exclusively on Milton.

Thorpe, James (ed.). *Milton Criticism: Selections from Four Centuries*. New York: Holt, Rinehart and Winston, 1950; repr. New York: Macmillan, 1969.

Historical and Theological Background

Barker, Arthur E. *Milton and the Puritan Dilemma, 1641–60*. Toronto: University of Toronto Press, 1942; repr. 1956.

Haller, William. *The Rise of Puritanism*. New York: Columbia University Press, 1938; repr. Philadelphia: University of Pennsylvania Press, 1972.

Hill, Christopher. *The Century of Revolution*. London: Thomas Nelson, 1961; repr. New York: W.W. Norton, 1966.

———. *Milton and the English Revolution*. New York: Viking, 1978.

Kelley, Maurice W. *This Great Argument: A Study of Milton's De doctrina christiana as a Gloss upon Paradise Lost*. Princeton: Princeton University Press, 1941.

Patrides, C.A. *Milton and the Christian Tradition*. Oxford: Clarendon Press, 1966.

Wolfe, Don M. *Milton in the Puritan Revolution*. New York and London: Thomas Nelson, 1941.